A
History of the
Black Death
in
Ireland

D0838798

MARIA KELLY is a freelance writer and historian. She is the author of *The Great Dying: The Black Death in Dublin*, also published by Tempus.

Praise for *The Great Dying: The Black Death in Dublin*

'An infectious chronicle... does a fine job reconstructing the plague era in calamitous detail' *The Sunday Times*

'Both scholarly and intensely readable... Maria Kelly has researched and drawn on a vast range of sources to recreate the sights, the sounds and the very feelings of Dublin during those dark days, and in so doing draws us into the pages of history itself' *The Irish Examiner*

A History of the Black Death in Ireland

MARIA KELLY

TEMPUS

Cover illustrations: (Front) *Burying the Dead.* By permission of the Koninklijke Bibliotheek/Bibliothèque Royale, Brussels. (Back) Detail from a German print of 1508, author's collection.

First published 2001
This edition first published 2004

Tempus Publishing Limited
The Mill, Brimscombe Port,
Stroud, Gloucestershire, GL5 2QG
www.tempus-publishing.com

British Library Cataloguing in Publication Data.
A catalogue record for this book is available from the British Library.

ISBN 0 7524 3185 4

Typesetting and origination by Tempus Publishing Limited
Printed and bound in Great Britain

Contents

Map of Ireland

Acknowledgements

My warmest thanks go to the many people who have helped me in preparing this book: to Dr Kevin Down for his kindness in allowing me to read his transcripts of the Ministers' Accounts in the Public Record Office in London; to Dr Pádraigín Riggs for pointing me towards the latest work being done in Irish literature; to Jonathan Reeve who first conceived the idea of publishing this and shepherded me through the process, and to his associates at Tempus Publishing, Holly Bennett and Joanna de Vries; to Patricia Kelly, Gerard Desmond and William Scobie for all their efforts in locating material; to Dan O'Connell who kindly supplied me with a very particular photograph of the Irish countryside; to István Nemeth and Lieve Dhaene for technical help with illustrations, graphs, maps and glitches. I am especially grateful to Dermot Kelly whose photographs help capture the world into which the Black Death erupted.

Finally, but not least, I am grateful to my family, William, Oisín, Hugh and Will who have had to put up with the virtual presence of the Black Death in their midst for a long time now. For their many bright ideas and abiding patience, much thanks. To them I dedicate this book.

Abbreviations

AC	*Annals of Connacht*
AFM	*Annals of the Kingdom of Ireland by the Four Masters*
AI	*Annals of Innisfallen*
ALC	*Annals of Loch Cé*
Anal. Hib.	*Analecta Hibernica*
Ann. Clon.	*Annals of Clonmacnoise*
AU	*Annals of Ulster*
Cal. Anc. Rec.	*Calendar of the Ancient Records of Dublin*
Cal. Carew MSS	*Calendar of Carew Manuscripts*
Cal. Close Rolls	*Calendar of the Close Rolls*
Cal. Doc. Ire.	*Calendar of Documents Relating to Ireland, 1171-1307*
Cal. Inq. Misc.	*Calendar of Inquisitions Miscellaneous*
Cal. Justic. Rolls	*Calendar of the Justiciary Rolls of Ireland*
Cal. Pat. Rolls	*Calendar of Patent Rolls*
Chart. St Mary's	*Chartularies of St Mary's Abbey, Dublin and Annals of Ireland*
Clyn, Annals	*The Annals of Ireland by Friar John Clyn and Thady Dowling, ed. R. Butler (Dublin, 1849)*
CPL	*Calendar of Entries in the Papal Registers relating to Great Britain and Ireland: Papal Letters*
CPP	*Calendar of Entries in the Papal Registers relating to Great Britain and Ireland: Papal Petitions*
Frag. Annals	*Fragmentary Annals from the West of Ireland*
Horrox	R. Horrox, trans. and ed., *The Black Death* (Manchester, 1994)
Hist. & Mun. Docs. Ire.	*Historic and Municipal Documents of Ireland 1172–1320*
IER	*Irish Ecclesiastical Record*
IHS	*Irish Historical Studies*
JRSAI	*Journal of the Royal Society of Antiquaries of Ireland*
NHI	*A New History of Ireland, vol. 2: Medieval Ireland 1169-1534, ed. A. Cosgrove* (Oxford, 1987)
PRIA	*Proceedings of the Royal Irish Academy*
PROI	*Public Record Office of Ireland*
Rot. Pat. et Claus. Cal.	*Rotulorum Patentium et Clausorum Cancellariae Hiberniae Calendarium*
SPD	*Calendar of State Papers and Letters, Domestic Series*

I

The Black Death

The Black Death erupted in Western Europe in 1347, inaugurating a period in European history when the plague would return intermittently to wreak its havoc. Not until the final decades of the seventeenth century did it finally disappear, though isolated outbreaks continued into the twentieth century. As is evident from contemporary chronicles, the Black Death was seen at the time as a cataclysmic event. Surprisingly, eighteenth- and early nineteenth-century historians did not reckon it an event worth considering and writers such as Hume, Henry and Green gave it but passing mention.[1] Later historians enthusiastically rediscovered the Black Death and endowed it with a shattering importance. B.G. Babington in 1844 described it as 'a convulsion of the human race, unequalled in violence and extent'. F. A. Gasquet in 1893 claimed that the Black Death took 50% of the population of England and brought about the end of the Middle Ages and of medieval monasticism. G.H. Trevalyan in his *English Social History* claimed it was 'a fortuitous obstruction fallen across the river of life and temporarily diverting it'; like many of his contemporaries, Trevalyan saw the Black Death as the crucible of the modern world.[2]

For long after, the Black Death was adopted as a symbol by historians mesmeexchequerd by Huizinga's concept of 'the waning of the Middle Ages' and it came to be seen as a watershed between the medieval and modern worlds. Late medieval human beings came to be presented as radically different from their predecessors; in Huizinga's famous words, they:

always oscillate between the fear of hell and the most naïve joy, between cruelty and tenderness, between harsh asceticism and insane attachments to the delights of this world, between hatred and goodness, always running to extremes.[3]

In the 1970s, the pendulum had swung the other way with the publication of J.F. Shrewsbury's very influential work, *A History of Bubonic Plague in the British Isles* which argued, on the basis of a study of the aetiology of bubonic plague, that the plague's importance had been greatly exaggerated, that descriptions of it 'sweeping like a pestilential storm over the country merely indicate a regrettable ignorance of the nature of the disease', and that claims of its killing up to 50% of the population of the British Isles 'are flights of fancy boosted by the age-old terror that the name "plague" still excites'. Shrewsbury instead presented the plague as a mainly urban phenomenon which, outside densely populated areas where mortality may have been as high as one-third, could not have taken even one-twentieth of the population. A somewhat later study by William McNeill returned the Black Death to the pantheon of major pandemics that radically affected human history and which, at least until the nineteenth century, remained impervious to human intervention.[4]

With the recent emergence of hitherto unknown and initially inexplicable diseases, interest has once again turned towards the Black Death. Recent studies have focused on particular regions, on demographic questions or on the epidemiology and bacteriology of plague. Some historians argue that environmental factors such as climate and rodent life cycles play a far more crucial role than human activities; others have emphasised the importance of other contagious diseases such as smallpox and influenza which raged concurrently with the plague. Yet others have claimed the 1348 outbreak was not of bubonic plague but some other disease such as pulmonary anthrax or some form of haemorrhagic viral disease perhaps similar to the Ebola virus. Another study relying on DNA testing techniques has confirmed that the medieval epidemic was caused by plague, while yet other studies again question this finding, arguing that the medieval plague was far too virulent to have been caused by the modern pathogen, *Yersinia pestis*, and that the causative agent must have been some ancestor that is now extinct or has evolved. Perhaps further scientific study will yield final conclusive answers as to the precise nature of the disease that devastated Europe in the Middle Ages. In the meantime, the debate has important implications for considerations of the human experience of the plague. In particular, the observations of contemporary chroniclers regarding the highly contagious nature of the epidemic, its rapid transmission and the huge numbers of people it killed are now increasingly being accepted as valid, where formerly they were dismissed as apocalyptic metaphors or the fabrications of innumerate men. Whatever its precise cause may have been, the outbreak of the Black Death is still considered to be one of the most significant events in the Middle Ages, and the weight of opinion has once again shifted to those historians who claim the Black Death was a crucial event in medieval history, causing a mortality of up to 50% in many countries. And with contemporary historians such as Herlihy pronouncing the Black Death to be the great watershed in the development of Western Europe, and Gottfried calling it 'the greatest biological-environmental event in human history', the pendulum of historical opinion has swung completely back again.[5]

The study of the social and economic history of medieval Ireland is hampered by the sparseness of source material, thanks in large measure to the destruction of the Public Record Office in Dublin in 1922 and to the neglect of medieval documentation until the later nineteenth century, when calendars and lists of documents were compiled and published. Sources for Gaelic Ireland are very scarce and while those for the Anglo-Irish colony are somewhat more plentiful, they do not compare with those available for England and the continent. Wills, rentals, records of entry fines, of transfers of land or of institutions to benefices, all of which historians in England and in continental Europe have effectively used to calculate plague mortality, at least among certain groups and in certain areas, are in Ireland either non-existent or totally inadequate. English historians such as Titow could rely on comprehensive account rolls such as those for the estates of the See of Winchester in their study of the plague's effects on the rural economy. Ireland does not have complete runs of manorial accounts and those that survive are quite limited, since they cover only the Irish estates of landowners resident in England. Moreover, like English manorial accounts, they are concerned principally with recording the profits and losses of the landowners and offer only very indirect information on the tenants or other people living on the estates. Nevertheless, through the painstaking trawling of surviving manorial and taxation records, much work has been done in recent years on records from the royal manors in Dublin and from the de Burgh/Clare and Ormond estates. Archaeological investigation has also done much to help reconstruct the late medieval period in Ireland, though as with the written records, evidence is particularly scarce for the later fourteenth century and much evidence is buried under modern towns and suburbs. Finally, dendochronological studies have shown that the environmental effect of the Black Death in Ireland was not inconsiderable: oak forests regenerated in the later fourteenth century, a process that can be explained only by a reduction in population.[6] Alas, however, the trees yield few further clues.

In evaluating the plague's effects and in re-enacting responses to it, historians elsewhere could always rely on contemporary chroniclers such as Boccaccio, Gilbert Li Muisis, Knighton, and many others who in varying degrees of detail describe the symptoms and progress of plague and the reactions it provoked. In fact, historians' treatment of the plague has, in the absence of other data, often been determined by the chroniclers' details. Irish annalists and chroniclers, however, give little information and this too has influenced much writing about the Black Death in Ireland, leading some to argue that the plague did not have the same effect in Ireland as elsewhere. Most of the Gaelic annals, though based on still-extant contemporary material, were not compiled until the sixteenth or seventeenth centuries and therefore do not have the vividness of the first-hand observer. Moreover, they generally are rather narrowly focused on particular areas, especially the north-west, where they were mostly compiled, and on ecclesiastical matters, reflecting the biases of their monastic compilers. The Black Death is reported merely in a succinct entry:

The great plague of the general pestilence that was throughout Ireland in Moy Luirg this year, so that a great number of people were destroyed by it (*In pláidh mór in galair coiteann do bí ar fud Eirinn a Magh Luirg in bliain sin co tucada ar mór daoine inntí*).

The plague is mentioned in the *Annals of Clonmacnoise* and in *Miscellaneous Irish Annals* in 1348 and in the *Annals of Connacht, Ulster* and *The Four Masters* in 1349, but the fact that the entry is virtually the same in all of them suggests the use of a common source, situated perhaps in the vicinity of Moylurg, Co. Roscommon.

The Anglo-Irish chroniclers offer more detail, but still nothing like the comprehensive coverage offered by contemporary chroniclers elsewhere. The *Chronicle of Pembridge* breaks off in the middle of the entries for 1347 with a parting, 'Here ends the Chronicle of Pembridge'. The *Annals of New Ross* end in 1346 and the *Annals of Nenagh* offer but a brief entry about the Black Death. John Clyn, a Franciscan friar from Kilkenny, gives us the only first-hand account we have of the plague in Ireland, yet his record, *Annals of Ireland,* finishes in 1349 on his own dramatically appropriate death, most likely of plague, which is noted by another hand in the laconic sentence, 'Here it seems that the author died'. Ecclesiastical records are equally scant. There are no extant episcopal registers for mid-fourteenth-century Ireland and very few documents of cathedral chapters. Fortunately, the chartularies and registers of some monastic houses have survived and offer some information on the period, though again they are often incomplete – the manorial documents from the Augustinian Priory of the Holy Trinity at Christ Church, Dublin, for example, end in 1346. *The Papal Registers of Letters* and of *Petitions* furnish some evidence of the effects of the plague on the church, though this record is not always complete.

Do literature and art yield any clues? One would wish for more help here, but surviving medieval literature, whether in Irish, English, Norman-French or Latin yields little information about the details of daily life. Very little survives of medieval decorative arts in Ireland, thanks to confiscations during the Reformation, war and various natural disasters. Medieval effigies, for example, which elsewhere have so often offered insight, are very scarce and most of those that have survived are military effigies.[7]

The historiography of the Black Death thus encapsulates all of the difficulties facing historians of the Middle Ages, whether in Ireland or elsewhere. The lack of explicit evidence is often frustrating for those seeking to re-enact the socio-economic world of fourteenth-century Ireland. However, medical science offers a source of non-historical knowledge which can be used to shed significant light on historical events. In this instance, it often enables one to see new significance in the observations of the chroniclers or a pattern in the plague's incidence that before had seemed inexplicable. The history of the rat, the flea and bacillus and an understanding of the plague's distribution patterns help to clarify the broad progress of the plague in Europe, but also the variations in its incidence and effects in individual countries. To understand the Black Death's progress then, we need to look first not at its victims, but at the bacillus that has traditionally been taken as the cause of plague and at its carriers, the flea and the rat.[8]

Plague has been for long widely accepted as a disease of wild rodents, which in western Europe happened to be the black rat or *Rattus rattus*. However, contemporary observers of the Black Death did not make any connection between rats and human illness.[9] Only with the scientific revolution of the seventeenth century and the discovery of the notion of germ theory were scientists led to some understanding of the plague. In 1894, Dr Alexander Yersin, a student at the Pasteur Institute, and Dr Shiba Saburo Kitasato discovered the bacillus that causes plague, subsequently named *Pasteurella pestis* or in more recent literature, *Yersinia pestis*. Then, in 1896 Dr Paul Simond identified the principal carrier of the bacillus from rats to humans, the rat-flea species known as the *Xenopsylla cheopis*. The human flea, *Pulex irritans*, can also be a carrier, but its effectiveness as a vector is debated. Thus the chain of transmission from rat to flea to human was mapped.

For reasons not fully understood, the bacilli multiply in the infected rodent's blood and are then passed into the digestive system of the flea feeding on the animal, forming a solid mass which blocks the flea's alimentary canals. The result is a hungry flea that has to regurgitate the bacilli into the blood stream of its host before it can begin to feed. When the infected rat dies of plague, the displaced flea, which itself remains immune, either goes into hibernation or finds another host. Rodent burrows provide the perfect hibernating environment for the plague bacillus where it can survive for at least six months, sometimes for years, even after the death of the rodent hosts. The displaced, infectious flea can also hibernate in grain or soft materials, such as wool, for up to three months and more. It finds its most ready – though not its only – host in burrowing rodents, such as rats. The black rat is semi-parasitic on the human population and burrows near grain reserves, in human dwellings or in ships. Humans are not the preferred hosts for rat fleas, but given the proximity of the black rat and the human populations, they are often the most accessible and are chosen only when all other possible hosts are dead. The transmission of the plague bacillus to humans then is an anomaly in that plague is a disease of rodents and their fleas, and humans enter the cycle only by chance. Finally, transmission to humans occurs either through a flea bite or else through contamination of skin abrasions. There is some evidence that it can also be transmitted by eating infected substances, such as infected wild animals, but this theory is not universally accepted.

The bacillus is transmitted over wide areas by the passive transport of the rat and flea, since the black rat is very sedentary and rarely travels from village to village or port to port. Ships carrying grain or cloth brought infected rats into the ports of Europe, and infected fleas travelled most likely in the merchandise of merchants and mariners. Another possible means of transmission was that as the black rat was carried into sea ports and market towns, its plague-bearing fleas may have also been transmitted to the brown or field rat (*Rattus norvegicus*) which dwells in fields and rural areas and can travel long distances, thereby carrying the bacillus further inland. Generally, brown rats could remain infected for up to ten years, though infected black rats died off more quickly. This time lag may explain the phenomenon so common in Ireland, as elsewhere, of certain areas being severely affected, while other areas escaped until some years later.

Finally, the extent of the plague's transmission was determined by the strains of the pathogen that dominated. There are three main forms: the bubonic, the pneumonic and the extremely rare form, the septicaemic. Most experts claim that the bubonic and pneumonic forms raged together in Europe in 1348, at least in the opening stages. Since pneumonic plague cannot survive long on its own, the bubonic form dominates. Bubonic plague is a contagion, is normally transmitted by the bite of an infected flea and rarely spreads directly between humans. Pneumonic plague is an infection of the lungs caused by the direct transmission of bacilli from an infected human to another primarily by airborne droplets, though contamination can also occur by inhaling the faeces of an infected flea. It would seem to occur only in cold weather. The septicaemic form is transmitted by a flea bite directly into the bloodstream, causing death within a few hours, without any symptoms. This form can also be transmitted very effectively by the human flea, *Pulex irritans*. However, since this form is so rare, it was not a significant factor in determining mortality.

The other two forms of plague differ significantly. Bubonic plague affects the lymphatic system first and is recognisable by painful swellings or buboes (usually only one) in the groin, armpits and upper neck, a sudden chill, a prickling sensation, hallucinations and delirium. Death occurs within a week for between 50% and 80% of those infected – the death rate is higher if infection occurs in the early stages of the outbreak. There is weighty epidemiological evidence that when plague invades virgin territory, it is particularly virulent and is apt to appear in its pneumonic form, at least in the first two or three months.[10] Since pneumonic plague attacks the lungs, its symptoms are expectoration, especially the spitting up of blood; death occurs within two to three days and case mortality is approximately 96%.

There are also significant variations in the transmission patterns of the two forms. In general, the distribution of bubonic plague in the human population is slow, as it depends on the prior infection of fleas by rats. This process in turn is influenced by the density of the rat and flea populations. Cold weather slows its rate of transmission, since the black rat needs warmth, the rat flea needs temperatures between 15°

and 20°C and the bacillus thrives in temperatures of about 25°. Furthermore, the flea needs relatively high humidity, between 90% and 95%, to propagate. Therefore, spring and early summer or late summer/early autumn were the times when it was at its most severe in Europe. However, bubonic plague can also be transmitted by the human flea which thrives in cold weather. Further, pneumonic plague and the very rare septicaemic form are not dependent on rat and flea density, but are dependent on certain environmental and climatic conditions and on a high degree of infection among humans. These forms are far more virulent and rapid, have a much higher infection rate and thrive in colder, damper climates. Accordingly, the accounts of many contemporary chroniclers emphasising the suddenness of some deaths and the wet weather are substantiated by what we have come to know about the epidemiology of plague and its variant forms.

Despite the increasing body of medical knowledge concerning the plague, there remains a number of contentious issues that further complicate any detailed analysis of historical sources.

Why the plague should have broken out at all is one issue. In Mongolia and Central Asia, where the bacillus had been endemic for centuries, people had protected themselves against the marmots (the flea carriers in those regions), and therefore survived even in the midst of the disease.[11] Ecological changes probably helped to disturb that balance. One theory holds that earthquakes, extremely dry weather in Mongolia, an increase in the rodent population and various other ecological changes disturbed the delicate balance between man and rodent, and caused the massive migration of infected rodents into regions closer to human settlements. This theory finds curious parallels in the work of contemporary chroniclers who also attribute the outbreak of plague to ecological disturbances, which they describe in somewhat apocalyptic terms. Louis Heyligen, a Flemish musician in Avignon, for instance, reported that the outbreak of the plague was preceded by first a shower of frogs, snakes, lizards and other poisonous animals, then huge, man-killing hailstones and finally flames of fire from the heavens. Today, some scientists suggest a relationship between the life cycles of rat colonies and sunspots determined the outbreak, that sunspots are linked with the fertility of rats and hence with that of fleas, though others deny any cyclic component in rats' biology.[12]

Why did the plague spread so quickly? Answers vary. Clearly changes in human commercial behaviour and improvements in the technology of transportation were partly responsible and led to what biologists call the microbial unification of the world. Ironically, the developments in trade that accounted for so much of the dynamism of the high Middle Ages were also the channels by which the plague entered and spread throughout Europe, helping to bring about the end of its booming growth. Another factor is that plague in the fourteenth century would seem to have been far more virulent than later outbreaks, as all epidemics tend to be when introduced into virgin territory. A final argument often proposed is that the plague spread quickly because the two variants, the bubonic and the extremely infectious pneumonic strains raged alongside each other in fourteenth-century Europe. This theory is not accepted by all experts, however, and some deny that the pneumonic variant could have caused the rapid infection evident in 1348-49.[13] However, contemporary chroniclers, including Ireland's Friar Clyn, clearly describe symptoms such as the coughing of blood that are peculiar to the pneumonic form of plague.

Expert opinion is even more divided on the issue of rat and human population density. The size of the rat population is an important factor in the spread of bubonic plague, as the density of the rat population generally follows the patterns of human population density. The historian of the plague, J.F. Shrewsbury emphasises that for an epidemic to develop it is necessary that 'the rodent must be present in such numbers that the density of the rat population is high enough to enable *P. pestis* to be distributed rapidly over the area of the epidemic by haphazard rat-contacts.' He adds that

> the distribution and density of the rat population governs the distribution and intensity of the human disease, and the rodent density is decisive because no serious outbreak of bubonic plague can take place in a locality supporting only a small or widely dispersed rat population.[14]

In his study of the Black Death, the zoologist Graham Twigg agrees, yet he emphasises the necessity of a concentration not only of rats but also fleas. Studies on the plague in Britain in the seventeenth and eighteenth centuries have also emphasised the importance of rat density. Because the plague affected some houses in a particular area and not others, and because mortality and household size were not always related, one researcher concluded that 'the frequency of human contact was much less significant than the numbers and movements of rodents carrying infection'.[15]

Others argue that the density of rats is not the dominating factor, as the transmission of plague to humans is dependent not on rats but on fleas, and that infected fleas carried in merchandise or food were and are the most effective vectors of plague.[16] In this case, transmission is determined by the extent and frequency of human contacts and communications. Moreover, though plague is initially transmitted only by fleas from infected rats, as the disease becomes established in the human population, given the right climatic and environmental conditions, direct transmission between humans can also occur. If, as some medical historians have argued, the plague can also be transmitted by the human flea, *Pulex irritans,* then transmission is even easier. The human flea can greatly accelerate transmission, as its range is not restricted by established trading routes and by the rat's preferred habitats: unlike the rat-borne flea, *Pulex irritans* can spread disease wherever its human host goes. Such a method of transmission could help explain why the plague moved rapidly through some sparsely populated regions. However, most evidence suggests that the human flea is not an effective carrier, except in the case of the septicaemic strain, and that this form of transmission was very rare.

In general then, population density was the major factor in the rapid transmission of plague, whatever its form. Nevertheless, it was not the sole determining factor and the issue of population density is not a clear-cut one. It would seem that settlements did not need to be large, but had to be clustered, and distances between settlements had to be traversible in medieval terms. However, complications remain, given the many instances of high mortality in sparsely populated areas:

Iceland experienced mortality in the region of 60%; the Scottish Highlands, a very sparsely populated region, was severely affected while densely populated Flanders escaped lightly. The plague spared some crowded urban centres like Milan and Ghent, while ravaging sparsely populated areas like Sardinia and Languedoc.[17]

A significant body of recent research has focused on the influence of climatic factors. Some experts, such as Shrewsbury and Twigg, have argued that the climate in most of England, and by extension Ireland, would have been too cold to permit the spread of plague fleas. However, some recent studies on climate point to a warming trend developing during the plague years. While the 1330s and 1340s were a time of generally colder and wetter weather, there is some evidence that in 1348-50 the warming winds of El Niño in Europe could have created higher than normal temperatures and more than normal rainfall even during the winter months. This would have created the optimal conditions for the rapid transmission of the bacillus: the rat flea prefers temperatures of 15° and 20°C with very high humidity and is killed by humidity under 70%. This theory adds new significance to the comments of so many contemporary chroniclers from Friar John Clyn in Ireland to Gilbert Li Muisis in Flanders and the Paris Medical Faculty, who all explicitly noted the temperate, wet weather during the years of the plague. Gilbert Li Muisis commented on the oddness of the winter when, as he put it, '…there was not so much ice as would support the weight of a goose,' yet so much rain that rivers burst their banks and 'meadows became seas'. The Paris Medical Faculty in its report on the plague in October 1348 also commented on the unseasonable weather: a mild winter, a windy and wet spring, a changeable summer and throughout all the seasons excessive rain leading to pestilential air, which it considered the cause of the plague.[18] Climatic studies have thus enabled historians to recognise the significance of what otherwise seem like the tangential observations of medieval chroniclers.

Mortality is another contentious issue: why did the huge numbers attested by the chroniclers die? Many factors determine mortality: the extent of exposure to infection, which is influenced by population density, public health, sanitation, and living standards; resistance to infection which can be influenced by nutrition levels, immunity and medical knowledge; and finally, the virulence and frequency of the pathogen which is affected by climate, as well as a host of other biological and zoological factors. Epidemiologists are not in agreement about the significance of any of these factors, some even arguing that diseases, like the Black Death, which are spread by animals have little to do with human behaviour and depend solely on exogenous factors such as climate and rodent life patterns. According to this view, the Black Death was completely independent of the human environment: as the demographic historian Livi-Bacci puts it,

> The ability of the plague to infect and kill bore no relation to one's state of health, age, or level of nutrition. It struck urban and rural populations with equal violence, and with the exception of a few isolated areas, density levels presented no obstacle to its spread.[19]

Other researchers look to the human factor to try to explain patterns of mortality and focus especially on living conditions. Clearly, overcrowding is connected with the higher mortality rates in towns than in rural areas. Some argue that the lack of sanitation in cities contributed to greater morbidity and point to the fact that improved public health in later centuries was crucial in bringing about the disappearance of plague in Europe. Others argue that sanitary measures are effective only against water and food-borne micro-organisms such as cholera.[20] Yet, this argument does not explain why some towns were affected and others not. Both Milan and Florence adopted some public health measures in 1348, yet Milan escaped with a mortality of only about 15% while Florence lost over 50% of its population.

Nutrition is another factor that has inspired an array of arguments. Prolonged malnutrition has clear connections with population levels. First, it causes amenorrhoea with all its consequences for fertility. Malnutrition is also connected in complex ways with higher mortality levels, though epidemiologists are not unanimous on the precise details. Some argue that malnutrition of the sort to be expected from the monoculture of medieval agriculture causes anaemias and a short-age of constituents in the blood that protect against infectious disease, including plague:

> Prolonged malnutrition heightens the chances of epidemics breaking out, infectious diseases take a heavier toll. This is the explanation of the havoc wrought by the Black Death and other epidemics of the four-teenth century.[21]

Food shortages also increase children's susceptibility to disease, since low body-weight increases susceptibility to diarrhoea which gradually undermines resistance to infection.[22] Moreover, severe malnutrition, such as in famine, can inhibit the proper biological development of children's immune systems. Dr W. Jordan in his study, *The Great Famine,* posits the hypothesis that at the time of the Black Death, those adults who had been young children during the famine years of 1315–18 were more susceptible to the plague than those who had been adults during the famine, or who had grown up earlier or later, in more prosperous times. The nutritionally induced immune prob-lems of adults who had suffered famine as children may have contributed to the high plague mortality thirty years later, Jordan argues. By contrast, the relatively low plague mortality in areas like Flanders may be explained by the fact that there, the famine of 1315–18 had claimed large numbers of children, so that those who were adults during the plague years would have been born later and there-fore would have been more able to resist the plague.[23] Records from some well-documented manors in England would seem to support this theory: on Halesowen manor near Birmingham, for example, mortality from the outbreak of 1348 was highest in the 30–59 age group, that is the group that would have been children in 1315, whereas those under 20 were hardly affected.[24] Other studies, while accepting that prolonged nutritional deficiency predisposes individu-als to disease, contend that plague is one of the infectious bacterial diseases that is only slightly influenced by nutritional status. Yet others argue, exactly opposite to Jordan, that malnutrition can actually help protect against disease.[25] In the end, definitive conclusions about the link between nutrition and plague mortality are not possible in view of the questions that have been raised about the nature of the bacillus that caused the Black Death.

Clearly, the fact that Europe was virgin territory contributed to its virulence. There is also evidence that the medieval plague was more morbid than later outbreaks, due probably to genetic changes in the bacillus.[26] But given its virulence, with a morbidity between 40-60%, why then did some people survive the plague and why were some areas not affected? As the historian R. Fossier writes: 'one has the feeling that the occasions when the plague failed to devastate rather than when it succeeded would explain its progress better'.[27] Bio-geography suggests some hypotheses. Sections of the population may have acquired genetic protection from Justinian's Plague centuries before. Others suggest that some people are naturally resistant because they are not liable to flea bites. In this vein, some scientists speculate that blood type may also play a part, with populations with a high percentage of blood group O, such as in Central Europe, being relatively spared.[28] Some argue that the disappearance of the plague in the seventeenth century was due to the build-up of immunity among the rodent and human population, and that survivors of the plague built up significant resistance. On the other hand, others question whether any immunity to plague is possible, and assert that survivors of the plague can at best acquire only short-term immunity. Many other theories also abound: that the plague flea is repelled by the smell of certain animals like horses, sheep and goats and by certain oils like olive and nut oils.[29]

Finally, and on this issue almost all historians are unanimous: the mortality caused by the Black Death must be seen in the context of the recurring outbreaks of plague. Because plague is a pandemic, it strikes in cyclic fashion, returning at least once every generation. The plague of 1348, therefore, was not an isolated incident and was part of a sequence of plague outbreaks throughout the next century. It returned in 1361 and periodically thereafter, every five to twelve years until it finally disappeared in the late seventeenth century. This recurrence was a crucial factor in determining demographic trends and, along with declining fertility, helps to account for the demographic slump that continued into the next century.[30]

Integrating historical details with scientific knowledge is not a straightforward task, given the sporadic nature of historical sources, the fact that data about modern outbreaks do not always apply to the medieval plague which was far more virulent than latter-day outbreaks, and the fact that despite gains in scientific knowledge, even still 'little is known of the biological and genetic determinants of exposure and resistance to disease'.[31] Still, whatever the biological and zoological details, the effect on the human population of widespread mortality remains undisputed. Or, to put it in a demographer's terms, exogenous occurrences provoke endogenous responses. It will be the varied endogenous, human responses that will occupy the rest of this study.

The plague's contours followed the history and geography of the countries it affected, even though certain patterns and responses were similar all over Europe. Thus the history of the Black Death in Ireland takes on a character peculiar to the Irish situation at the time. The later medieval period in Ireland is not an easy one to read as military, economic and political developments are inextricably intertwined. Constant warfare is a leitmotif throughout this whole period as a beleaguered administration in Dublin strove to retain its hold on the Anglo-Irish colony in Ireland and as Anglo-Irish and Gaelic-Irish lords tussled for control. As the fourteenth century progressed, a welter of events propelled the colony towards decline: warfare, the Bruce Invasion in 1315, the increasing fragmentation of political authority, a sequence of climatic disasters, famines and economic recession. The 1330s and 1340s in particular saw an intensification of what has been traditionally termed the 'Gaelic Resurgence'. The Black Death was a fitting part of this continuum, marking neither its beginning nor its end.

In the succeeding chapters I will examine the different contexts of the plague in Ireland. First, I will consider the factors governing the transmission of the plague to Ireland and around the country, both in rural and urban areas, in the Anglo-Irish colony and in Gaelic areas. I will then map the known progress of the plague and consider its overall impact on the country's population. Then, since the immediate effect of the plague was a psychological one, I will consider what we know of people's reactions to the plague as expressed in their daily, non-working lives. The next two chapters focus on how the plague affected the rhythms of life and work in rural areas and in the towns and cities of Ireland. However, since records for Gaelic Ireland are so scant, these chapters will perforce concentrate more on the colony of Ireland and the feudal economy. The Church played an important role in medieval Ireland and its records, being more extensive, offer us further clues as to how the ecclesiastical establishment, secular and regular as well as lay, responded to this incursion of sudden and inescapable death. In the final chapter, I consider the possible effect of the Black Death on the changing political and military situation of the Anglo-Irish colony and Gaelic Ireland.

The effects of the Black Death were manifold but, given the sparse sources, they elude quantification. Nor is it easy to disentangle the effects of plague from those of warfare. In fact, its survivors didn't distinguish between them either: time and again in contemporary records 'war and pestilence' are cited in tandem as the causes of the troubles in late medieval Ireland. The many changes cannot be attributed to the plague alone; it was one of many factors at play. This is not to downgrade the importance of the plague but rather to see it in its proper context, not as a phenomenon divorced from local conditions, but as one which, though characterised by general biological and medical characteristics, nevertheless played out differently in different places, depending on local geographical, political, economic and social conditions. In Ireland it helped intensify processes already in process, and its aftershocks were felt long after the terror it first inspired had faded away.

The Coming of the Black Death to Ireland

Plague was not unknown in early medieval Ireland. The nature of these 'plagues', however, is a matter of some conjecture, since plague or in Irish *pláig* was a non-specific term. Sometimes the cause was smallpox, sometimes jaundice, known as the *buídhe chonaill*. In 545 the *Annals of Ulster* recorded a plague which it called 'blefed'. Its noble victims included three kings, an abbot and a saint, together with many other princes, bishops and abbots. In the seventh century, a wave of pestilences swept the country which have been linked to the outbreak of bubonic plague in Europe in 540, known as 'Justinian's Plague'.[1] There were recurrent outbreaks throughout the century and it then seems to have abated. Later, 'pestilences' were more likely outbreaks of other diseases, though the mortality was still noteworthy. In AD 1094, for example, an unprecedented pestilence is recorded which carried off many nobles 'with infinite numbers of the meaner sort'. In 1116, there was

> a great famine and pestilence in the half of Mogh among Leinstermen and Munstermen, so that it desolated churches and forts and districts and spread throughout Ireland and over sea and caused destruction to an inconceivable degree.

Pestilences are again recorded in 1271 and periodically until 1317, when there:

…came a marvellous plague unto Ulster upon the Scots, which did prey and did much exceeding hurt in Ireland.

The effects of this 'hurt' are graphically recorded:

for a very vengeance men did eat flesh in Lent without need. Therefore, God sent a great plague upon them, which was that one did eat another, so that of ten thousand men there remained but a few.[2]

However, bubonic plague returned, though that of 1348 was of a different order. Linguistic usage reflects the history: in Irish, it was referred to as *an pláig mór*, or in English 'the great plague' or 'great pestilence'.

The story of the plague's transmission to and general devastation of Western Europe is well known.[3] The outbreak of 1348 would seem to have originated in the Yunan peninsula of China and in the steppes of Central Asia and Mongolia, where *Yersinia pestis* is endemic. Epidemics usually follow commercial trade routes, and the Black Death was no exception. With the opening up of trade routes in the East the bacillus was brought westward to the Eurasian steppes. This could have happened in two ways. The bacilli may have been carried by infected rats who travelled in ships or migrated overland towards Central Asia, then moved inland and burrowed near human habitations, especially in places where grain and cloth were stored. Alternatively, bacillus-laden fleas travelled in the merchandise of Mongol nomads from Eastern into Central Asia in the late 1320s. The disease then spread from Central Asia to the Black Sea and Southern Russia in 1345-6. From there it travelled over land or by sea to the Crimea and then, according to some sources, in Genoese trading vessels from the port of Caffa in the Crimea to Italy and Egypt in 1347, though other routes were also very likely. It then spread rapidly.

The opening up of trade throughout Europe in the medieval period meant that even the most remote parts had become part of a single disease pool. Once the plague had reached Europe, its progress was steady and rapid: spread over sea and land, along the trading routes, it reached Sicily in October 1347 and Marseilles and other Mediterranean ports by December of the same year. From there it spread westwards to Bordeaux, and north to Paris and the northern French coast. It quickly spread through France, Italy, Austria, Switzerland, Southern Germany and the Netherlands. From either the Bordeaux area or from Calais, the plague travelled in ships to Southern England around the end of June 1348, with Melcombe Regis (Weymouth) on the south-west coast, Southampton and Bristol named as the points of entry. It had reached Bristol by mid-August. By November, it had swept through the south-western counties, as far east as London. By February or March 1349 it had reached Cornwall and South Wales.[4] Ireland was struck at about the same time as Bristol, probably in July or early August 1348.

The Transmission of the Plague
Strong trading links between Ireland and the ports on the western coast of England, especially Bristol, as well as with south-west France and the Low Countries, meant that the plague would inevitably filter into Ireland. Overseas trade, principally in grain and wool, was concentrated in the eastern and southern ports, particularly in New Ross, Waterford, Cork, Drogheda, Dublin and Youghal.[5] New Ross was the main centre for the trade in grain, thanks to its location on the Barrow and Suir rivers which offered easy access to the manors of the south-east. However, considerable business was carried on in all the ports from Carrickfergus in the north to Kinsale in the south, since Ireland was a valuable source of provisions for the king's army in the Scottish and French wars. Drogheda, Cork and Youghal purveyed to the King's armies in Scotland, Wales and Gascony as well as to England, the Low Countries and France. In addition, there was a certain amount of direct import and export trade with Spain, Portugal, Bordeaux, Gascony and Flanders through ports such as Dublin, Waterford, Youghal, and Cork. Archaeological investigations have revealed contacts with many areas of England and Europe: excavations at Trim Castle, Co. Meath, at Wood Quay in Dublin, and

in Cork city for example, have unearthed shards of pottery imported from Bristol and from North-Western France.[6]

Summer was undoubtedly the period of briskest trade, when weather and maritime conditions would have been most favourable to shipping; this is also the period when bubonic plague is at its most virulent. Consequently, given a raging epidemic on the continent and in England, it was inevitable that *Yersinia pestis* would have been conveyed to Ireland in the strongholds of trading vessels or in the goods of merchants. According to Friar Clyn, it reached Ireland in July or early August 1348, entering through ports on the east coast. It had reached Bristol at the earliest on 24 June and at the latest on 1 August. The close timing between its arrival in Bristol and in Dublin and Drogheda suggests that the plague could have been brought to Ireland directly from the continent. Whether or not it also entered through ports in the south and south-east we don't know, but trading contacts were such that it could have. How it spread from these ports and why it spread as it did is a rather complex subject.

Once in port, the black rat abandons the ships and burrows in the port areas. Or, if the infected fleas are man-carried, the fleas quickly move into the local colonies of rats, their natural hosts, and transmit the bacillus to the rats. This process may take only up to two weeks. However, it is very likely that the plague in Ireland assumed a pneumonic form, possibly in the autumn months, and both strains of the plague, the bubonic and pneumonic, seem to have existed simultaneously. Friar Clyn's graphic description of plague deaths in Ireland incorporates the symptoms of both forms: he describes the eruptions on the groin or under the armpit characteristic of bubonic plague, but also the headaches and spitting of blood that distinguish pneumonic plague. We know from other sources that 1348 was particularly wet and cool, therefore presenting the conditions conducive to pneumonia and pneumonic plague. Epidemiological evidence, as we have seen, indicates that plague in invading virgin territory often assumes its pneumonic form and is particularly virulent, at least in the first months. Moreover, pneumonic plague is highly infectious and is transmitted directly between humans. This too is described by Clyn:

the pestilence was so contagious that whosoever touched the sick or the dead was immediately infected and died, so that penitent and confessor were carried together to the grave.

Transmission by direct contact was quite likely then in Dublin and Drogheda in the first more virulent phases of the plague's outbreak in Ireland. As it moved beyond these first stages out to the surrounding countryside, it is not likely that it continued in its pneumonic form, especially once it moved away from the larger towns and areas of densest settlement. Its transmission to the rest of the country would have mainly depended on a creeping epizootic of rat and flea contacts, which in turn would have been dependent on the density of the rat and flea populations. These in turn were contingent on the density of the human population and, more important, on the frequency and extent of trading and other contacts between different areas.

As happened throughout Europe, the plague was most likely spread by infected fleas travelling in merchandise or by infected rats and their fleas travelling in cargo boats. The paths of transmission were along the overland routes between the ports and market towns and villages, along the rivers connecting market towns and seaports especially in the east and south, and by sea-traffic between ports on the east and south coasts. Clearly, Dublin and Drogheda formed one nucleus of the disease. Whether the disease spread from there overland to the rest of the country is a debatable point. Given the rapidity with which the plague moved in Ireland, in the opening months at least, and the general slowness of overland travel, it is quite likely that the plague was introduced into the south directly from England or the continent through the trading activities of ports such as Waterford, Youghal and Cork. But in the hinterland of these ports, particularly in the more heavily settled parts of the east and south, transmission could have occurred along overland routes between towns and villages, since the distances were not great. That there were many and frequent contacts is clear from contemporary evidence. Medieval communications were governed by the needs of daily life, war and trade, administration and not least by pilgrimages. Most particularly, the outbreak of a plague without known cause or cure led many to go on pilgrimage. Friar Clyn writes that the onset of plague brought on pilgrimage

> from divers parts of Ireland, bishops and prelates, churchmen and religious, lords and others, and commonly all persons of both sexes… in troops and multitudes, so that you could see many thousands there at the same time for many days together.[7]

Such excursions, of course, as we know from elsewhere in Europe, acted as ideal occasions for the transmission of plague.

There was, moreover, considerable contact through trade, both coastal and overland. Much of the trade was in grain and wool, perfect habitats for the plague-carrying fleas and their rat hosts. There was constant shipping from Dublin to northern ports and to southern ports such as Youghal, Waterford and Cork. Navigable rivers also would have acted as the principal means of cargo transport. By the fourteenth century trade had reached deep, though unevenly, into the hinterland, extending particularly along the Barrow, Suir and Slaney rivers to the great manors of eastern Leinster, and along the Blackwater and the Lee rivers to the southern hinterland. It is very probable, for example, that river-traffic on the Barrow brought the plague inland to parts of Leinster, such as Kilkenny. However, within particular regions, plague travelled along overland routes. There was a well-established and often-used system of roads. Three roads are known to have emanated from Leinster: a highway from Dublin through Thomastown to Kilkenny, a royal road passing through Kells in Co. Kilkenny and another through Athy into Munster. Another well-established route linked Cork city and Kilmallock in Co. Limerick.[8] Merchants travelled the country plying their wares in the many markets held in even the most remote parts of Ireland, though the densest concentration was in the eastern and southern regions. A selection of references will indicate how widespread the market system was: annual fairs in Kilmallock, Adare, Waterford, Dublin…; weekly markets in Ballymore-Eustace, Drogheda, in various places in counties Meath and Louth, in Buttevant, Co. Cork, in Irystown near

Kilkenny. There is also evidence of marketing circuits within the colony: in certain areas markets rotated between different boroughs on different days, so that there would have been considerable travelling by traders between these markets.[9] Distances between these markets would not have been much more than the twenty-five miles that has been calculated as the distance of an average day's journey in fourteenth-century England, itself a very conservative estimate.[10] Moreover, normal manorial business required frequent journeys to all parts of the country: records for the manor of Duleek, Co. Meath in 1351-52, for example, mention journeys to Kilkenny and Dundalk on 'the lord's business'. Considerable travelling must have been occasioned by the administration of the scattered estates of the larger abbeys; to cite just one instance, the Hospital of St John of Jerusalem in Dublin had property in Kildare, Wexford, Meath, Down, Waterford, Cork, Limerick, Galway, Carlow, Louth, Tipperary and Sligo.[11]

While rivers, roads and fairs all contributed to the spread of plague, its progress was not unhindered. First, stretches of unpopulated marshland, bog and forest acted as effective barriers against the spread of epidemic activity. Most notably, the Bog of Allen would have effectively hindered the overland dispersion of the plague from Leinster to the south. Approximately 15%-20% of medieval Ireland was forested. Moreover, the Anglo-Irish colonists were concentrated mostly in land below 600 feet, leaving mountainous and hilly areas to the Gaelic-Irish.[12] This may be one of the explanations why the Gaelic-Irish population, which lived largely on more hilly land and in less accessible regions, was spared the worst effects of this outbreak of the plague. Other places would have been spared thanks to the effects of warfare, particularly from 1315 onwards, which hindered travel and with it the transmission of plague. To illustrate the precariousness of the times: in 1311 the Mayor of Waterford was allowed to take the oath of office in his home town rather than travel to Dublin as had been the custom hitherto, because of the hazardous nature of the journey; in 1340, merchants were afraid to travel in Co. Kilkenny and there are numerous other contemporary references to the dangers of overland travel from the south to Dublin.[13] Records such as these suggest that travel between certain areas had become restricted in the decades just preceding the Black Death. This factor would have limited the transmission of infected fleas and again could help account for what seems like the uneven nature of the plague's incidence in some areas. Because river traffic wasn't similarly affected, it is even more likely to have been the route of the plague's transmission in the south and south-east.

Factors Governing the Incidence of Plague

The issue of rat and population density is, as already noted, a contentious issue in the literature on the Black Death. Evidence from modern outbreaks indicates that the incidence of the bubonic strain of plague was, above all, determined by population density and insofar as that density was uneven, so was the incidence of plague. There are no reliable figures for the population density necessary to sustain an epidemic of plague. J.F. Shrewsbury calculated that population density in England in 1348 was at most sixty-nine persons to the square mile, and that there were large areas of the country where both the human and rat population density was too low to allow for an epizootic of rat-plague on a countrywide scale. Local concentrations of house-rats could have allowed for localised epizootics and local epidemics, but only towns provided a sufficiently large population of rats to allow for dangerous epizootics of rat-plague to develop. However, he insisted that the long distances between such urban settlements, whether large or small, would not have allowed for the plague's transmission over wide areas. Shrewsbury's arguments were based solely on his theories regarding the aetiology of bubonic plague and not all experts agree. He ignores the incidence of pneumonic plague, minimizes the role of the flea in favour of the rat and does not accept the possibility of the human flea as vector. Recent historical studies have shown that, in fact, during the Black Death, counties in England with densities as low as nineteen persons per square mile were severely affected, and parts of the very sparsely populated Scottish Highlands suffered as high a mortality as more densely populated areas in lowland

England.[14] Such variations may be attributed to many causes, including the virulence of the medieval plague, its transmission by human flea, or to the possibility that the pneumonic strain dominated here. Moreover, settlement in these areas, though sparse, was clustered, and the distances between these settlements were short enough to permit the quite rapid transportation of infected fleas.

These notable variations have to be borne in mind in looking at the plague in Ireland, where population density was extremely uneven and where settlement patterns varied from region to region. Settlement generally in medieval Ireland was likely much more dispersed than in England and continental countries, and differed radically between Gaelic Ireland and the Anglo-Irish colony.[15] Simply put, the Gaelic-Irish did not live in towns and villages, the Anglo-Irish did. Consequently, outside of Leinster, Munster and Ulster east of the Bann, population was sparse and in many respects would have been similar to what had prevailed in other European countries more than a hundred years previously, before the spate of town building in the thirteenth century. Since Gaelic society was mainly pastoral and settlement was based on the pre-conquest townland system, settlements were very scattered, either in irregular nucleated rural settlements or individual farmsteads. There may have been considerable settlements of at least a quasi-urban nature around some of the most important ecclesiastical centres, but these were very rare.[16] In keeping with the pastoral nature of the economy, trade was sporadic. The chronicler Froissart wrote that

> the inhabitants of the more remote parts of Ireland neither know nor wish to know anything about commerce, since they live, quite simply, like wild beasts.[17]

Froissart, of course, exaggerated in more ways than one. All but the most remote parts of Gaelic Ireland maintained some contact with the principal towns, through fairs, trading and even warfare. Gaelic areas were therefore not protected from the incursions of plague, except in the most inaccessible mountainous or boggy regions. However, the absence of a network of towns and villages and the sparseness of the population in all but those areas closest to the colony militated against the rapid spread of the disease.

Parts of the colony exhibited the same scattered settlement patterns. Colonial settlement in Connacht was sparse, few towns had been founded there and the number of settlers was low.[18] Most of Ulster had not been colonised in any systematic fashion and no attempts had been made to found towns between Sligo and Coleraine; nor was there any network of nucleated villages in the colony of Ulster where farming was largely carried on by Irish tenants living in townlands away from the manorial centres.[19] This form of settlement also characterised frontier regions of the colony. Even in Leinster settlement could be quite dispersed also, not only on the marches, but even in the centre of the medieval lordship. On many manors, different groups of tenants farmed holdings in separate townlands within the manor. This has been shown in investigations of the manor of Newcastle Lyons, Co. Dublin, where in the fourteenth century many free tenants lived not in the manorial village but in dispersed settlements within the manor's boundaries. Evidence from other parts of the country, such as the manor of Lisronagh in Co. Tipperary where the betagh holdings were on the periphery, suggests similar patterns.[20] If this kind of dispersed settlement was typical, it would have meant villages in the colony were not as large as in England and that the population density typical in rural England could not have characterised settlement in the Irish colony. As a result, the incidence of plague could have been very irregular. However, this same finding about the dispersed nature of rural settlement in the medieval colony also points in the opposite direction: scattered settlements of tenants living in outlying farms also imply scattered colonies of rats and fleas, thus providing the links necessary for the transmission of bubonic plague. Moreover, such a settlement pattern allows for more frequent human contacts and trade, another factor in determining the plague's incidence.

However, there is also evidence that nucleated village settlements characterised much of the colony at this time and provided the density necessary for the transmission of bubonic plague. Excavations at Caherguillamore, Co. Limerick, a rural area, revealed quite a large and thriving settlement, centered on a cluster of some twelve houses.[21] Even though some of these villages were quite small, they were numerous, and the estimated numbers keep increasing according as historical evidence accumulates and as investigative techniques become more sophisticated. There were twenty-five mercantile towns involved in external trade. The Anglo-Irish colony was studded with at least 330 chartered boroughs in about 1300, some of which were far more populated than are those areas even today.[22] Settlement was particularly dense around the principal towns of Drogheda, Dublin, Kilkenny, New Ross, Waterford, and Cork and in the counties of Louth, Kildare and Dublin, with the other counties of Leinster as well as Tipperary, Cork and Limerick forming a somewhat less densely settled area. A large number of towns were situated along the east and south coasts and in inland centres, especially along the valleys of the Nore, Suir and Barrow Rivers. In Co. Wexford, for example, some fifty-four village sites have been positively identified, and most of these were situated in the south of the county. In medieval Kildare there were at least fifteen towns and at least twenty-three villages were located between the river Barrow and the Blackstairs Mountains. Co. Cork in the late thirteenth century had at least thirty-eight market towns and ports, and there were approximately forty-four other villages. Co. Tipperary had at least thirty-five boroughs and there were at least about ninety-eight villages in Co. Meath.[23] So, while the nature of settlement in the colony is still not completely known, it is clear that there was an extensive network of towns and villages, which with their trading activities and fairs provided the means for transmission of the plague. Distances between these towns and villages were not great, easily traversible in a day's journey. While some of them were little more than agricultural villages or rural boroughs, nevertheless with their fairs and markets they acted as trading hubs for the surrounding countryside and would have therefore served as centres for the trans-mission of plague.

In the more densely settled areas, principally around the larger towns, environmental conditions were conducive to the propagation of plague fleas and black rats, which burrow close to human sites. Grain-growing areas were especially vulnerable and many manors and manorial villages had a mill and some also a brew house, obvious attractions for burrowing rats. Especially vulnerable were priories and abbeys, in particular Cistercian abbeys and Augustinian priories, which usually included large grain storehouses, a factor cited by historians as an explanation for the heavy mortality in priories and abbeys in rural areas all over Europe. Fleas also thrived. A poet of the thirteenth or fourteenth century, in a highly ironic tone, writes of Ireland in 'The Land of Cokaygne':

> The land is full of every good,
> There is no fly, flea, nor louse
> In cloth, in farm, in bed, nor house.[24]

The prevalence of dirt and vermin was the first observation made by Elizabethan commentators on Ireland, such as Dr Andrew Boorde who illustrated the Irish with a woodcut depicting an Irishwoman delousing a soldier's head. Around 1590, Dr Thomas Moffat wrote, 'all Ireland is noted for this that it swarms almost with lice'. In this he was in agreement with Giraldus Cambrensis who, some centuries before, had noted that 'the whole of Ireland is infested with lice'.[25] Towns with their inadequate sanitation facilities offered the perfect environmental conditions for the spread of plague. However, the rural population particularly in Gaelic areas were likely spared the unhygienic conditions of the medieval town-dweller and would not have had that close contact with plague fleas and rats necessary for the transmission of bubonic plague.

Prevailing housing conditions, especially among the poor, offered very little protection against plague. One might perhaps in this context note the testimony of John of Fordun, the Scottish chronicler, who in his *Scotichronicon* noted that 'this sickness befell people everywhere, but especially the middling and lower classes, rarely the great'. This observation is supported by modern research which has shown that, in general, plague is a disease of the poor because rats cannot burrow through hard materials such as stone, whereas houses of soft materials and with thatched roofs provide ideal habitats for rats and fleas.[26] Evidence of housing conditions in Ireland supports the view that in general it affected the poorer classes more. Since Ireland's wealthier classes lived either in stone castles such as at Trim or Kilkenny or in stone houses, they were far more likely to escape contact with infected rats and fleas; moreover the more substantial houses were two-storeyed and this also offered some protection. Most peasant houses, however, both in the colony and Gaelic Ireland, as elsewhere in contemporary Europe, were one-storeyed, timber-framed constructions with wattle-and-daub walls, while roofing was of turf or thatch. However, generalisations are difficult as human habitations seem to have been very varied: in some manors, such as at Clonkeen in Co. Dublin, one of the manors of Holy Trinity Priory at Christ Church, manorial buildings had thatched roofs and wattle-and-daub walls and excavations in Dublin itself have revealed similar construction materials used in houses from as late as the fourteenth century. On the other hand, some earlier thirteenth-century peasant houses had walls of stone, as archaeological excavations have revealed. And the evidence from Cork excavations indicates that many post-and-wattle houses of the earlier Middle Ages were, from about 1300 onwards, replaced by stone buildings with slate roofs. Still, Cork was severely affected by the Black Death and it seems likely that stone houses were probably still too few to have hindered the spread of plague in towns.[27]

Crowded conditions within the houses, both rural and urban, further facilitated transmission. Most peasant dwellings consisted of two rooms, one for humans and the other a byre for cattle. Though houses in cities were somewhat larger, the use of thatch for roofs and brushwood as a floor covering provided ideal breeding grounds for rats and fleas. In Shrewsbury's graphic reconstruction,

> under the floor and in the thickness of the wattle-and-daub or mud walls the house-rat could construct burrows in which it could climb to its resting and breeding nests in the thatch, whence it could emerge at any time between sunset and sunrise safely hidden by the gloom which

obscured the interior of the dwelling, whereas it dared venture outside the dwelling only on dry, warm nights. [28]

However, the houses of the upper classes may not have offered significantly different conditions as suggested by a description of the interior of an Irish castle in 1644:

> The castles or houses of the nobility consist of four walls extremely high, thatched with straw; but to tell the truth, they are nothing but square towers without windows, or at least having such small apertures as to give no more light than a prison. They have little furniture, and cover their rooms with rushes, of which they make their beds in summer, and of straw in winter. They put rushes a foot deep on their floors and on their windows, and many ornament the ceilings with branches.[29]

Climatic conditions at the time also facilitated the spread of plague. The decade was in general characterised by colder and wetter weather, not only in Ireland but in England and throughout Europe. Higden's *Polychronicon* written in Chester describes the period between Midsummer and Christmas 1348 as a period when 'scarcely a day went by without rain at some time in the day or night'. This observation is repeated by Thomas Walsingham in St Albans Abbey and by John of Reading writing from Westminster, who both record the extensive damage caused in low-lying coastal areas by storms and unusual flooding.[30] The later fourteenth century in Ireland was also beset by wetter and colder weather and frequent storms, a catalogue of exogenous disasters culminating in, though not ending with, the Black Death.[31] In more recent outbreaks of plague, cold weather halted its progress, and some commentators have argued on this basis that the Irish winter would have been too cold to permit the transmission of plague. However, contemporary evidence indicates that 1348 in Ireland, as elsewhere in Europe, was a mild albeit wet year; Clyn writes of it as being an extraordinarily fertile and plentiful year, suggesting the kind of warmth and humidity in which the plague bacillus thrives. Furthermore, the Black Death would seem to have been far more virulent than modern outbreaks of bubonic plague, and consequently was not affected by weather conditions to the same degree. If anything, cold weather added to its virulence by favouring the outbreak of its pneumonic form, which flourishes in cold weather and climates when people are more likely to be in close proximity indoors.

Bad weather caused widespread crop failure and poor harvests, with consequent famine and chronic malnutrition. Famines are recorded in Ireland in 1294-96, in 1308-10 and culminated in the Great Famine of 1315-18, which was compounded in Ireland by the Bruce Invasion. The result was not only a higher mortality but prolonged malnutrition which has been claimed to affect plague morbidity.[32] This could be considered a crucial factor in the incidence of plague in Ireland where many rural dwellers lived at or below subsistence and where famines were common. Here, one might also speculate as to whether the diet of the Gaelic population offered them protection against plague. Their diet wasn't as reliant on grain and seems to have been higher in protein, as was suggested by Richard FitzRalph, Archbishop of Armagh in a sermon of 1350 who said the Irish lived 'from flesh and milk products, and did not deal with merchants'. Perhaps this is also a factor in the relatively mild effect of the Black Death of 1348 on the Gaelic population. A similar diet in the Low Countries has been cited by some historians as protecting the population from the worst effects of the Black Death.[33]

Another possible factor in the varying incidence of plague in Ireland may lie in the theory that populations with a high proportion of blood group O were more immune to plague. Investigators have shown that in Ireland the highest proportion with this blood group, about 77%, is concentrated in Connacht and Munster; the lowest, 72%, is to be found in the east and south-east and 73% in the north-east. The lowest percentage of all, 71.1%, is to be found in the extreme south-east. The most important factor posited for these variations is that these were the areas dominated by Anglo-Norman settlers from England and Wales who had lower proportions of this blood group than the native Irish.[34] These were also the areas most affected by the plague. Perhaps this is a factor in the progress of the plague through Ireland. The connection is an intriguing one, albeit hypothetical.

We could also speculate about the role played by their living patterns. Many of the Gaelic-Irish lived in impermanent post-and-wattle houses and migrated seasonally with their cattle between grazing sites. Sources indicate that transient settlements associated with this custom of 'booleying' widely characterised Gaelic society in the later Middle Ages.[35] This factor too may have played its part in saving the Gaelic-Irish from the worst effects of the plague in 1348-50. Studies on the plague in Egypt, where records are far more comprehensive than those for Ireland, have shown that the nomadic habits of the Bedouins kept them removed from the centres of the epidemic, helping to explain why they were hardly affected by the plague of 1347-48, which yet severely affected the rest of the country. The Nile Valley peasants fled to the cities and death, with the result that the settled population declined while the nomadic population remained constant.[36] The analogy is perhaps apt for Ireland where the Gaelic-Irish would also seem to have been hardly affected, a factor that may be connected to wide-ranging social, political and cultural consequences in the succeeding centuries.

In general then, while conditions in Gaelic Ireland would not allow for the even or rapid transmission of plague, this was not the case for the colony concentrated in the east and south which presented all the conditions favourable to the transmission of the plague bacillus: an extensive network of communications, areas of clustered settlements, appropriate housing, a suitable climate and a vulnerable population. And if, as is possible, the plague took a pneumonic form in the autumn/winter of 1348, transmission would have been even easier and more rapid, mortality even higher. The records that are extant regarding the transmission of plague in Ireland are therefore credible, while the extent of the plague was probably greater than the paucity of records would suggest. Dendrochronological studies certainly suggest considerable disruption. In constructing a tree-ring chronology covering Ireland in the last millennium, the fourteenth century proved particularly difficult and researchers concluded that the decrease of population consequent on the Black Death in Ireland was apparently sufficiently severe to lead to a regeneration phase for oak forests.[37]

The Plague's Progress

Whether from England or France, the plague reached the east coast of Ireland in July–August 1348. Contemporary witnesses do not wholly agree on the exact points of entry. According to Friar Clyn, the Kilkenny chronicler, the plague started either at Howth or Dalkey and then reached Dublin and Drogheda almost simultaneously. The Nenagh annalist notes it as beginning in Drogheda and then spreading to Dublin and the surrounding countryside.[38]

It raged in Dublin between August and December, setting a pattern for the terror it would spread through other parts of the country. 'There was hardly a house in which one only had died,' writes Friar Clyn, 'but as a rule man and wife with their children and all the family went the common way of death'. He noted that abbeys and friaries were particularly hard-hit with twenty-five Franciscan friars dying in Drogheda and twenty-three in Dublin. Clyn records vividly the horrors of the deaths:

> many died of boils and abcesses and pustules which erupted on their shins or under their armpits; others died frantic with pain in their head and others spitting blood.

Its progress throughout the rest of the country has to be pieced together from scattered sources. From Dublin, the Nenagh annalist tells us, this 'unheard of mortality' spread to surrounding towns and villages, many of which were left without inhabitants. Clyn adds that they were stripped so thoroughly of their inhabitants 'that there was scarcely anyone left alive in them'. The dense concentration of towns and villages in areas surrounding Dublin aided the rapid spread of the plague into the hinterland. Before the end of the year 1348, the plague had penetrated overland into Louth, Meath and Kildare. Public functions were cancelled as is suggested by the unprecedented break in the sermons of Archbishop FitzRalph of Armagh between 11 May 1348, when he preached in Mansfieldstown, Co. Louth, and his next sermon on 25 March 1349 in Drogheda, and then again until his departure from the country in June 1349.[39] The onset of colder weather did not bring about any diminution in the virulence of the plague, not at least until December. In this it seems to have followed the patterns recorded elsewhere. In France and Germany the onset of winter arrested its progress, as happened also in England. For example, in England on the well-documented manor of Farnham, south-east of Reading, the plague also arrived in autumn 1348, raged until the end of the year, abated in the first six months of 1349, picked up during the summer and reached its peak in autumn 1349.[40] The plague in Ireland seems to have followed a somewhat similar schedule. By 25 December 1348, Friar Clyn notes, the pestilence had reached Kilkenny. Allowing for the fact that the plague had arrived in Dublin at the latest by the beginning of August, and in Kilkenny at the earliest by the end of November, the Black Death would have covered the 100-mile distance between Dublin and Kilkenny at the rate of .8 miles per day. Such a rate is too slow for even the tardiest medieval cart, so that it seems more likely that the plague was transported to Kilkenny via river-traffic from the south-eastern ports. However, it didn't stop then. Clyn tells us that the pestilence was rife in Kilkenny between Christmas and March, and took a toll of eight Dominican friars in one March day alone. Clyn doesn't record any more deaths, most likely because he was himself among the first victims of the plague in Kilkenny. But given its contagious nature, the plague would have inevitably spread among others of Friar Clyn's Franciscan community as well as among the town's inhabitants.

Whether or not the plague abated in the early months of 1349 has not been noted. We have no record of the plague again until June 1349 when the Prior of the Augustinian monastery of St Catherine's in Waterford died of it and July 1349 when the death of the Bishop of Meath is recorded. The plague spread all along the south-east and south, to New Ross, Clonmel, Cashel, Cork and Youghal, though we don't know the precise dates. The Nenagh annalist is our only direct source for its transmission in the south and he focuses only on those deaths of interest to the Franciscan order. He records the deaths on 10 August and 19 August of two friars in the Franciscan community at Nenagh. By 1 November, the plague had reached Limerick, where the death of one friar is noted. It then spread to Ennis in Co. Clare where the death of a lay patron of the Franciscans, Matthew Caoch MacConmara, is recorded. The following year the annalist notes the death of Traolach, son of Donncha O' Brien, who was buried at Nenagh. Though the cause of these deaths is not explicitly mentioned, the fact that these notices are juxtaposed with the entry recording the coming of the plague to Ireland strongly suggests that they were plague deaths.[41]

Drogheda, Dublin, New Ross, Waterford, Youghal, Cork: the catalogue of port towns testifies to the fact that coastal areas bore the brunt of the disease. The English chronicler Ralph Higden in his entry for 1348 in *Polychronicon,* writes that the plague was 'especially violent in and around the Roman Curia at Avignon and around the coastal towns of England and Ireland'. Archbishop FitzRalph in his address to the Pope in 1349 stated that 'the plague had fallen most heavily on those who lived near the sea and has found more victims among fisherfolk and sailors than among any other class of men'. The seventeenth-century historian, Barnes, echoes this – 'the plague made great havoc among the Englishmen of those parts, especially about the seacoasts' – as does Marlborough, another later chronicler.[42]

However, the less populated areas of the north and west did not escape entirely. The plague is recorded in Ulster in 1349 when 'great destruction of people was inflicted therein'. However, the only two victims named were aristocratic: Matthew, son of Cathal O'Rourke from the area of Co. Leitrim and Richard O'Reilly, King of East Breifne in Cavan. The exact date of its entry into Ulster is not known but it was probably late in 1349, transported there most likely by overland traffic from Leinster or else as a creeping epizootic. The plague raged in Connacht and, according to the annals, especially in Moylurg in Co. Roscommon in 1349, again probably in late November or early December; the *Four Masters* merely record that 'great numbers were carried off'. The *Annals of Clonmacnoise* also record the Black Death in Roscommon in 1348, though this is probably a scribal error since the plague would most likely have taken longer to reach the west of Ireland. The *Annals of Connacht* record the plague in Moylurg and all Ireland in 1349 and, like the *Annals of Ulster*, note the same deaths of Matthew MacCathail (son of Cathal), and Richard O'Reilly, King of Breifne. The disease was active in Mayo as late as 1350 and the annalist there writes of the deaths of William Ó Dúda, Bishop of Killala, Concubhar Ó Lochlainn, Cathal Ó Flathartaigh, the son of Dónal Mac Gearranagastair and his brothers who all died 'within six days because of the pestilence'. The *Annals of Loch Cé* record the deaths of five persons, including the Bishop of Killala, in 1350. The cause of death is not specified, but since we know from the Mayo annalist that the Bishop of Killala died of plague, we may perhaps assume that the other four died of the same cause.[43]

It is difficult to say to what extent the Black Death affected the Gaelic population. The foregoing evidence shows that the plague penetrated all regions of the country between 1348 and 1350, though some localities undoubtedly escaped. Our only sources for Gaelic Ireland are the annalists who, however, are most aristocratic in their evidence; for every *obit* of magnate, chieftain or bishop they record, there are in all likelihood numerous deaths of people of lesser note whom they do not mention. Still, the fact that the *Annals of Ulster*, *Loch Cé*, the *Four Masters* and *Clonmacnoise* all record virtually the same entry suggests they were relying on a common secondary source, not observation. The brevity of the entry also supports the view that the plague did not affect the Gaelic-Irish population to the same extent as it affected the colony. Other contemporary evidence supports this view. Geoffrey Le Baker, the contemporary English chronicler, writes that the plague in Ireland 'killed the English inhabitants there in great numbers, but the native Irish, living in the mountains and uplands, were scarcely touched'. In a sermon to the Pope in summer 1349, Richard FitzRalph, Bishop of Armagh, asserted that the plague had not yet reached the 'Irish nation', by which he meant the Gaelic-Irish population. The Great Council in a complaint to the King in July 1360 moaned of a plague that was 'so great and so hideous among the English lieges and not among the Irish'.[44] Finally, Barnes writing his history some centuries later notes that the plague:

> made great havoc among the Englishmen of those parts… But as for those who were true Irishmen born and dwelling in hilly countries, it scarce just saluted them so that they suffered little or no loss thereby.[45]

These observations are in line with contemporary epidemiological assertions that bubonic plague, in general, follows the patterns of greatest density of human populations. Clearly, the dispersed and isolated settlements of the Irish would not offer congenial breeding grounds for colonies of rats and their fleas and would have hampered transmission of the plague bacillus. Nor can one discount the importance of the fact that the majority of the Gaelic-Irish population did not live in urban settlements and didn't share the crowded and insanitary conditions of life typical of a medieval town.

By contrast with Gaelic Ireland, rural areas in the Anglo-Irish colony suffered severely. Here, in well-settled regions with a network of towns and markets or on religious estates, there are numerous records of high mortality: in Co. Dublin, the royal manors of Newcastle Lyons, Saggart, Crumlin, Oughterard and Castlewarny; in Co. Tipperary, the estates of the Archbishop of Cashel and the manor of Lisronagh; numerous manors in Kilkenny and Meath by 1351 were left with vacant cottages, untilled lands, fallen rents because of the deaths by plague of tenants. The priory of Lismullin in Co. Meath suffered grievously from the plague and its successor of 1361, its inmates being reduced from fifty-four to thirty-two as did the monastery of Llanthony Secunda in Duleek, Co. Meath, whose tenants fled leaving their holdings vacant.[46] Population density and the frequency of trading contacts account for the widespread incidence of the plague in the colony by contrast with Gaelic Ireland. The historian J.Z. Titow has estimated mortality among the rural population of

England to have been as high as 50% in more densely populated areas, an estimate that many more recent studies have corroborated.[47] A similar figure is not impossible for the more densely populated areas of the colony in Ireland.

The Plague's Recurrence

By 1351 this outbreak of the plague had run its course. But it did not disappear and would return repeatedly in years to come. In many respects a study of the overall demographic effects of the plague of 1348-50 cannot be considered apart from these later, related outbreaks. Had the outbreak of 1348 been the only one, the population of the colony in Ireland, though not robust in the years before the plague, would have recovered. However, the recurring nature of plague meant that sustained recovery wasn't possible and a chronic pattern of crisis mortality set in. Admittedly, later outbreaks were likely less virulent though research in other countries has shown that areas which escaped the plague in 1347-49 were affected severely in later outbreaks, perhaps as new colonies of rodents became infected. This happened, for example, in the Southern Netherlands. In the second half of 1349 the western regions were affected by the plague, though only a few towns, such as Tournai, were severely affected. In subsequent outbreaks, the eastern and north-eastern regions of the Northern Netherlands bore the brunt of the plague. Throughout the whole epidemic, the central regions were largely spared.[48] Geoffrey Le Baker made a similar observation about Ireland, claiming that the native Irish, while escaping in 1349, were severely affected in 1357 when the plague 'took them unawares and annihilated them everywhere'.[49]

Moreover, the effect of the later outbreaks was not restricted to mortality, but also affected fertility. Many chroniclers especially note that later outbreaks often affected young people and children particularly. This observation is corroborated by recent medical research which supports the view that plague can become age- and gender-specific within a few years of its first outbreak, often even affecting a region's pregnant women, who in turn can transmit the plague to their unborn children.[50] A plague affecting children is recorded in 1350 and again in 1361, the latter popularly known as the *mortalité des enfants*. In 1370, the *Annals of St Mary's Abbey* record a great pestilence, 'of which many nobles and citizens and especially young people and children died'. In 1390, the English chronicler Walsingham recorded 'incredible numbers' of adolescents dying of plague.[51] The recurrence of plague meant that generations of children would never reach child-bearing age, ensuring that a population's chances of recovering from plague mortality were further damaged. The effects of this development are revealed in the records from Halesowen manor near Birmingham. While the mortality from the outbreak of 1348 was highest in the thirty to fifty-nine age group and hardly affected those under twenty, such was not the case in subsequent outbreaks when mortality among children was catastrophic. The result in that particular manor was that the population in the final decades of the fourteenth century was dominated by the middle-aged and elderly, leading to long-term demographic stagnation.[52] There are no such records for Ireland, but there is no reason to suppose that arable areas with clustered settlements and a network of villages and towns would not have experienced similar demographic patterns.

The plague continued to recur throughout the rest of the fourteenth century and after. In 1361 there was 'a great mortality of people, consuming many men, but few women' and 1363 brought a 'great mortality in Ireland and especially in Connacht, Thomond, Kerry and Desmond'. In 1365, the *Annals of Ulster* record the death by plague in Trim Castle of Feilimidh, grandson of Philip O'Reilly, and in the Franciscan friary at Nenagh only two people remained alive. There were outbreaks in 1370, 1383, 1390-93, 1398 and periodically thereafter. And these are just the outbreaks that have been recorded; there may have been other localised outbreaks that were not noted in official records. The recurrence of the plague was in effect the single, most significant effect of the Black Death. Studies have shown that these recurring outbreaks had a profound effect on slowing population recovery in Europe generally, above all since these later outbreaks affected not only mortality levels but were also connected to fertility and replacement rates. The long-term result was continuing crisis mortality and lower fertility, if not zero population growth, for many years. As Dr John Hatcher has written of post-plague England:

> …it must be stressed that it is mistaken to assume that demographic decline could only be effected by national epidemics of spectacular proportions. On the contrary there is every reason to believe that the cumulative impact of lesser and local epidemics could be decisive, the more so if the young were afflicted in disproportionately high numbers. [53]

Plague Mortality in Ireland

Large-scale demographic decline has multiple origins. But whatever the causes, the results are undoubted. In Ireland, recurring outbreaks of the plague in the fourteenth century, as well as famine and warfare, created population changes that had profound effects for the English colony in Ireland and for Gaelic Ireland. The decline continued for many years. The parameters of this decline elsewhere are a subject of much debate, with some arguing for at least a stagnating population until well into the next century, others holding that decline was over by the end of the fourteenth century, yet others restricting it to the period between 1348 and 1369. [54] The general consensus, however, is that elsewhere in Europe mortality rates began to decline around 1450, allowing for limited demographic recovery in the earlier decades of the sixteenth century. This did not happen until the seventeenth century in Ireland, where the continuation of warfare and frontier conditions, coupled with recurring outbreaks of plague, especially in towns, ensured continuing population loss.

The Black Death's contribution to this demographic decline eludes quantification. The continuation of natural mortality as well as of other diseases and our ignorance of contemporary population figures makes the task of estimating well-nigh impossible. J.F. Shrewsbury, in his study of the plague in the British Isles, concluded that it may have destroyed as much as one-thirtieth of the populations of Ireland and Scotland, and this he considered 'a generous assumption'.[55] However, this estimate is much too low, given what is known about the aetiology of plague and about medieval settlement in Ireland. At the opposite end of the scale is the estimate of Richard FitzRalph, Archbishop of Armagh, who stated that it had destroyed more than two-thirds of the English nation in Ireland.[56] This figure, though probably exaggerated, points to an unusually high mortality among the Anglo-Irish colonists. But such estimates are difficult to corroborate. Part of the difficulty in trying to assess the plague's mortality is that there are no pre-plague population figures and historians' estimates vary widely. A.J. Otway-Ruthven calculated the population of Ireland in the twelfth century to have been about 1,375,000, the same as that estimated for England a few generations before in 1086 at the time of the Domesday Book. J. C. Russell suggested the population of Ireland in the later thirteenth century may have been about 650,000 and that by 1348 it would have reached about 800,000.[57] Russell's estimates, like those he cited for contemporary England, are unfortunately too low. More recent estimates posit a much higher figure for England's population: 1.75-2.25 million at the time of Domesday in 1086, 2.75-3 million in 1327 at the time of the Poll Tax in 1377 and, allowing for a decline of 40%-50% for the Black Death and subsequent plague outbreaks, a figure of 5-6 million in 1347. Another more recent study even argues that the population of England before 1310 was over 6 million, a level not again reached until the eighteenth century, while yet another historian posits a figure of 5 million in 1300 and up to 7 million in 1348.[58] The population of parts of the colony in Ireland was undoubtedly also high, though few places would have had the same density as had parts of England like the Fens. While there is no way to calculate the population of Gaelic Ireland in the late Middle Ages, the historian Kenneth Nicholls concludes that it was low because of the very low value of land shown in contemporary land transfer deeds.[59]

In estimating general figures for plague mortality, historians have often extrapolated on the basis of known mortality figures for specific areas or specific groups. Particular religious houses in Ireland claimed death rates over 50%, while figures for the death rate among tenants on some manors were equally high. One could attempt to adjust this figure downward to account for those areas which were not affected by the plague and then come up with a countrywide mortality rate. There are difficulties however with this approach. Not all recorded deaths are plague deaths. Moreover in the case of Ireland, it is difficult even to come up with satisfactory figures for specific groups or areas as the records are not comprehensive or consistent. And, as Dr Z. Razi notes in his study of Halesowen manor, 'there is no reason to suppose that the average of low and high estimates of mortality provides a more reliable estimate'.[60]

One could also make inferences on the basis of evidence from other countries, but historians' estimates here also vary widely from Shrewsbury's 5% to Ziegler's 33%. More recent estimates, especially for England, are much higher, with some arguing for an estimate of 30%-45% mortality in 1348, others claiming that a mortality of 40%-50% was common in many areas, with a probable average mortality of around 47%-48% during the first eighteen months of the plague.[61] Evidence from other countries in Europe indicates clearly that the plague's incidence varied. Mortality in densely populated Flanders was in the region of 15%-25%, but in rural Holland it exceeded 30%, in the rural Midi of France 45%, in sparsely populated Scandanavia 45% and in Iceland over 50%.[62] Some figures put Europe's and England's population at 50% lower in 1430 than it had been at the end of the thirteenth century, and argue that the pre-plague population levels were not reached again until the 1600s. The demographer Livi-Bacci is somewhat more cautious: on the basis of studies in Italy, he suggests that between 1347 and the first half of the fifteenth century, Europe lost between 30% and 40% of its population, and regained its pre-plague population of 74 million in the 1550s.[63] A rough consensus of historians' estimates of overall mortality in Europe would be a figure ranging from 35% to 45%, with the preference being for rates at the higher end of the scale. Such a mortality rate for the plague of 1348 and its successors may be conservatively inferred for parts of the Anglo-Irish colony. This is particularly so since surviving manorial accounts mention holdings being vacant 'for lack of tenants' right into the late fifteenth century, indicating that Ireland's experience of plague was not unique and that in broad outline it followed the same patterns as elsewhere.

However, generalisations must remain tentative in the absence of substantiating evidence. Moreover, there is the important consideration that Ireland in general had not experienced the same population growth rate in the thirteenth century as had England and other European countries and Irish towns, in particular, were not as overcrowded as their European counterparts. Since there wasn't any surplus of population, Malthusian interpretations of plague mortality are not relevant to Ireland. Nevertheless, the plague's overall effect on demographic decline in Ireland in the later Middle Ages was a cumulative one. Thanks to famines and warfare, the population of the colony in Ireland, as in Europe generally, had already been declining for some decades before the Black Death broke out. The effect of the plague, this new, unpredictable, inescapable and recurring disease, was crucial in finalising the downward demographic trend, and many epidemiologists argue that exogenous factors such as pestilence are, in the end, ultimately responsible for large-scale demographic downturns. Ireland was to remain seriously underpopulated for the next two centuries. One estimate puts its population in the early sixteenth century at ½ million or below, a level maintained until 1600 and beyond.[64]

In England and in Europe generally, demographic decline had stopped by the end of the fourteenth century and society had somewhat recovered by the early fifteenth century, even though demographic recovery took longer. In Ireland, the thirteenth-century position was irrevocably lost and chronic depopulation continued. This had widespread repercussions in the agricultural sector and, as elsewhere, led to a redistribution of power and wealth. Ireland experienced that same re-alignment that characterised post-plague England and Europe. Some towns, manors and religious houses declined, others recovered, others again came to the fore. In general, the Anglo-Irish colony declined, Gaelic Ireland recouped. As elsewhere then, though in different ways, the long-term effects of the plague in Ireland helped to change the social fabric, sometimes radically, sometimes imperceptibly. But in the immediate aftermath of the plague also, the human reactions to the terror of plague were everywhere very similar.

3

Plague: The Human Response

Life in medieval Ireland, as elsewhere in contemporary Europe, was hard and brief. People were ready victims of disease, and typhoid, tuberculosis, influenza, smallpox, skin diseases as well as childbirth all exacted a heavy toll. The average lifespan was short: in excavations of a medieval cemetery in Cork, of 216 skeletons examined, 24% died before their early twenties, with 48% of these dying between sixteen and twenty years of age; the rest were adults, with the largest number, 36.5% dying between twenty and thirty years old.[1] Excavations of church cemeteries in York yielded similar results: 56% of women and 36% of men died before their mid-thirties, and 27% of the population were dead by the age of fourteen, figures supported by written sources.[2] All of this was aggravated in Ireland by the endemic violence. From the late thirteenth century particularly there reigned

> an age of violence, when life was as uncertain as it is always under frontier conditions and the fear of death was ever present. Raids by Irish enemies or English rebels, not to mention the activities of 'common thieves' and criminals who roamed the countryside made terror a common experience in many a community.[3]

Conditions became especially chaotic in the decades preceding the outbreak of the Black Death, as the central government became increasingly unable to control the lawlessness. There were numerous reports of nobility robbing merchants or requisitioning provisions. The tension created by such conditions may be surmised from a statement in 1349 that 'if a large number of inhabitants of either kingdom [Anglo- and Gaelic-Irish] should leave their houses, the opposing nation will at once enter their holdings and kill their women and children'.[4]

Moreover, the typical medieval peasant lacked the resources to withstand such warfare. Many were living at or below subsistence level. Hunger and want were constant hazards in an economy that was still largely a closed one. Poor harvests were frequent, famines familiar, such that, according to a contemporary annalist, 'multitudes of poor people died of cold and hunger, and the rich suffered hardship'.[5] Just as in the rest of Europe, a pattern of disaster forms the history of Ireland in the later fourteenth century. Apart from human warfare, the earlier decades of the century are studded with climactic irregulari- ties, storms, murrains of cattle, bad harvests, famine, diseases and floods. Ireland seems to have experienced the same sequence of climatic disasters as elsewhere. An abbreviated list of these disasters in the years before the Black Death gives an indication of what the conditions of everyday life were like: a murrain of cattle in 1302 and again in 1308, storms in 1308, famine in 1308-10, violent winds in 1310, famine in 1315-18, storms in 1317, the Bruce Invasion in 1315-18, a murrain of sheep in 1315-17, crop failures in the 1320s and 1330s, cattle murrains in the 1320s, smallpox in 1327, flooding and hard winters in 1330, 1338 and 1339, crop failure in autumn 1339, a murrain of sheep in 1338, famine in 1339.[6] Yet, because many of these disasters were recurrent and often on a small scale, they could therefore be more easily tolerated. The unprecedented onslaught of plague represented something far more sinister and enigmatic.

In attempting to re-enact the psychological and cultural responses to the plague in Ireland, it is important to emphasise that responses would at least to some extent have been affected by the extent of the mortality: the more virulent the disease, the more intense the reaction. Sources are very scarce in this area, once again raising many questions. Nevertheless, people's reactions were undoubtedly similar to those of their European counterparts, since the inadequate understanding of medieval man regarding the nature of disease transcended all national, religious, economic and social boundaries.

Explanations and Remedies for Plague

The Black Death was inexplicable, its nature and tactics shrouded in a veil of myth and mystery. Such 'natural' disasters were regarded as being of the same fabric as military and political oppression and human sin, and the ultimate cause was God's anger. For example, on the death of the unpopular Justiciar, Sir Thomas de Rokeby in 1346, one annalist wrote: 'at [his] death the floods ceased and the distemperature of the air had an end and in one word, the common sort truly and heartily praise the only Son of God'.[7]

Human excess, whether moral or political, was linked to natural disasters and ultimately to God's wrath. Similar tales of prodigious events and earthquakes were common currency, and an angry God was often cited as the cause of disease and hardship. So too with the plague. God was the ultimate cause as the respected Andalusian doctor, Ibn Khatimah wrote in 1349:

> This [plague] is an example of the wonderful deeds and power of God, because never before has a catastrophe of such extent and duration occurred. No satisfactory reports have been given about it, because the disease is new… God only knows when it will leave the earth.[8]

Christians in particular believed it to be God's punishment for man's wickedness: the Italian chronicler Gabriele de' Mussis saw it as God's punishment on 'the entire human race wallowing in the mire of manifold wickedness'. The English chronicler, Henry Knighton, added a familiar twist, that it was God's remedy for the vanity, immodesty and wantonness of women. The tradition of seeing plague as punishment for sin is of course an old one: in Homer's *Iliad* it is the punishment meted out for Agamemnon's sin in carrying off Chryseis and is frequently a consequence of God's anger in the Old Testament.[9] It is a particularly strong tradition in Christian cultures since death itself is seen as punishment for Adam's sin.

Since plague was such an unknown disease, medical understanding of it was very limited. One Arabic doctor, Ilyas Ibn Ibrahim, acknowledged this and described the physician trying to treat plague patients as being like 'a blind man, trying to find his way in the darkness'.[10] Others attempted to give explanations. There was some understanding of contagion among a few Arabic doctors, but in general medical men, trained in the traditions of Galen, believed disease was caused either by afflictions in the soul or by a corruption in the air, a miasma, which released poisonous fumes that caused an imbalance in the bodily humours. In 1348, the medical faculty at the University of Paris in a lengthy argument attributed the plague to a conjunction on 24 March 1345 of Saturn, Jupiter and Mars in the house of Aquarius: the unusual event created changes in the atmosphere of the earth and caused imbalances in the body, which in turn were manifested in the buboes of the plague. This anonymous contemporary English commentator managed to synthesise many explanations:

> If I am asked what is the cause of pestilence, what is its physical cause and by what means can someone save himself from it, I answer to the first question that sin is the cause. To the second question, I say that it arises from the sea, as the evangelist says: 'There shall be signs in the sun and in the moon and in the stars; and upon the earth distress of nations, by reason of the confusion of the roaring of the sea and waves.' For the devil, by the power committed to him when the seas rise up high, is voiding his poison, sending it forth to be added to the poison in the air, and that air spreads gradually from place to place and enters man through the ears, eyes, nose, mouth, pores and other orifices. Then, if the man has a strong constitution, nature can expel the poison through ulcers, and if the ulcers putrefy, are strangled and fully run their course, the patient will be saved, as can be clearly seen. But if the poison should be stronger than his nature, so that his constitution cannot prevail against it, then the poison instantly lays siege to the heart and the patient dies within a short time, without the relief that comes from the formation of ulcers.[11]

Medicine in Ireland was most likely based on similar theories, since the medical treatises extant are largely translations of well-known European works: the texts of the twelfth-century Renaissance, the works of Galen, Avicenna and Hippocrates. Some fifty-eight translations of late thirteenth- and fourteenth-century works survive, indicating their widespread use.[12] Medicine was a mixture of superstition, moralising and religious faith with the addition of some folk medicine and homeopathic remedies, as is evidenced in a medieval Irish manuscript written by a doctor:

> May the merciful God have mercy on us all. I have collected practical notes from several works for the honour of God, for the benefit of the Irish people, for the instruction of any pupil and for the love of my friends and of my kindred. I have translated from Latin into Gaelic, from the authority of Galen, in the last book of his *Practical Pantheon* and from the book of *Prognostics* of Hippocrates. These are things, gentle, sweet and profitable, and of little evil, things which have often been tested by us and by our instructors. I pray God to bless those doctors who will use this book, and I lay it on their souls, as an injunction, that they extract the practical rules (herein contained) and more especially, that they do their duty devotedly in cases where they receive no pay. Moreover let him not be in mortal sin, and let him implore the patient to be also free from grievous sin. Let him offer up a secret prayer for the sick person, and implore the Heavenly Father, the Physician and Balm-Giver of all mankind to prosper the work he is entering upon.[13]

A catastrophe such as plague was beyond the ken of Irish medicine, as much as it was for contemporary European experts, and even a century later plague in Dublin was still being attributed to 'pestilential exhalations' in the air.[14]

Remedies for the plague were few. Bloodletting was a common procedure used to alleviate plague and may have been used also in Ireland, given the survival of a poem 'On Bloodletting' from the end of the fourteenth century. Other contemporary remedies included improving the surrounding air, smelling roses or other fragrances to drive away the stench of the plague, eating prescribed herbs and vegetables, drinking good wine, phlebotomy, staying indoors; and there was also the remedy of the English poet, Lydgate, for the man who '…would resiste the strok of pestilence/Let him be glad, and voide al hevynesse'. Others would have stressed repentance and prayer, since plague was seen as arising from people's sinful ways. Richard Ledrede, Bishop of Ossory during the plague years, in one of his poems reveals what would have been the attitude of many non-experts to disease; he advises that

> the wound of Christ's side is medicine above all others…
> For the fevered, the chilled, the withered, the dropsical,
>   cripples, paralytics, the broken-limbed, the swollen,
> Lepers, demoniacs, the desperate, the dead – it cures their
>   every ill, it is the healing art for doctors.

Prayer to a favourite saint was also seen as a possible remedy and Mary, Christ's mother, was a particularly favourite intercessor during the plague. In another poem Ledrede speaks of Mary as a healer who can 'make level what is swollen', words strongly suggestive of skin eruptions like buboes.[15]

Responses: Terror, Flight and Pilgrimage
The absence of known remedies had the effect of heightening people's fear. Terror and shock were everywhere the primary reactions to sudden and inescapable death. The Welsh poet, Jeuan Gethin, most graphically captures the horror of people in 1349:

> We see death coming into our midst like black smoke, a plague which cuts off the young, a rootless phantom which has no mercy for fair countenance. Woe is me of the shilling in the arm-pit; it is seething, terrible, wherever it may come, a head that gives pain and causes a loud cry, a burden carried under the arms, a painful angry knob, a white lump. It is of the form of an apple, like the head of an onion, a small

boil that spares no-one. Great is its seething, like a burning cinder, a grievous thing of an ashy colour. It is an ugly eruption that comes with unseemly haste. …It is a grievous ornament that breaks out in a rash. They are like a shower of peas, the early ornaments of black death… [16]

His terror must have come out of first-hand experience, as he died in March or April 1349. The Irish chronicler, Friar John Clyn, is not quite so graphic and speaks plainly of 'boils, abscesses and pustules which erupted on the legs and in the armpits. Others died in frenzy, brought on by an affliction of the head, or vomiting blood'.

Perhaps there is no more moving testimony that that of the young Irishman, Aedh Mac Aodhagáin, writing in 1350 of his fear of dying:

One thousand three hundred and fifty years until tonight since J.C. Amen was born and in the second year after the coming of the plague into Ireland that was written. And I myself am full twenty-one years old, that is Aedh, son of Concubhar Mac Aodhagáin, and let everyone who shall read this utter a prayer of mercy for my soul; Christmas Eve tonight and under the safeguard of the King of Heaven and earth who is here tonight I place myself and may Heaven be the end of my life and may He put this great Plague past me and past my friends and may we be once more in joy and happiness. Amen, Pater Noster. [17]

Aedh Mac Aodhagáin in fact outlived the plague, but John Clyn did not survive. He never completed his chronicle, and his closing words must rank among the most poignant of last words ever recorded:

And I, Brother John Clyn of the Friars Minor in Kilkenny have written in this book the notable events which befell in my time, which I saw myself or have learned from men worthy of belief. So that notable deeds shall not perish with time, and be lost from the memory of future generations I, seeing these many ills, and the whole world lying, as it were, in the wicked one among the dead, waiting for death till it come, have committed to writing what I have truly heard and examined; and lest the writing perish with the writer or the work with the workman,

> I leave parchment for continuing the work, if haply any man survive or
> any of the race of Adam escape this pestilence and continue the work
> which I have commenced.

As noted already, Clyn died of plague and another hand closed his
annals with the terse *obit*: 'Here, it seems, the author died'.[18]

There were many who, in the face of such overwhelming mutability, shared Clyn's sense that written records should be made. It had
been a response in Ireland in the middle of the seventh century
when the outbreak of plague led to the first recording of ancient
Irish sagas, poetry and genealogies because, as the historian Michael
Richter writes, 'the community seems to have sensed that this catastrophe marked a caesura in Irish history'.[19] Another way in which
medieval writers made sense of the unprecedented mortality was to
place it in the context of the history of the human race as foretold in
the Book of Revelation: they linked this plague with those biblical
plagues that will signal the end of history. Not surprisingly then,
chroniclers present the plague in traditionally apocalyptic images
and Friar Clyn is no exception:

> There will be many battles and much slaughter, unrelenting famine and
> widespread mortality of men, revolutions in kingdoms; the land of the
> heathens will be converted.... More people in the world have died in such
> a short time of plague, hunger or other infirmity than has been heard of
> since the beginning of time. An earthquake, which extended for miles, has
> overwhelmed, swallowed and destroyed cities, villages and castles.

Clearly, one must suspect such an account as owing its details more to
the influence of Revelation than to eyewitness accounts of actual
happenings. Yet, these images were the common currency of the time
and capture the horror that people felt and the ways in which they
tried to make sense of events. For many, such as John of Reading, the
plague signalled an end to normal life: 'there was in those days death
without sorrow, marriage without affection, self-imposed penance,
want without poverty and flight without escape'. Interestingly, one of

the French chroniclers, self-styled prophet John of Bassigny, prophesied that the plague would be followed not only by such dreadful events, but would also have positive effects, such as that the Irish and Scots would invade England and annihilate the 'sons of Brutus'- a reference to the legend that London had been founded by Brutus, grandson of the Roman hero, Aeneas. John of Bassigny's prophecies however post-date the plague.[20]

Responses to this intimation of a final end spanned the gamut of human emotions. Flight was a common reaction on the European continent, particularly among the wealthy, many following the advice of the Arabic physician Rhasis:

> Three things by which each simple man
> From plague escape and sickness can,
> Start soon, flee far from town or land
> On which the plague has laid its hand,
> Return but late to such a place
> Where pestilence has stayed its pace.[21]

Another common reaction was precisely the opposite: to come together for public processions or pilgrimages intended to propitiate an angry God and to pray for deliverance from the horrors of the plague and of a sudden, painful death. Particular saints were favoured in different places: on the continent, cults grew up around St Roch who had miraculously survived the plague in Rome and St Sebastian, the early Christian martyr who had been killed by arrows. Arrows had been associated with plague since late antiquity and Sebastian's suffering from the pricks of the arrows that killed him was compared to the pricking sensation that preceded the outbreak of buboes. In Ireland, however, Saints Roch and Sebastian did not figure among the pantheon of plague intercessors. In surviving tomb surrounds, for example, neither makes an appearance and the only known surviving representation of Sebastian is in the Cistercian Knockmoy Abbey in Co. Galway. The most popular saints in Ireland as evidenced by the figures on surviving tombstones were St Michael the Archangel, the apostles, St Francis, St John the Baptist, St Catherine of Alexandria, St Margaret of Antioch, and above all St Thomas of Canterbury.[22] All point to the more sober, conservative hue of religious practice in Ireland.

In Ireland too, according to Friar Clyn, in the first months of the plague the number of pilgrims soared and in his area the favoured supplicant was St Moling:

> In this year [1348] and particularly in the months of September and October there came together from diverse parts of Ireland, bishops and prelates, churchmen and religious, lords and others to the pilgrimage and wading of the water at Thath Molyngis, in troops and multitudes, so that you could see many thousands there at the same time for many days together. Some came from feelings of devotion, but others and they the majority from dread of the plague, which then grew very rife.[23]

St Moling (also known as Mullins) was a seventh-century monk at Glendalough, Co. Wicklow who went on to found a monastery near the present St Mullins in Co. Carlow, on the border with Co. Kilkenny, though there are other sites also associated with him, including *Tobar Moling*, or Moling's Well, at Mullinakill, in Rosbercon parish in Co. Kilkenny.[24] Clyn was referring to the site in Co. Carlow, on the river Barrow, which was home to the original house of the saint, in Irish *Teach Moling*, or as Clyn transposes it, Thaht-Molyngis. It was a revered site, closely associated with the Gaelic chieftains of Leinster and throughout the medieval period was the burial ground of the MicMhurchadha clan. The monastery had been recently rebuilt in 1347, having been burned in 1323. In Friar Clyn's time, many legends were associated with this place in which pagan, Christian and folk-loric elements were all interwoven. Its roots lay deep in Ireland's legendary past: it is connected with the mythical hero, Fionn Mac Cumhaill and the folklorist Máire MacNeill argues that this site was very likely originally associated with Lughnasa, the Celtic harvest festival. MacNeill recounts a legend associated with the site that carries overtones more reminiscent of death than harvest and that bears strong resemblance to John Keats' 'La Belle Dame Sans Merci' and other such medieval-inspired legends of Lady Death:

> From the old grave-yard at this place, a lady clothed in a long and flowing white dress has sometimes been known to proceed, when a solitary horseman may happen to be riding, at a late hour of the night, and along these roads, leading from St Mullins in various directions. She seats herself behind the rider, and grasps him around the waist. He becomes chilled with this cold embrace, and then, after riding with him for some time, the goblin lady disappears. Soon afterwards, the rider begins to decline in health, until death ensues, when it is thought the white lady claims him as a future tenant of that ancient burial ground which she haunts.

By medieval times, the site had become christianized and had become a pilgrimage site popular throughout Leinster. St Moling himself was known as a prolific poet in Irish and was reputed to have a special relationship with animals, both tame and wild – an early St Francis. More relevant to Clyn's testimony is that the saint had single-handedly built a watermill nearby to bring water to his monastery and did so by diverting water from a spring one mile away. The site came to be known as St Moling's Well, one of the 'holy' wells of Ireland, the waters of which were famed for their curative properties. Moling promised healing and salvation until the end of time to all who would wade upstream against the current. St Moling was deemed to be particularly effective in curing skin diseases, since he is said to have cured his own skin ulcers by wading upstream. Throughout the Middle Ages and until as late as the nineteenth century great crowds came there on pilgrimage and waded in the waters to cure their ailments. This is clearly the 'wading of the water', the *vadacionem aque* to which Clyn refers. Pilgrimages normally took place either on the Sunday before the feast day on July 25th of the locality's patron, St James (who, parenthetically is often portrayed as a pilgrim in medieval illustration), or on June 17th, the feast day of St Moling. Clearly then, pilgrimages in September and October, such as are recorded by Clyn, were exceptional.

Many other local places of pilgrimage were no doubt equally thronged in the immediate aftermath of the plague. Pilgrimages were common in fourteenth-century Ireland: the Augustinian Church at Trim, Co. Meath was a favourite because of a famous statue of Our Lady, which later came to be known as the 'Idol of Trim', so-named by Cromwell's Chancellor in the sixteenth century. Other popular pilgrimage sites included Navan, Raphoe, Ballintubber, Cork, Thurles, Lough Derg, Christ Church and St Patrick's in Dublin; in Dublin alone there were about thirty-five places with shrines of some kind.[25] However, in some areas, going on pilgrimage wasn't possible because of troubled conditions, especially on the marches. Archbishop FitzRalph of Armagh in a sermon suggested that many wished to go on pilgrimage to Rome but in the dangerous conditions of the times, feared letting their property and families unprotected.[26]

Breaking the Mould

Terror and dread of the plague led to a disruption in normal patterns of human behaviour and conventional values, as contemporary chroniclers everywhere testify. Boccaccio and many other chroniclers eloquently record that in the panic engendered by plague the normal ties of kinship were forgotten. Boccaccio writes:

> It was not merely a question of one citizen avoiding another, and of people almost invariably neglecting their neighbours and rarely or never visiting their relatives, addressing them only from a distance; this scourge had implanted so great a terror in the hearts of men and women that brothers abandoned brothers, uncles their nephews, sisters their brothers, and in many cases wives their husbands. But even worse, and almost incredible, was the fact that fathers and mothers refused to nurse and assist their own children, as though they didn't belong to them.

In Siena, Agnolo di Tura wrote that the dead were left unburied or thrown into pits so poorly covered that the dogs gnawed their bones, adding:

and I, Agnolo di Tura, called the Fat, buried my five children with my own hands, and so did many others likewise ... So many died that everyone thought that the end of the world had come.

And in Scotland, John of Fordun in his *Scotichronicon* wrote that the plague

generated such horror that children did not dare to visit their dying parents, or parents their children, but fled for fear of contagion as if from leprosy or a serpent.[27]

Friar Clyn also speaks, albeit more soberly, of the fear and horror that so affected people they 'hardly dared to perform works of piety and mercy; that is, visiting the sick and burying the dead'. However, the high mortality figures Clyn cited for the mendicant friars in Dublin, Drogheda and Kilkenny indicate that they cannot have shirked performing works of piety and mercy. The fear of burying the dead, as well as other factors, led elsewhere to mass, open pit graves where the dead were piled in layers, as described by a Florentine commentator with a simile that would do justice to John Donne, illustrating how quickly the extraordinary can become part of the normal order of things:

At every church they dug deep pits down to the water level; and thus those who were poor who died during the night were bundled up quickly and thrown into the pit. In the morning when a large number of bodies were found in the pit, they took some earth and shovelled it down on top of them; and later others were placed on top of them and then another layer of earth, just as one makes lasagne with layers of pasta and cheese.[28]

In Ireland, however, to date archaeologists have not found any plague cemeteries such as these or those uncovered in Spitalfields in London. But if Clyn's mortality figures are any indication, then special plague cemeteries may well have been created in the larger towns to deal with the unusual demand (see Plates 9 and 10).

Contemporary chronicles also repeatedly emphasise the decadence and vice prevalent in the post-plague era. A certain caution must be exercised in judging these accounts: they are at times almost formulaic and may owe much to an imitation of Thucydides' accounts of the outbreaks of disease in Athens in 427 BC when, he wrote, people realised that 'life and riches were alike transitory and they resolved to enjoy themselves while they could and to think only of pleasure'.

Yet, these similarities can also be seen as testifying to the commonality of human responses that emerge in crisis moments in history. According to Boccaccio, some people responded to the horror of the plague by drinking and carousing and enjoying life to the full. The monastic chronicler of Neuberg in Austria describes this merrymaking more sympathetically as an effort to overcome depression and to kindle 'a sort of half-happiness' even in the face of despair, though he goes on to add also that 'the best wine was easily come by, and all those who indulged in it to excess behaved as if they were mad, beating and abusing people for no reason'.[29]

Unfortunately, medieval Ireland has no Boccaccio, and we have to rely on ecclesiastical records to get a sense of people's behaviour. Immorality seems to have become a pressing problem for churchmen, and in 1373 the Pope ordered the Archbishops and Bishops of Ireland 'to assemble within six months, and yearly in future, a provincial council … to treat and draw up statutes for the reformation of the life and manners of clergy and people'.[30] Most of the surviving evidence in Ireland focuses on an increase in greed and injustice. This, too, echoes experiences recorded elsewhere. The contemporary French chronicler, Jean de Venette, wrote that after the Black Death,

> people became more miserly and grasping, although many owned more than they had before. They were also more greedy and quarrelsome, involving themselves in brawls, disputes and lawsuits… Also from that time charity began to grow cold, and wrongdoing flourished, along with sinfulness and ignorance.[31]

Richard Ledrede, in one of his Latin poems, begs for Christ's mercy and redemption since

> Avarice increases, deception and malice,
> Love and justice are in flight from our land,
> Everywhere rapine flourishes, hatred and arson.

Other poems from the mid-fourteenth century decry the prevalence of greed, dishonesty, cheating and abuse of power at all levels of society, always at the expense of the poor.[32]

These themes also dominate in the thirty-one surviving sermons of Archbishop FitzRalph of Armagh from the periods 1348-49 and 1351-56. Between 1348 and 1355, he inveighed repeatedly against the wickedness of men and their ignorance. Above all, his sermons reflect what must have been a growing concern with property and profit, not surprisingly in the post-plague context where the pickings were all the greater for the survivors. In the five sermons FitzRalph gave in Ireland soon after his arrival around April 1348 and before the outbreak of the Black Death, he focused on the themes of usury, temptation, sin (lust, avarice, lack of charity), the necessity of penance, reparation, restitution and prayer, themes that had been the stuff of his sermons in England before he was appointed to Armagh. A gap of one year ensued, until March 1349, while the plague raged in Louth and throughout Leinster. Yet, though FitzRalph had stayed in Ireland during this period, he made only a brief reference to the plague in his next sermon delivered in the Carmelite church in Drogheda on 25 March 1349. He offered his listeners little comfort, other than an injunction to trust in the Virgin Mary. Instead, he quickly segued into contrasting Mary's sinless state with the injustice and dishonesty of his listeners. Whether his emphasis on the faults of his listeners reflected worsening conduct among his congregation or his own growing awareness of local conditions is a moot point. From then until 1 June 1349 when he left for Avignon, he delivered no sermons. On his return in 1351, his sermons continued to emphasise man's sinfulness and the necessity for confession, restitution, and contrition, and he harked frequently on the vanity of possessions and the sinfulness of hoarding wealth. He spoke out against theft, cupidity, the trickery of merchants both in their dealings with the clergy as with the people, the dishonesty of lawyers, usury, extortion and the seizure of church property. In a charge that addressed what must have been a common occurrence in the wake of the Black Death, he condemned those who interfered with the inheritance rights of women and minors. In examining these remarks, Dr Katherine Walsh asks, somewhat rhetorically, whether the Black Death offered

> an even more effective opportunity for a relatively sophisticated merchant community to engage in plunder and extortion at the expense of the more helpless sections of the population such as widows, orphans, and minors deprived of their guardians?

In other sermons, FitzRalph betrayed a concern for the more vulnerable in society and repeatedly castigated the wealthy for neglecting their social obligations and for not distributing their superfluous wealth. He emphasised, perhaps not always objectively, the lack of charity evident in people's dealings with each other, and especially with the Church. At the opening of a synod in 1352, he complained that in his diocese were 'many usurers, many perjurers, many hostile to the church and priests'.[33]

Moreover, it is not unreasonable to suggest that the already violent nature of Irish society was further aggravated, given that the plague's effects were generally to intensify features already existing. An increase in crime had been reported in previous times of stress and particularly so at times of famine. In 1228, an annalist wrote of churches and property being plundered during a famine in Connacht. The trial in October 1310 of a man accused of robbery may be taken as typical: the jurors said that the accused had robbed 'from excessive poverty and hunger, which…they had in the summer last past, when there was a great dearth in this land.' In the period 1310-12, there were numerous trials of men who had turned criminal 'because of great poverty'. The famine of 1315-18 had also led to an increase in murder.[34] The plague of 1348 may well have aroused a similar spate of criminal activity. Some isolated references certainly suggest so: Archbishop FitzRalph, in a sermon in November 1357 before the Pope, claimed that more than 2,000 serious crimes were committed every year in his diocese.[35] In 1359, Papal faculty was given to the Archbishop of Dublin to absolve those clerks and laymen,

> who in that distant part of the world, where wars are almost continually being waged, have incurred excommunication by taking part in the destruction of churches, towns and other places, burnings, slayings of ecclesiastics and public spoliations.[36]

However, the Irish annalists do not record any instance of the plundering or burning of churches in the period 1316-60, even though thirteen instances are recorded for the period 1200-60, six for 1260-1310, four in 1310-16 and five in 1360-1402.[37] One could hazard many explanations for this gap for the period 1316-1360, but whatever the explanation, in general one may safely surmise that the frontier conditions prevailing in many parts of medieval Ireland may have sublimated much of the violent emotion aroused by plague that elsewhere found other forms of expression.

Richard FitzRalph's sermons again eloquently speak to the ways in which tension between the English and the Irish may have been used as justification for all manner of injustice, and suggest that incidents of the illegal seizure of land and property were on the increase at least in his Diocese of Armagh in the aftermath of the plague. In a sermon in the Carmelite church in Drogheda on 25 March 1349, some eight months after the plague's arrival there, he condemned those who 'seize hold of land that belongs to another using the judgements of an earthly court, but acting against their own conscience and against the plain law of God'. His remarks seem rather uncaring of his audience's troubles, but as historian Aubrey Gwynn writes:

> The audience to whom these stern warnings were addressed in March 1349 were not the few broken survivors of an almost annihilated

population, but rather, hard-pressed English colonists [who] were very capable of very vigorous aggression, in spite of – or perhaps because of – their heavy losses during the past winter.

FitzRalph continued in subsequent sermons in 1348-49 and in 1351-56 to condemn the violence in Ireland, the way in which each community robbed and even killed those of the opposite community, so that, as he said, 'many died without grace or charity'.[38]

Religious Responses: Flagellants, Heresy, Theology

Disasters like the Black Death challenged the most fundamental values and attitudes of society. That this challenge was most evident in the religious sphere is not surprising, since people's lives and world-view centred on their faith. The Black Death on the continent aroused strains and tensions between different groups, which found expression in anti-semitism, anti-papalism, anti-clericalism, hysteria, heresy, milleniarism, susperstition and the like. It led to widespread burning of Jews who were accused of poisoning the wells; in Strasbourg, for example almost a thousand Jewish people were burned alive in 1349 as a precautionary measure. In Ireland, as in England, there are hardly any records of such extimist millenarian reactions, as was also the case in Egypt and other Muslim countries where contemporary human responses to plague have been more fully described. Ireland and England largely escaped the excesses recorded in continental countries; as Dr Maurice Keen says of England, in words that could also be applied to Ireland, 'all seems to be in rather a minor key when it comes to reaction'. Why? The historian J.F. Lydon believes that in medieval Ireland religion 'sat lightly on the people, cleric as well as lay, and was not either oppressive nor an inhibiting factor in their lives', and he surmises that 'it was probably because they were not so morbid about their religion that the excesses so noticeable elsewhere are not a prominent feature of life in Ireland at this time'. In illustrating his hypothesis, he quotes Archbishop Minot of Dublin who, in reducing the number of feast-days in 1367, complained that they were occasions of sin to workmen,

> many of whom never or rarely enter their parish church at hours when
> masses are celebrated but spend almost all of the feast-day or at least the
> greater part thereof, in taverns and drunkenness and other illicit acts of
> pleasure.

Since the church was used as a hall for dances, games and storing valu-
ables, Lydon concludes that the Irish had 'an easy familiarity with
their Church which was in a very real sense the centre of their
community'.[39]

That same familiarity could also be taken as evidence of a deep,
almost instinctive faith which offered ways of responding to sudden
death that avoided the emotional extremes and could explain the relative absence of any reference to widespread milleniarist movements in
post-plague Ireland. One cannot discount that a deep religious faith
could have led people to accept what would have been seen as God's
will. The absence of widespread hysteria could also perhaps be linked
to the absence of an apocalyptic imagination in medieval Irish religion. In his study of the plague in Egypt, Michael Dols argues that the
controlled reaction to plague in Muslim countries and Eastern
Europe may be linked to Muslim theology and to the absence of an
apocalyptic mind-set.[40] There were no milleniarist responses in
Muslim society, perhaps because there is not a doctrine of the apoca-
lypse in orthodox Islam; similarly Byzantine chronicles of the Black
Death do not offer any evidence of messianic movements because the
Book of Revelation and apocalyptic ideas were not favoured by the
Orthodox Church. While Clyn uses apocalyptic images in his account
of the Black Death, they are relatively muted, even controlled, by
contrast with accounts by his contemporaries elsewhere.

Ireland doesn't seem to have escaped entirely, however. There are a
few references to flagellants in Ireland. In August 1349 the Pope,
Clement VI, ordered the Archbishops of Armagh, Dublin, Cashel and
Tuam 'to warn and induce certain persons calling themselves
Flagellantes to leave their vain religion', and this before he officially
banned the movement in Europe in a Bill issued 20 October 1349. In
his communication to the Irish bishops, the Pope claimed that some

mendicants were responsible for encouraging the flagellants, and most likely he had the Franciscans in mind. Some years later Richard FitzRalph in a sermon in Kells, Co. Meath on 14 May 1355, warned against the excesses of the Flagellants.[41] So perhaps certain towns and cities in Ireland saw scenes such as those described by Louis Heyligen in Avignon where

> men and women alike, many barefoot, others wearing hairshirts or smeared with ashes … processed with lamentations and tears, and with loose hair, [and] they beat themselves with cruel whips until the blood ran.

We find a less apocalyptic description offered by the chronicler of the monastery of Neuberg in Austria:

> Men gathered together from cities and towns and went devoutly in procession from church to church, walking two by two, totally naked except for a white cloth covering them from their loins to their ankles, singing beautiful hymns in honour of the Passion in their mother tongue and beating themselves so hard with knotted whips that drops of blood spattered the roadway. When the chapels closed after vespers, women humbly followed them.[42]

These processions usually lasted thirty-three days in memory of the length of the life of Christ and on the continent were initially welcomed by the public, but as their actions became ever more excessive, while clearly failing to halt the plague, opinion turned against them and they were outlawed. By the time we encounter references to flagellants in Ireland, the movement was already on the wane. In general, religious responses in Ireland betrayed a traditionalism and conservatism not evident in post-plague movements in continental countries.

Plague challenged religious belief in other ways and historians have long attributed to the Black Death the increasing questioning of authority and religious doctrine prevalent in the later fourteenth century. Heresy had not been unknown in pre-plague Ireland. In the early fourteenth century, Philip de Braibrok, a canon of Christ Church, was excommunicated for heresy; in 1324 a witchcraft scandal rocked Kilkenny and in 1335, in a letter to King Edward III, the Pope asserted that certain heretics had arisen in Ireland, some of whom asserted that Jesus Christ was a man, a sinner and deserved his crucifixion. Heresy seems to have been rife in the Diocese of Ossory in mid-century, and one contemporary source related that the heretics had spread into the Diocese of Dublin in 1352. Some four years later there was a case of heresy in Bunratty, Co. Clare when two Irishmen were burnt 'for casting contumely on the Blessed Virgin', a heresy that may not be unrelated to the increase in Marian devotion evident in Ireland, as throughout Europe, in the wake of the plague.[43] Of course, many of these 'heretics' were perhaps more victims of political expediency rather than religious dissenters. Nevertheless, the numerous references would suggest that heresy was even more prevalent in the 1340s and 1350s, even though details of these are scarce. In Ireland, however, religious dissent does not seem to have manifested itself violently as it did on the continent. Heretical persons are always mentioned singly or in twos or threes, never with a mass following. Lollardry, lay mysticism and the other manifestations of religious fervour which swept across Europe in the later Middle Ages, seem to have left Ireland untouched. Consequently, some historians would argue, Ireland was unprepared for the Reformation of the sixteenth century: 'there had been no *preparatio evangelica* as there had been in Germany before Luther's time or as in England in the days of Wycliffe'.[44]

While one cannot attribute developments in philosophical and theological thought directly to the influence of events such as the Black Death, the atmosphere of fourteenth-century thought does catch something of the popular pessimism and scepticism. The plague seems to have undermined medieval man's trust in authority and many have seen it as contributing to the growing scepticism that characterises European philosophy in the later Middle Ages. Above all, the plague contributed to a certain fatalism which seems to have possessed artists and philosophers alike and to a bleak view of man's sinfulness. This found intellectual expression in a revival of Augustinian doctrines, which emphasised the power and will of God and played a crucial part in the debates about justification through faith or good works. Because of the absence of universities and limited access to translations of philosophical and theological works, theology and philosophy did not attract the same attention in Ireland as in England or on the continent. This may also account for the general conservatism of religion in England and Ireland, and makes it difficult to ascertain whether contemporary doctrines gained any adherents in Ireland. One of the few we know to have engaged in the contemporary debate was Richard FitzRalph. In the debate on justification, he emphasised the sovereignty of conscience and the supremacy of an omnipotent and predestinating God in election and salvation. In this he deviated from the official emphasis on freewill and the efficacy of good works. FitzRalph's theological orientation is an interesting sidelight on contemporary attitudes, but how he was received in Ireland we do not know. What is clear is that he foreshadows Wycliffe and the puritan theology of the Lollards, some of whom looked to him for inspiration.[45]

Lay Piety: Indulgences, Bequests and Confraternities

There is no doubt, however, that the plague deepened the waves of orthodox lay piety and devotion which was at that time spreading all over Europe, as people turned increasingly to familiar religious practices. What we see here is not perhaps as dramatic or novel as the flagellants and other such milleniarist movements.

And whether these practices betray a deep faith or a form of superstition is not at issue here. They are revealing of people's fears and of the more usual ways they attempted to cope with the prospect of sudden death which had become so much a feature of daily life. Pope Clement VI in 1348-49 authorised a special plague mass, the '*Missa pro Mortalitate Evitanda*' or 'Mass against pestilence' which promised to safeguard from sudden death all those who heard it on five consecutive days. But above all, people were concerned that they would die a happy death, which primarily meant that they received absolution for their sins before death. The great fear was purgatory, that place to which are sent those who, though not condemned to hell, still need to do penance for sin. The horrors of purgatory were well-known: in the words of historian Eamonn Duffy, purgatory was seen as 'an out-patient department of Hell rather than the ante-chamber of Heaven'.[46] Consequently, the sacraments of penance and communion became particularly valued, understandable in conditions when people didn't know when death might take them. However, given the heavy toll on the clergy, often there were not sufficient clergy to administer the sacraments. This was of concern to the contemporary Bishop of Bath and Wells, Ralph of Shrewsbury:

> The contagious pestilence, which is now [10 January 1349] spreading everywhere, has left many parish churches and other benefices in our diocese without an incumbent, so that their inhabitants are bereft of a priest. And because priests cannot be found for love or money to take on the responsibility for those places and visit the sick and administer the sacraments of the church to them – perhaps because they fear that they will catch the disease themselves – we understand that many people are dying without the sacrament of penance…Therefore… we order and firmly enjoin you…to make it known…to everybody, but particularly to those who have already fallen sick, that if when on the point of death people cannot secure the services of a properly ordained priest, they should make confession of their sins, according to the teaching of the apostle, to any lay person, even to a woman if a man is not available.[47]

While there isn't any record of an Irish bishop speaking so directly, or of authorising women confessors, the issue of confession and penance had become urgent, as is indicated by the increasing number of refer-ences to petitions for plenary indulgences. A plenary indulgence in traditional Catholic doctrine means the remission of the entire temporal punishment due to sin, so that no further expiation is required in Purgatory. Initially, only the Pope could grant plenary indulgences, and this on the occasion of going on crusade; even the power of the bishop was limited to the granting of one year's indulgence on the occasion of the dedication of a church, and of forty days on other occasions. From 1300 on, and especially from the time of the Black Death, the requirements for indulgences were relaxed. Plenary indulgences were granted on the occasion of the Jubilee year every hundred years to all those who visited certain basilicas in Rome. Then, during the plague years (at the urging of the Italian poet Petrarch among others), Pope Clement VI in 1350 shortened the span for Jubilee years on the grounds that the average span of a human life at that time was too short a time to allow people the chance of enjoying a Jubilee in their own lifetimes.[48] That the indulgence associated with the Jubilee was sought by many is borne out by the fact that Archbishop FitzRalph of Armagh travelled to Avignon in June 1349 expressly to request of the Pope a plenary indulgence for the people of England and Ireland, without their being obliged to make the hazardous journey to Rome.[49] Given the Black Death, among other factors, it was clearly not possible for people to travel to Rome; yet the possibility of sudden death had become so real that the prospect of being granted complete remission of sin was a solacing one.

Another form of indulgence prevalent in these years was for full absolution of sin at the hour of death. Hitherto only the Pope could exercise this right, but from the second quarter of the fourteenth century the Pope granted to various petitioners the right of *confessionale*, that is the right to choose their own confessors who would grant them full remission at the hour of death. This is remarked upon in numerous chronicles both in England and on the continent. Evidence for Ireland comes from the *Calendar of Papal Letters*, which notes that the plague of 1348-62

> led to a very large demand for plenary remissions at the hour of death. The Pope, with his usual generosity, granted such remissions to whole dioceses at once as the plague spread, but the private demand was none the less stimulated, as the more comprehensive indults were usually limited to short periods.[50]

These requests were clearly inspired by the beliefs and fears of lay people, not by any ecclesiastical requirements. The sharp rise in the number of requests may not be explained solely by reference to the developing efficiency of the Curia at this time, nor to the practice of requiring a fee for indulgences which became increasingly common during the Avignon Papacy. There is an evident decline in such demands after 1352, as a graph indicates (see Figure 1, p.199). Clearly the increase was occasioned by the shortage of priests and by the terror caused by unpredictable, sudden and likely death by plague.

Nor are all such petitions represented here as the other Papal register, the *Calendar of Papal Petitions* records many others. In 1343, three people requested the right to choose their own confessor; in 1351, the Archbishop of Armagh made a similar request for an unspecified number of people, while some years later, in 1363, there was only one such petition, when on the occasion of the second outbreak of plague in Ireland, the Pope granted to the Bishop of Iniscathaigh the power to absolve in the hour of death 'all who labour in the said lands so long as the mortality lasts' as well as permission to absolve Irish labourers in time of pestilence for a limited period of four months.[51]

Purgatory, however, was seen as unavoidable for all but the most saintly. But in various ways one could shorten the time spent there. Charitable giving was one such way. Giving to the Church had always been a response in times of trouble. For example, after the great mortality of 1094, we read:

> the King and his subjects … were strucken with great terrour, for appeasing of which plague the Clergie of Ireland thought good to cause all the inhabitants of the kingdome in generall to fast from Wednesday to Sunday once every month for the space of one year, except solmne and great festivall days, they also appointed certain prayers to be dayly said. The King, the noblemen, and all the subjects of the kingdome were very benefitiall towards the Church and poore men this yeare, whereby God's wrath was aswaged. The king of his great bounty gave great immunities and freedom to churches that were then before charged with Cess and other extraordinary contry-charges with many other large and bountifull gifts.[52]

Bequests to the Church could range from gifts to religious orders, donations for the maintenance of churches, or for masses and prayers to be said for the deceased to speed him or her on the journey through Purgatory. Many chroniclers, themselves clerics, complain in the post-plague era of the lack of charity and the fall-off in donations, which of course may have been occasioned simply by the fact that there were fewer donors after the plague. Clearly, Archbishop FitzRalph of Armagh was troubled by what he saw as the lack of charity among the merchants and rich people of Drogheda, and by the tendency to postpone giving until after death. Post-mortem giving, he argued, wasn't as meritorius as giving during life. FitzRalph's problem was compounded by the fact that what charity was being given was going largely to the mendicant orders and especially the Franciscans, who were particularly popular everywhere, especially as confessors.

Much of the evidence of lay piety in Ireland in the post-plague years centres on the Franciscans. It is revealed in the increasing number of Franciscan friaries that were founded by Gaelic leaders in their own territories, and particularly by the large number of houses of the Third Order of St Francis that sprang up everywhere and especially in the west.[53] There is some evidence also of an increase in the number of lay religious confraternities, akin to the guilds and fraternities that developed in England and all over Europe in the later fourteenth century. The Third Order Secular consisted of loosely knit groups of lay people who lived in their own homes, pursued their own occupations but followed a certain semi-monastic rule, participated in the order's religious activities and were often responsible for the care of the churches.[54] It was a practice that arose in the mid-thirteenth century and became increasingly common in the fourteenth century. According to Friar Clyn, one such confraternity was instituted in the Franciscan church in Kilkenny in 1347, with responsibility for repairs to the church and the erection of a new belltower. The Black Death interrupted its construction. But the still-standing corbel figures on the church's tower are modelled, according to legend, on members of this confraternity. There were quite likely many of these confraternities throughout Ireland in the later fourteenth century, since many of the later foundations of the Third Order Regular were outgrowths of the secular confraternities. One of the rights granted to members of such confraternities, and also to other benefactors, was the right to be buried in the Franciscan habit and in a Franciscan cemetery, privileges considered to be an aid on the way to heaven. There are a number of extant references in Irish Franciscan records to such practices among lay people. In recording two plague deaths in Ennis in 1349-50, the annalist notes that Matthew Caoch McConmara was buried in the Franciscan habit at Ennis, and Traolach, son of Donncha O' Brien, was buried with the Franciscans at Nenagh.[55]

The Black Death in Art and Literature

The artist, above all, gave expression to the fears and insecurity of late medieval, plague-stricken man. Faced not only with the prospect of sudden death, but also the suffering and deaths of family members – and this not just once as in 1348, but repeatedly throughout the later fourteenth century – people's thoughts and imagination, not surprisingly, turned frequently to dying and death. This is reflected in the art and devotion of the period. Artists concerned themselves with the figure of the suffering pathetic Christ or with the image of the Pieta; Mary is increasingly represented as the *mater dolorosa*; instruction manuals in the *ars moriendi*, the art of dying well, became popular; the Stations of the Cross commemorating Christ's journey to Calvary became a regular devotion. Then there were the more morbid expressions such as the *danse macabre* and the cadaver tombstones that also appear with more frequency in the years after the plague. The themes of suffering and death are evident in the surviving art not only of this period, but of succeeding centuries.[56] Some historians have attributed this death-oriented art to the impact of the Black Death, but as Eamonn Duffy in *The Stripping of the Altars* notes 'reflections on the inescapable fate of all flesh were common long before: the later Middle Ages saw the unfolding of the theme, not its invention'.[57]

The effect of the plague on people's image of death has been exaggerated, as has been the extent of the religious pessimism. In many ways, the art and literature of the post-plague era is of a piece with what preceded it, and images of death and decay, which some have seen as peculiar to the post-plague era, characterise the art of the whole medieval period. Siegfried Wenzel in an analysis of the post-plague poems on death written in 1372 by the English friar, John Grimestone, couldn't find any significant changes in either theme or tone from the lyrics that predate the plague.[58] At least some of the Huizinga-style pronouncements on the Black Death inducing an obsession with death have arisen because of the mis-dating of artistic works, such as the 'Triumph of Death' in Pisa which, among other macabre images, portrays death as an old woman with a scythe swooping on her victims. This work was thought to have been painted after the Black Death, possibly in 1350, but has now been shown to have been painted before the plague.[59] If there is a change, it is more one of emphasis than of theme: an emphasis on the mutability of all things – Fortune's wheel – the unpredictability of death, the corruptibility of the body, always casting a shadow on life. Moreover, the surviving representations both in England and Ireland suggest some cultural differences from France and Germany, where the cult of death seems to have been more extreme. The *danse macabre*, *Totentanz* or Dance of Death, focusing on the egalitarianism of death and its inevitability, with death presented as a skeleton either dancing or playing an instrument, was far more popular on the continent in the fifteenth century than it was in England, and there are no known surviving representations of it in Ireland.

Whatever may have been the case in France and Germany then, late fourteenth-century Irish literature, in Latin, English and Irish, is quite conservative in its focus on traditional Christian themes: the Nativity, sorrow for sin, prayers for help, conflicts between soul and body, Judgement Day, Resurrection, Mary. The Latin poems of Richard Ledrede, for example, are considered to be far more traditional and austere than those of his contemporary Franciscan poets elsewhere: whereas Franciscan poets in continental countries focus on the Passion and details of Christ's suffering, Ledrede's poems deal more with themes relating to the Nativity and Resurrection.[60] In the group of poems known as the Kildare poems dating from the second quarter of the fourteenth century, more typically late-medieval themes dominate. Some are satirical, anti-clerical and anti-establishment in tone, particularly critical of the rich who amass wealth at the expense of the poor. In the poem 'Hymn' by Friar Michael of Kildare, death is presented as the Great Leveller:

> Be thou baron or knight
> Thou shalt be a sorrowful wight,
> When thou liest on bier itight
> In fulli poor weed.

The futility of riches is repeatedly stressed: 'all is fenne/The chattel of this life'. The poet denounces the folly of hoarding, emphasising that man enters and exits the world in poverty; therefore, he warns the rich man that 'Thou shalt not of all thy thing/A Penny bear to mould'.[61] In one of his poems, Richard Ledrede repeats the theme:

> the man who is rich in earthly lordship, poised on top of the
>   world,
> is like a bladder full of wind when we see him reduced to the dust of
>   death.[62]

Other themes are the standard themes of orthodox Christianity and even of western thought: the story of creation, Christ's Passion, the transitoriness of human life, the mutability of all things, Judgement Day…, all presented with a strongly moralistic overtone. Against the fear of death is always the consolation of religion, Christ's sacrifice and the promise of salvation. Whether the plague wrought any significant change in this attitude is difficult to say. Negative evidence speaks more loudly than the surviving evidence: from about the middle of the fourteenth century no more original work was produced in English in Ireland, a development that owed much to the growing domination of Gaelic-Irish culture and the Irish language, and the growing contraction of the English colony in Ireland.[63]

By contrast, there seems to have been a revival in Irish literature in the later fourteenth century as suggested by the large number of manuscripts in Irish surviving from that period. Irish poetry and particularly the official bardic poetry at this time is highly conservative, preserving medieval themes and attitudes even in poetry written in the sixteenth century. So poetry written even in the sixteenth and seventeenth centuries can be very revealing of the medieval religious mind, of what the historian J. Watt describes as

> the brooding sense of the proximity of death, the sense of conflict between man's spirit and flesh ('let me and my body consort not'), an awareness of the perils of judgement and especially of Christ's love shown in his Passion, with a strong sense of his physical suffering.

Even late medieval love poems in Irish, collected by Ó Rathile in 1925 in a volume entitled *Dánta Grádha,* carry echoes of *memento mori* themes. The male speaker gives frequent injunctions to remember the proximity of the grave, the brevity of life, the fleeting nature of beauty, though always in the context of love. The earliest of these poems date from the fourteenth century, though many are most likely from the sixteenth and seventeenth centuries and reflect the renaissance in contemporary Europe of late medieval attitudes to themes of mutability, ideas which infiltrated Irish literature through the many clerical students who studied abroad.[64]

Of even more immediate interest in the context of the Black Death is the echo in this poetry of that great image from post-plague Europe, the *danse macabre*. Scholars have usually assumed that the persona in these poems was a man speaking of his love of woman in both its more positive and negative aspects, but Cathal Ó Háinle in a recent article argues that in at least one of these, No. 103 (in the Ó Rathile collection), the speaker is in fact Death addressing a young girl, reminding her of her inevitable death, her beauty and youth, urging her to avoid marriage and to wait for him ('Remember me and don't marry/*Cuimhnigh oram, ná pós fear*'). In a careful analysis of the poem's metre and rhythm, Ó Háinle has shown that the poem, departing from the variable meter traditional in such poems, uses the regular 4/4 rhythm of dance music and an insistent trochaic meter. The result, argues Ó Háinle, is a rhythm that suggests the beating of a drum, and so is 'consonant with the notion that Death is speaking here, and that, as in the *danse macabre/Totentanz*, Death comes beating a drum, as he does when inviting people to join in the Dance of Death.'[65] The very form of the poem then re-enacts the speaker's invitation to the young girl to wait and follow him, a standard feature of the Dance of Death motif.

Such *memento mori* themes haunt late medieval sermons. They made, writes Huizinga, 'the eternal admonition to remember death swell into a sombre chorus ringing throughout the world' and in that vein have often been read to reflect the post-plague consciousness.[66] Very little sermon literature, however, survives in Ireland from this period. The sermons still extant focus on the themes common in late medieval sermon literature in England: the ten commandments, the life of Christ, the conflict of body and soul, the transitoriness of life, the sinfulness of man, the vanity of earthly possessions.[67] The sermons of Archbishop FitzRalph of Armagh, as we have seen, do not address the more human sorrows of people, but focus on the moral failings of his congregation. Other surviving literary evidence indicates that emotions and responses in Ireland took a similar form to those on the continent. Surviving translations into Irish of popular European works were often of current mystical works; one of the most popular devotional works throughout Europe in the fourteenth century was the *Meditationes vitae Christi* which was translated into Irish in the fifteenth century as *Smaointe Beatha Chríostí* and proved equally popular.

The visual arts also mirror the religious and artistic images popular in the post-plague era in continental Europe though, as already noted, very little medieval art survives in Ireland. One surviving sculpture, however, perhaps best captures the most general emotion felt in 1349 on the outbreak of plague. One of the corbel figures under the vaulting of the tower in the Church of St Francis in Kilkenny carries an expression suggestive of the surprise and horror and infinite sadness felt by the people of Kilkenny in 1349 (see Plate 6).

There are no illustrations of the Black Death itself such as are to be found in the annals of Gilbert Li Muisis in Flanders, nor any later plague illustrations such as are to be found in France and Germany. The few works that survive betray the same vision as is to be found in contemporary English and continental art, focusing on the themes of the suffering Christ, judgement, mutability: again, the themes of traditional Christianity. A late medieval wood sculpture from Fethard in Co. Tipperary depicts a popular theme in late-medieval art: the *Ecce Homo* Christ with a bleeding, scourged body and a drooping head caught at the moment before the Crucifixion. Images of the Passion of Christ were also frequently depicted on tombs of the period, and a number of late medieval Pieta sculptures have also survived, all suggesting a greater sensitivity to the theme of human suffering. This focus on Christ's suffering is also evident in the metal processional crosses and crucifixes that survive from the late medieval period, some from the 1340s though most from the early and mid-fifteenth century. As elsewhere in Europe, the Christ figure appears twisted and in pain, perhaps reflecting the sensitivity of a plague-stricken people. However, such perceptions gradually changed accordingly as plague came to be accepted as yet another disease in the medieval pantheon. As Dr Colm Hourihane in his study of these crosses writes, those of the fifteenth century begin to evince a change of focus:

> By the early fifteenth century the body lacks the distorted position of the previous century and has a stronger focus on realism and victory. Christ is shown in death with his arms upraised and his head resting on his shoulder. By the mid- to late-fifteenth century the victory of Christ over death was being depicted. He is still shown with all the agony of the Crucifixion, ranging from the wound in the side to the hollow of the stomach and the exaggerated ribcage, but his head is more vertical and confident in posture.

What paintings survive often depict images of the last judgement and crucifixions. Whereas contemporary European artistic survivals frequently depict the plague saints Roch and Sebastian, or Mary in the guise of protectress against plague, there are none such extant in Ireland, with one notable exception. In the church of the Cistercian Knockmoy Abbey in Co. Galway on the chancel's north wall is a faded fresco depicting the martyrdom of St Sebastian, one of the patron saints of the plague. Above it is that image which is almost a cliché in late medieval art, an outline of the very popular narrative morality, 'the three living and the three dead', of three young kings coming upon their own crowned skeletons. Underneath is the inscription, 'we have been as you are, you shall be as we are'. The fresco has been dated to around 1400, when it was commissioned by two Gaelic-Irish chieftains. The motif is in fact a Roman one, but gained currency in the wake of the plague and post-plague depictions of the motif tend to a greater realism. The image stresses that in the midst of life is death, though its thrust is generally not pessimistic but didactic.[68]

Surviving sepulchral slabs might perhaps be seen to carry some suggestions of a changing perception of death from the earlier to the later Middle Ages. In general, pre-plague effigies in Ireland, like other northern European effigies, emphasise not death but life, with images of the resurrected Christ or of the deceased not as dead but alive. An example is the group of effigies of the Hackett family in Cashel where the figures are portrayed cross-legged, an image according to E.C. Rae suggestive not 'of dying nor of death but of vitality'. If there is a change, it is that in the fifteenth century large funerary monuments became more popular, and in particular cadaver tombs, such as the Beaulieu Cadaver, in which the deceased is portrayed as a corpse, with the emphasis on decay and finality. The eyesockets are empty, the body realistically become food for worms (see Plates 14 and 18). This is evident in the tomb erected about 1482 for James Rice (a former Mayor of Waterford City) and his wife. The figures are cadaverous and are intended not to shock, but as a *memento mori*, to remind the viewer of his or her own mortality and of the need for repentance. And as the accompanying inscription reveals, there is always the hope that the prayers of the living will aid the dead in the journey beyond death:

> Here lie James Rice, onetime citizen of this city, founder of this chapel, and Catherine Broun, his wife. Whoever you may be, passerby, stop, weep as you read. I am what you are going to be, and I was what you are. I beg of you, pray for me! It is our lot to pass through the jaws of death. Lord Christ, we beg of thee, we implore thee, be merciful to us! Thou who has come to redeem the lost condemn not the redeemed![69]

We can say then that if there is an alteration in artistic consciousness in the post-plague era, it is more one of emphasis than of any radical change: death's more macabre details are foregrounded, death is presented as a grim threat, pervasive and beyond human control. But in general this alteration, subtle as it is, does not become evident, either in Ireland or England, until the fifteenth century. Moreover, very few monuments from the later fourteenth century survive in Ireland, again pointing to a dislocation caused by plague and other factors.

It is significant that when recovery emerged in the fifteenth century, it emerged most particularly in the funerary sculpture that developed particularly in the Meath, Kilkenny and Dublin areas. Perhaps here, more than in any other area, is the pervasive consciousness of death most evident. In general, one could argue for a general shift away from the simple, uninscribed and unadorned tombs common in the earlier Middle Ages to the ornate tombs in the fifteenth century, which high-light the personal details of the deceased. Some have argued that the proliferation of these tombs reflects people's reaction to the unceremonious, impersonal mass burials that took place during the plague era.[70] But this shift may also owe something to the vagaries of fashion, the growth of towns and the increasing prosperity among the new elites that led them to erect such monuments. The practice of decorating the sides of tombs was not a new one in Ireland, but became more common in the later fourteenth century. An example of this shifting fashion is the tomb stone near St Erc's Hermitage in Slane, Co Meath which the art historian John Hunt dates to the late fourteenth or early fifteenth century and singles out as foreshadowing the tombs with weepers which became popular in the Dublin area in the mid-fifteenth century (See Plate 12).[71] Tombs were decorated along the sides with weepers mourning the deceased, usually favourite saints and patrons, with the apostles becoming more common at the turn of the century. Again, one might argue that these new tombs emphasise the finality and human pathos of death, more than had been the case in tombs of earlier times: death is portrayed more as an end of a human's life than the beginning of new life.

What we can say of the post-plague artistic and architectural landscape in Ireland is marked above all by negative evidence. Few monuments or works can be dated to the latter half of the fourteenth century, not surprisingly given the recession that occurred in the aftermath of the plague. This is particularly evident in the more densely populated areas of the east and south where no new monasteries were built in this period, and castle-building largely stopped. Clearly, with the lower rents and higher wages consequent on the Black Death, few patrons could afford any architectural or artistic expenditure. Building programmes already started were interrupted. The tower in the church of St Francis in Kilkenny was begun in 1347, but its completion seems to have been delayed for a number of years by the Black Death which severely affected Kilkenny. Such a hiatus is not peculiar to Ireland; it was also evident elsewhere in England and Europe, as for example in Florence, where the Black Death interrupted the refurbishment of the city which had started with Giotto earlier in the century, or in Siena where the building of the Duomo was interrupted by the plague and never fully resumed.[72]

Perhaps, too, this negative evidence speaks to a high rate of mortality among sculptors and masons in Ireland; in Europe at large this section of the population was badly hit by the plague outbreaks of 1348 and 1361.[73] Since most masons' and sculptors' workshops were in the cities and towns of Leinster most affected by the plague, their work was also interrupted. This is particularly evident – ironically given the number who died in some of those towns – in the relative dearth of funerary sculpture. Whereas in England many tombs survive from this period, in Ireland there are only about nine funerary monuments extant for the period 1350-1450. The reasons may be sought in the Black Death's effect on the towns of Ireland, the contraction of the colony and the unsettled and warlike conditions in Ireland at this time. And there could be reasons other than the Black Death. In examining the medieval tombs at St Canice's Cathedral in Kilkenny, Dr John Bradley discovered that many medieval tombs and memorials which had existed in the seventeenth and even in the nineteenth centuries are now missing. Possibly this is a consequence of disused medieval memorials being quarried for stone, while many were destroyed during the Cromwellian sack of the cathedral in 1650.[74]

While artistic life elsewhere in Europe resumed quickly enough, in Ireland recovery took longer, thanks to continuing warfare and the increasingly perilous state of the colony. When recovery took place, it did so initially under the patronage of Gaelic or Gaelicised Anglo-Irish chieftains, particularly in the west. Friaries and churches were built, tower-houses were erected. Architectural styles changed as Irish masons developed their own Irish late-Gothic style. The art historian Roger Stalley sums up the change:

> About 1350 a stylistic watershed was reached following which the isolation of Irish architecture became more marked… It was an era of retrenchment that must have had a devastating impact on the masons' yards and it is hard to see how any continuity of training or apprenticeship could have survived.[75]

In the following century, the new sculpture evinces more Gaelic-Irish characteristics, reflecting the domination of the Gaelic-Irish generally.

If the plague evoked fear and terror in those it immediately affected, the extent to which it created a new consciousness is very debatable. Apocalyptic statements about it changing the medieval mind are highly suspect. Such changes take more than decades, and even then human responses to tragedies haven't radically changed throughout the centuries. Death is a perennial human concern and in a predominantly Christian culture is always perceived with some ambivalence, at once the end of life and the beginning of eternal life. The responses to plague revealed the extremes of frailty, cruelty and gullibility; others responded courageously and with faith. Some, especially people in those parts of Ireland not affected by plague, no doubt continued unaware of the disasters happening elsewhere. Those who did know of events elsewhere probably simply felt sorrow, loss, gratitude and relief and continued living more or less as before, sharing the sentiments of Aedh Mac Aodhagáin, who earlier in his diary had given poignant expression to a young man's fear of dying. He survived the plague and in his diary entry for Christmas Eve 1351 wrote,

> a year ago this night since I wrote these lines on the margin below and may I by God's will reach the anniversary of this night. Many changes. Amen, Pater Noster.[76]

4

The Black Death and the Countryside

In the world of work the effects of the plague are more readily identifiable, if only because most of the population lived in villages and rural areas and because sources are somewhat more revealing. The rhythms of rural life were disrupted by the plague's mortality, but at the same time its demands – sowing and harvesting, farming land and tending livestock – meant that people had to readapt quickly to changing conditions. However, the rural economy was ill-equipped to weather the onslaughts of sudden mortality because of the decline that had been progressing since at least the beginning of the century.

The thirteenth century had been a period of exuberant economic development and demographic growth all over Europe. Ireland too participated in this expansion: after 1169, forests were cleared, new methods of agriculture were introduced, boroughs founded, castles and churches built. Manorial revenues increased thanks to more efficient management, some political stability and more intensive farming of demesne lands. Demographic growth, though never on a par with that in England or on the continent, was nevertheless sufficient to cause a rise in the prices for agricultural produce and a growing demand for land which helped further increase manorial profits. The first century of feudalism in Ireland brought great wealth to landowners and made Ireland the granary of Britain. Moreover, the colony in many respects came to play an important role in maintaining England's well-being. Ireland offered new frontiers for an expanding population, for younger sons and for the surplus of tenants for whom there were no holdings in England. The shortage of land in England, its easy availability in Ireland, together with the offer of attractive terms of tenure, led many landless English and Welsh peasants to emigrate to Ireland and to continue coming well into the late thirteenth century.[1]

By 1348, however, the medieval rural economy had everywhere contracted and the later fourteenth century was a time of falling productivity and a declining population. This decline or malaise is a contentious subject and historians do not agree on its origins, some claiming it originated with the famines of 1315-18, others with the Black Death, yet others even earlier in flaws inherent in the manorial economy itself.[2] A consideration of the causes of this decline in Ireland is necessary to an understanding of the Black Death's effects.

Pre-plague Decline

Endogenous factors have long been cited as the fundamental cause of the late medieval decline, and in particular what are seen as the fatal flaws at the heart of the medieval agrarian economy itself. Much of the land reclaimed in the later thirteenth century was poor, marginal land, particularly that reclaimed as free tenants moved away from manorial centres to outlying farms on the edges of manors. The cultivation of what was often poorer land, along with intensive grain production, which had led to prosperity for Ireland in the thirteenth century, inevitably resulted in a certain amount of soil exhaustion. This is the widely accepted explanation for the general European recession in the fourteenth century:

> The honeymoon of high yields was succeeded by long periods of reckoning, when the marginal lands, no longer new, punished the men who tilled them with recurrent inundations, dessications and dust-storms.[3]

By the early fourteenth century, a widespread contraction had set in with settlements – especially on the frontiers of the colony and in marginal areas – being abandoned. This happened, for example, on manors in the northern parts of Co. Tipperary. In the 1330s and 1340s the value of tenements in the manors of Nenagh and Thurles fell by 75% and never recovered, partly because the lands were not valuable, partly because these were the very lands also subject to attack from the Gaelic-Irish.[4] Many early fourteenth-century Irish manorial extents also make frequent reference to lands lying tenantless because they are 'poor and too much used'. This abandonment of poor or marginal land in the pre-plague area is not peculiar to Ireland. And, as happened elsewhere, it was a process that was accelerated by the plague. In the straitened circumstances of the years after the plague, and given the abundance of land available, tenants had no interest in farming poorer, marginal and unprofitable holdings.

Moreover, the proportion between the total population and the amount of available arable land was always a precarious one in Northern Europe, and the continuing increase of population into the late thirteenth century led to a contraction in the size of holdings, some of which were too small to support a family. Consequently, many peasants lived close to subsistence and did not have the resources to withstand natural disasters.[5] The extent to which this process was also true of Ireland varied from region to region. The colony in Ireland did not experience the same pressure on land evident elsewhere, but as the colony contracted with the Gaelic resurgence of the fourteenth century, the size of holdings in some areas contracted also as tenants withdrew from outlying farms and marcher lands. There is evidence that betaghs (unfree tenants, the equivalent of villeins, who were often Gaelic-Irish) in some areas were able to acquire land or increase their holdings by taking over lands abandoned due to war. Nevertheless, in general, the majority of peasant holdings would seem to have been smaller than in England. A sample of Co. Dublin tenants from the second half of the fifteenth century shows them tilling together an area averaging eighteen acres, whereas a holding of a quarter-virgate (about seven acres) is considered by historians to be the minimum holding capable of affording basic subsistence to a single family.[6] Conditions for agricultural labourers were also depressed as wages stayed at a steady level, even falling in real terms, well into the fourteenth century; for example, wages paid on the Earl of Norfolk's Irish manors in 1279-86 were very similar to those paid on the farms of Holy Trinity Priory, Dublin, around 1344.[7] Generally, the crop yield per acre was low, though this was not peculiar to Ireland, and declined further in the late thirteenth and early fourteenth centuries, thanks to warfare. The frequent references to the poverty of tenants and to the low quality of peasant land also suggest the possibility that the quantity of food produced per head of the Anglo-Irish population must have been dwindling.[8] Every failed harvest then meant malnutrition, if not starvation.

However, many historians suggest that the difficulties experienced in Europe at the beginning of the fourteenth century cannot in the end be satisfactorily attributed to any primary endogenous factor. But for external factors, and in particular the Black Death, the difficulties of the early fourteenth century could have been just 'a passing phase, a period of adjustment as population sought a more favourable balance with resources'.[9] Exogenous factors include the Europe-wide climatic changes from the early decades of the fourteenth century that caused the weather to turn colder and wetter. Many argue that this change was the cause of the poor harvests, food shortages and famines, and not any fundamental flaw in the economy itself. Studies have shown that from the end of the thirteenth century the weather, even in summer, became wetter and colder, and conditions worsened in the 1330s and 1340s, with storms and floods wreaking havoc especially in some low-lying areas in England. Ireland's experience mirrors this. Storms and floods were common, with particularly hard winters recorded in 1338 and 1339, often with unusually wet weather. This weather pattern continued right into the 1340s, providing conditions that would favour the spread of pneumonic plague which thrives in colder temperatures. Evidence of pollen analysis also indicates that cereal growing began to contract around 1300, probably because of the wetter and colder weather. Harvests were ruined and crop failures are reported repeatedly throughout the 1320s and 1330s. Famine became almost endemic, beginning with the great famine of 1294-96, which was followed by another in 1308-10. The Great European Famine of 1315-18 decimated the population in many areas, led to an increase in the number of subtenants and landless and accelerated the process of demographic decline. Finally, all this was further aggravated by a series of cattle and sheep murrains which caused untold hardship, as well as by epidemics of smallpox, typhoid and a myriad other diseases. By the time the Black Death struck in 1348, the rural economy had been battered and the rural population was declining. People not only lacked the reserves to withstand the further onslaughts of plague, but in all likelihood were immunologically weakened and therefore even more vulnerable to plague.[10]

Though much of this recession is part of a wider European phenomenon, local and regional factors were crucial everywhere, and especially so in Ireland. The Irish situation is distinguished by the endemic warfare that continually threatened economic stability, gave further impetus to economic recession and prevented recovery from natural disasters. Recent studies in England and Europe suggest that the recession had steadied by the 1330s and 1340s, that population decline had halted and that manorial incomes had stabilised by the time the Black Death struck, as landlords pursued policies of cutting costs, reimposing labour services and raising rents.[11] Colonial Ireland, by contrast, did not share in this recovery, thanks to local conditions prevailing in the years prior to the plague, the worsening warfare in the country and the Bruce Invasion of 1315-18 which inflicted considerable destruction on the countryside, devastating some areas.[12]

Even before 1315, warfare had caused a contraction in the colony. At a time when land was still available for colonisation, settlements, especially in outlying areas, were deserted or lost to the Irish. Tenants fled and some areas (particularly marcher lands) were devastated, in many cases lying waste for years to come. Lands were often reported as 'waste', not because the soil was exhausted but because they had either been destroyed during some military campaign or had returned to Irish use. A few instances indicate the extent of the contraction in the Anglo-Irish colony, even in Dublin, the centre of the colony, long before the advent of the plague. An inquisition of 1305 revealed that a tenement near the Abbey of St Thomas, 'for thirty years past answered nothing to the city because no one dwelt there nor brewed ale for sale'.[13] In south Co. Dublin, the manor of Castlekevin was wholly lost by 1326 and many of the betaghs had disappeared; on the Archbishop of Dublin's manor of Tallaght only four betaghs remained and three townlands were alleged to be uninhabitable; on the manor of Clondalkin, fifty-two acres of betagh land were unoccupied and much of the land in the manors of Rathcoole and Ballymore was in the hands of the Irish.[14] In the early fourteenth century the tenants of the royal demesnes of Saggart, Co. Dublin, claimed they were so impoverished by war that 'they have become vagrants, begging their bread' and holdings in the other royal manors of Newcastle Lyons and Crumlin were reported as waste due to war.[15] At the other end of the country, in Munster, on the manor of Grean in Co. Limerick, a 1331 extent revealed that both demesne and betagh lands rendered nothing because they were in Irish hands, while court fees rendered nothing because there were no tenants; in 1331 on the manor of Adare, 1,391 acres of demesne lay waste and tenantless, another 4,006 acres rendered nothing, and betaghs in Kerry returned nothing, all due to war.[16] In Connacht an inquisition in 1304 on the lands of Edmund de Butiller revealed that little or nothing could be got of the issues of those lands, 'on account of the power of the Irish in those parts, who prostrated castles, burned and wasted the lands'.[17] These details all come in the context of petitions for rent relief and so were couched in suitably exaggerated terms. Nevertheless, they may be taken as indicative of general trends and of the widespread contraction in those areas that had not been heavily colonised.

Then there were the many other factors peculiar to Ireland, such as landlord absenteeism and the emigration of farmers and labourers. The result was the desertion of marginal rural settlements, a common feature in contemporary Europe and especially Germany. However, whereas economic crises elsewhere led rural dwellers to move to larger towns and manors, in Ireland the cause was most often war or the fear of war. The persistence of warfare forced settlers, particularly in the more exposed march areas or on the outer reaches of manorial settlements, to retreat further and further, leaving their lands tenant-less. This was true even of the Dublin area where we read of

> certain persons holding lands both in the Irish marches and in peaceful places [who] flee to live in the latter, leaving the former waste and undefended and to the detriment of their English inhabitants.[18]

Demesne lands were leased as landlords began to lose all interest in direct cultivation and some demesne castles were allowed to fall into ruin. So from the early decades of the fourteenth century, the 'lack of tenants because of war' is repeatedly echoed in contemporary documents as an explanation for lands lying waste.

However, it is important to emphasise that the retrogression was not uniform and varied between different parts of the country, depending on the intensity of the initial colonisation and the strength of the local Gaelic-Irish leaders. In east Ulster, for example, colonising activities were continued and castles were built there until well into the fourteenth century, while in the well-settled manors of south Leinster and south-east Munster, contraction was limited.[19] To what extent a decline is evident in the rural economy of Gaelic Ireland is not possible to determine due to lack of sources. Certainly, the military resurgence of Gaelic Ireland in the fourteenth century would suggest that this sector of Ireland was experiencing a certain economic well-being, or at least was in a position to capitalise on the difficulties of the colony.

Rural Ireland then proved a complex host for the plague of 1348. While the colony's manors would have presented many of the same conditions as those pertaining on similar manors in England, the constant presence of war is the crucial factor that makes any direct comparison of the plague's effects in the two countries difficult. To a degree unparalleled in England, the colony in Ireland was declining for many decades before the advent of plague, and the plague intensified this decline. Distinguishing the effects of war from those of the plague is virtually impossible in the Irish situation: both worked in tandem, even in the view of contemporaries assessing their own economic predicaments.

Mortality

The mortality caused in 1348–50 was the most significant effect of the Black Death on the Irish feudal countryside; it is also the issue that is the most elusive and the most contentious. There are no population figures for medieval rural Ireland, nor are there any figures for plague deaths beyond a few isolated references. Nevertheless, some indication of the extent of the mortality can be discerned from these references and through analogy with mortality elsewhere. Figures from well-documented English manors can function as a guide and indicate that mortality was very high in certain rural areas. For example, the average mortality for twenty-two manors on the estates of Glastonbury Abbey was 54.6%. In one of the best-documented manors of England, Halesowen near Birmingham in the West Midlands, plague mortality has been calculated as having been in the region of 44%, a figure matched by mortality figures for a neighbouring manor in the See of Worcester. On the manors of Bishop's Waltham in Hampshire with a total population of 404 persons, 264 deaths were recorded between Michaelmas 1348 and Michaelmas 1349, a mortality rate of 65%. On the manor of Farnham to the south-east of Reading in Wiltshire, an estimated 1,436 died out of a total rural population of about 3,000 – a mortality of between a third and a half of the population. Studies of other manors in Wiltshire have posited similar figures. A study of Coltishall manor in Norfolk – which, perhaps not coincidentally, had a population density of approximately 500 per square mile – showed that the population declined by 80% as a result of the plagues of 1348, 1361 and 1369.[20]

While such precise figures are hard to come by for Ireland, there is no reason to suppose that they are not significantly different for at least some rural areas. Its incidence was greatest in the rural parts of the colony, especially in the east and south. These would in general have been arable areas with some population density, though it is doubtful that any areas in Ireland would have reached the population density of Coltishall manor. Surviving records either refer directly to plague mortality or to lands lying tenantless, a clear indication of a falling manorial population. The references to high mortality are scattered, and many do not distinguish between the effects of the different outbreaks of plague. In 1351 a report on the estates of the See of Cashel alleged that the 'lands and rents had been all but totally destroyed by the king's Irish enemies and by the mortality of their tenants in the last plague'. The royal manors of Newcastle Lyons, Tassagard, Crumlin, Oughterard and Castlewarny were severely affected by plague. Numerous manors in Meath, Tipperary and Kilkenny by 1351 were left with vacant holdings, indicating the deaths of the tenants and of their heirs. The only area for which we have any precise figures, however, is the township of Colemanstown in the manor of Newcastle Lyons, Dublin where, according to a later petition from the tenants to the king, only three tenants remained, sixteen of the tenants having been 'cut off by the late pestilence'.[21] If these figures are correct, then total mortality from the Black Death and later outbreaks in this township was in the region of 84%. What is also significant here is that this manor was on the marches and was therefore less densely populated than other manors in more secure areas; however, studies have indicated that many tenants lived at a distance from the manorial centre, in outlying farm settlements which provided the necessary links for the transmission of plague.[22] Such a high mortality from accumulated outbreaks of the plague is not unbelievable. But to what extent this instance can be taken as typical of total rural mortality in Ireland is a debatable point. A mortality rate of 84% throughout even Co. Dublin would have left the economy far more shattered than surviving evidence corroborates.

One of the problems encountered by historians in trying to calculate overall plague morbidity figures is what seems like its inexplicably irregular incidence. Some have argued that generalised mortality figures are impossible in view of the instance in one English village where 747 died in 1349, whereas in a neighbouring village with a similar population, only five died.[23] Levett's final conclusion in 1916 on estimating plague mortality on the estates of the See of Winchester was that 'extremely little is gained by making out an average death rate. The mortality varied widely, not only from manor to manor, but from tithing to tithing'. And though the average mortality for twenty-two manors on the estates of Glastonbury Abbey was 54.6%, the range varied from 33.3% to 69.4%. However, some more recent studies in England argue that there is little evidence to support claims that the plague could severely affect one rural settlement and leave a neighbouring village unaffected, and that in fact the plague's incidence was, in general, quite regular within defined areas: mortality in the manor of Halesowen in 1348-50, for example, was evenly spread throughout, averaging 40%, with a high of 57% and a low of 33%.[24]

Another crucial factor however in examining the plague's incidence is the nature of the farming and the terrain of the affected areas. The most severely affected regions were those low-lying areas which pursued arable farming and were, in general, quite densely settled; pastoral or highland areas suffered less. A striking instance of this is afforded by patterns of mortality recorded in three deaneries in the Diocese of York: Bulmer, the populous arable district, experienced a mortality of about 50%, Ryedale, a hill-farming community, lost 28% and Cleveland, which is located in the high moors, lost 22%.[25] This kind of variation would have been particularly pertinent in Ireland. The Normans had settled mainly in well-drained, lower-lying land east of a line from Skibbereen to Galway to Coleraine. This was also the area in which the Black Death wrought its havoc. The colony's network of village settlements also contributed to the rapid transmission of the plague in the rural areas. However, rural settlement even in the colony was more scattered than in England. The dispersed nature of settlement, together with geographical obstacles such as bogs and mountains, and variations in agriculture would have meant that some rural areas in all likelihood escaped, particularly those in hilly and mountainous regions, or those in non-arable areas. Gaelic-Irish settlements by contrast were largely on higher, often impassable ground; even as late as the seventeenth century, the Gaelic-dominated areas in Leinster were the boggy and hilly regions which were forested on their perimeters.[26] Their location as well as their largely pastoral agricultural help account for the fact that they were spared the worst effects of the plague of the Black Death, as contemporary observers emphasised. However, in the absence of more complete data, all conclusions are tentative. Definitive statements are just not possible in view of the fact that death rates in parts of the sparsely populated Scottish Highlands were as high as in the more densely settled areas of Eastern England.[27]

To infer a percentage of the rural mortality in Ireland on the basis of rural mortality elsewhere then is difficult, given the bewildering array of estimates presented by historians of rural society. Figures range from 15% to 25% for heavily populated Flanders to over 30% for rural Holland and a minimum of 45% for Languedoc.[28] Even the figures for overall rural mortality in England are widely diverging: Shrewsbury insists on a figure not more than 5%, Russell posits a figure of 27%, Levett about 33%, Titow suggests a minimum of 50%. On examination, however, it is clear that the lower calculations were often based on an under-estimation of the level of population density. Recent research in England favours an average figure for Black Death mortality closer to 40%–45%, with an average net decline as a result of later outbreaks estimated as being between 40%–50%.[29] Since, warfare aside, conditions in the manors of the colony would have been similar to those in rural England, there is every good reason to suppose that such figures can by analogy also be applied to Ireland. If generalisations must be made, the conservative estimate is that the Black Death and its successors probably reduced the rural population of the colony by some 40% through mortality and emigration, while its effects on Gaelic Ireland are impossible to estimate. But the incidence of the plague was irregular, or at least followed paths that have not been fully detected, and many areas escaped altogether. In view of its uneven incidence and the complex terrain, both geographical and political, of medieval Ireland, any general figure for plague mortality can be highly misleading.

Effects on the Manorial Economy
In the immediate aftermath of the plague in England and on the continent, many places exhibited some resilience and recovered quickly largely because of the surplus of people living on the land.

Levett's study of the Black Death on the estates of the Bishopric of Winchester typifies what occurred on many English manors: despite a mortality of approximately 39%, after 1349 there was 'no sign of chaos or complete depopulation' and 'no revolution either in agriculture or tenure'; there were enough surplus tenants to take up the vacant holdings. In Bridbury's famous phrase, the Black Death in England was 'more purgative than toxic'. The only immediate effects of the plague were first to raise the price of commodities and labour, thereby increasing manorial expenditure, which in turn was offset by the other immediate effect of the plague, the increase in death duties and entry fines. The plague then did not bring about any radical shift in the economic changes already afoot. Similarly, on the manor of Halesowen holdings were quickly taken over and the pre-plague patterns of life resumed though land became cheaper. On the manor of Farnham there were no great economic changes: even though about 740 people died in the first year of the plague and between a third and a half died during the course of the whole plague, revenues increased, tenements were eventually filled and the manor survived. Change did come however, though not until the 1370s, when after successive outbreaks of plague and declining fertility levels, a deep recession became much more visible on the estate, as on many estates throughout England. Population continued to decline and by 1487 the population had declined to 2,000, the level it had been in 1300, and continued to decline, reaching 1,000 in 1548.[30] While this manor's records are not necessarily a blueprint for what happened elsewhere, they offer a broad outline of the changes that took place in many rural areas in these decades.

These repercussions are supported by extant evidence from Irish manors. Irish manorial records are too few in number and do not cover a sufficiently extended period to warrant any statistical survey of the decline in Anglo-Irish manorial incomes. However, the ministers' accounts that have survived indicate that the plague affected many Anglo-Irish manors, some heavily, others lightly, and all the available evidence points to the plague having its most severe effects in the east, south-east and south of the country. This is particularly evident in the surviving accounts for the Irish estates of Elizabeth de Burgh; since her estates were spread throughout the country, in Counties Meath, Kilkenny, Tipperary and in Connacht and Ulster, the accounts give an indication of the plague's effects on different parts of the colony.[31]

The plague did not put a stop to normal manorial life which seemed to have proceeded with its normal rhythms: courts continued to be held, rents to be collected, presumably harvests to be gathered and in general no great changes are evident in 1348-49, the first year of the plague. But clearly disruption was felt, as indicated by the fact that accounts were now drawn up twice a year instead of annually as had previously been the case.[32] More changes are clear by 1350. In all the manors mortality was clearly high enough that holdings fell tenantless and remained 'in the lady's hand' through 1351, because tenants could not be found. This indicates not only that the sitting tenant had died, but also either that his heirs had also died or that neither they nor anybody else was willing to take over the holding, perhaps because the land was too marginal or the terms of tenure uninviting. This situation particularly prevailed on the manors in Co. Kilkenny which was one of the centres of the plague. The list of land and holdings lying vacant is long: on the manor of Latthedran over sixty acres of land were still reported to be waste in 1352; over 127 acres and three cottages on the manor of Loughmoran were reported as vacant in Easter 1350 because of pestilence; on the manor of Callan, over ninety-five acres out of a total of over 548 acres lay tenantless in 1348-49 and by the following year this had risen with over 302 acres, as well as other holdings, reported as vacant. Though by 1351 vacant holdings had dropped to twenty-six acres, the fact that the manor's revenues still continued to fall suggests that the number of reported vacancies may not be accurate, or that some tenants had enlarged their holdings to include the vacant lands. The manor of Palmerstown showed only one holding as lying vacant in 1351, but this was also the manor where tenants had to be induced to stay with lower rents.[33]

In Co. Meath, also one of the areas severely afflicted by plague, a similar pattern emerges: in Duleek manor in 1350 only three acres and one plot, which formerly had yielded rents, were recorded as waste, but in 1351 this rose to twelve acres and three plots, and in 1352 to over twenty-eight acres and two plots; other rents could not be levied and the mills were ruined. However, the total receipts of the manor show an increase, and it is quite likely that these lands were marginal and hadn't ever yielded much. In Coolock, total receipts dropped by a third between 1348-49 and 1350-51, though some recovery was evident by 1351, mainly because demesne land was rented to tenants that year. Nearby Kells manor, however, was only slightly affected with only two plots left vacant in 1352 because of the lack of tenants; however, because of the pestilence as well as war, other rents could not be levied.[34] Further south in the manor of Lisronagh in Co. Tipperary, in 1350-51 about 730 acres lay untilled for lack of tenants. This included the land both of free tenants as well as of betaghs, suggesting that not only marginal land fell into disuse, but also lands that had formerly been cultivated and yielded revenue. Rents were reduced, perhaps to attract tenants, perhaps to dissuade them from moving away.[35]

What is clear from reports on the de Burgh estates is that the plague's impact varied from region to region, depending on the nature of the terrain and communications. And even after the plague's disappearance in 1350-51, the speed of recovery also varied. In general, the estates in Leinster and Munster suffered most and longest, with manors such as Lisronagh continuing to report vacant lands in the succeeding years. But the details vary. The total receipts for the manor of Palmerstown in Kilkenny in 1344-45 totalled £12 6s 5d; in 1348-49 this dropped only slightly, to £12 0s 2d; by 1351-52 receipts rose again to £12 4s ½d and only one tenement lay vacant. Perhaps the quick recovery here was due to more vigilant management, as indicated by the twice-yearly reports and by measures such as rent reductions. This pattern of a quick recovery echoes what happened also on many of the wealthier, well-run manors of East Anglia, Monmouthshire and Somerset where, by the 1370s, revenues were only 10% lower than they had been in the 1340s.[36] However, as also in so many estates in England, this seemingly quick recovery was not to continue in Palmerstown or Callan, suggesting that the recovery in manorial revenues could have been artificially boosted by higher entry fines in the wake of the plague, or that as land values continued to decline and tenant shortages to worsen, the surviving tenants were increasingly unwilling to pay the same rents. Tenants on these estates in Leinster were in a bargaining position, all the more so as recurring outbreaks of the plague would have continued to make inroads on the tenant population.

In other areas, the plague's incidence was more sporadic, and this is echoed in the records of the de Burgh estates in Connacht and Ulster. Those in Ulster recovered quickly, not surprising given that the plague seems to have had little effect there. In Connacht however, some manors such as Clancoscry were severely affected, whereas the manor of Strothir survived.[37] In many of these manors holdings that fell vacant in 1348 stayed vacant and land went out of use. Again, the contrast with England is striking: on most English manors, even those reporting mortality of up to 45%, vacancies were filled quickly and labour shortages were not felt until the 1370s, thanks in the main to the population surplus. In Ireland, however, pre-plague population levels didn't allow any comfort margins. There wasn't any shortage of land or surplus of tenants. Consequently, labour and tenant shortages are reported as early as 1348, and clearly were not resolved in the succeeding years. Lands falling tenantless in 1348 remained so in many areas, and went out of use, particularly those marginal lands that hadn't yielded much revenue even prior to the plague. In many cases these lands returned to Gaelic-Irish use.

Somewhat similar patterns emerge in the records of other manors, though in general difficulties are not reported until the 1350s and 1360s. In 1354, the demesne tenants and farmers of the king's manors in Co. Dublin petitioned for help, claiming that

> as well because of the late pestilence in that land as on account of the excessive prises of the king's ministers in Ireland, they are so entirely impoverished that, unless a remedy be applied, they will not be able to maintain themselves and pay the farm due to the king.

Tenant shortages continued to be felt into the 1360s on these royal manors in Dublin and reached such a pitch that in 1362 orders were issued to lease vacant lands to all willing takers, a clear indication of the crisis being faced by landowners in certain areas. Nor was there any respite: rent reductions and vacant lands are still reported for the royal demesnes into the 1360s.[38] Loss of rents, waste land and empty tenements were also the lot of manors in other parts of the country in the aftermath of the plagues, such as in Co. Kilkenny on the manors of Damma, Latthedran and Loughmoran and on the manor of Duleek in Co. Meath.[39] One could generalise then that by comparison with estates in England, Irish manorial estates were unable to recoup their plague losses because of low pre-plague population levels, the recurrence of the plague and the endemic state of warfare in the country.

Migrations and Rural Desertion

In all areas of life, the plague disrupted the established patterns of work and living. One of its most visible effects on rural life in general in the post-plague era was the human migrations it engendered, as rural dwellers left for larger manors, towns and cities in pursuit of work and better opportunities. Demographic decline is not necessarily then the only explanation for the desertion of marginal rural settlements; internal migration is equally so, as tenants abandoned outlying areas for the larger manors and towns. In this of course, one must note that Ireland was not unique: all across Europe, especially in Germany, a progressive *Wüstungen* or depopulation of the small villages and countryside set in. In Ireland however, the effects of the plague on migration were reinforced by those of war. This happened also in Egypt, where peripheral regions of the Mamluk empire were abandoned in the post-plague era. Absentee landlords refused to reclaim land deserted by peasants fleeing the plague, and they refused to attract new settlers, particularly since those lands were under continual attack from the nomadic Bedouins.[40] However, in the Irish colony, movement was largely out of the country altogether. It seems very likely that in the aftermath of plague, the problem of landowner absenteeism worsened, if the increasing number of statutes dealing with the problem is any indication: statutes were passed in 1350, 1351,

1353, 1359, 1360, 1368 and 1380.[41] To an increasing degree, absentee landlords lost interest in their Irish estates; it was no longer profitable for them to farm or even supervise their lands, and in the 1370s many sold their manors in Ireland altogether, including the de Verdon lands in Meath and Louth.[42]

Furthermore, in the years after 1348 labourers and small tenants fled the country in increasing numbers, leaving large areas of land lying waste. The Statutes of Kilkenny attempted to legislate on the problems caused by the shortage of common labourers who 'are for a great part absent and fly out of the said land' by threatening a year's imprisonment to all who would attempt to leave.[43]

These measures were clearly not effective. In the period 1391-99, numerous exemptions from the Statute of Absentees were granted to labourers, while many English towns such as Bristol and Coventry encountered significant problems in the later part of the century from influxes of Irish immigrants.[44] Emigration continued into the next century with parliament noting in 1410 that so many labourers and servants had gone abroad that 'the husbandry and tillage of the same land is on the point of being destroyed and wasted'. The petition is repeated in a complaint to the king in 1421 that 'artificers and labourers...daily depart in great numbers... to your kingdom of England and remain there, whereby the husbandry of your said land is greatly injured and disused'.[45] Clearly, conditions for labourers were much more attractive in post-plague England, which at least in the initial decades after the plague had experienced a quicker recovery than Ireland where continuing warfare rendered life in the colony and its marches increasingly insecure and unprofitable.

Sources for similar migration and movement in Gaelic Ireland are scarce, and existing sources suggest reasons other than the dislocation caused by the Black Death. Mobility and impermanent settlement had for long been a feature of Gaelic society particularly among certain classes, such as the bards who had the right to wander with their herds of cattle even through hostile territory. The custom of moving with herds of cattle into unoccupied lands, or 'booleying', was especially common in the more mountainous areas of Ulster, and by the sixteenth and seventeenth centuries it had become a characteristic feature of Gaelic society in general. Some linguistic evidence suggests that this phenomenon first became more widespread in Gaelic Ireland towards the end of the fourteenth century. Dr Katherine Simms has pointed out that the Irish term *caoraigheacht*, anglicised as 'creaght', the term used to refer to the large herds of livestock owned by lords and their herdsmen, begins to appear sometime in the later fourteenth century.[46] The 'creaght' was often formed by a settled population which had been displaced and exiled and was led by either Gaelic-Irish or Anglo-Irish lords. If such migration were common in Gaelic Ireland in the later fourteenth century, it would present a similar picture to that of many other countries in Europe in the post-plague era when large groups of people were on the move, though the actual causes for such movements in Gaelic Ireland are not known.

Changing Conditions for Peasants

Declining population, whether through mortality or migration, has often been proposed as the cause for accelerating fundamental changes in the feudal system, such as the decline of villeinage and the commutation of labour services to money payments. This was the view of the historian Edmund Curtis who attributed wide-ranging economic changes in Ireland to the agency of the plague of 1348. He argued that it

> altered the earlier medieval economic structure and began modern several farming. Free labour and free rent-farming paid better. The growth of freedom was marked by the limitation of services and commutation. Villeinage ceased to pay and it was against the spirit of a freer age.[47]

Curtis' view was shared by many historians of his time, but more recent studies do not attribute such radical changes to the plague.[48] The plague did not bring about commutation or the end of villeinage, since these phenomena had already been changing from the beginning of the fourteenth century. This is particularly true in Ireland where the duties of the villein or betagh do not seem to have been as onerous as elsewhere: labour services were never as heavy as they were in England, partly because such services were often not included in the type of tenure offered to attract settlers to Ireland. Furthermore, from quite early on any services that had existed had been commuted, either partially or completely, to money payments; for example, on the manor of Senede in 1298 it was stated that 'there are no works of betaghs because they are charged with rent for works, gifts and presents'.[49] The process of commutation had already gone far by 1299 as is suggested by a law passed in that year, one of exceptional harvests and therefore greater demand for agricultural labour, that sought to freeze wages and reimpose services. The reasons cited foreshadow the conditions that would pertain also in the aftermath of the Black Death:

> complaints having been made that servants, ploughmen, carters, thresh-
> ers and others, on account of the fertility of the year, refused to serve as
> accustomed, it was provided…that such servants should serve as they
> were accustomed to do and stay with their lord and receive the same
> liveries and wages as in other years, and that no lord should give greater
> liveries or larger wages than heretofore, or draw away the servants of
> another without his will.[50]

Long before the end of the thirteenth century, duties such as might be expected of betaghs were no longer unlimited: on the manor of Holy Trinity Priory, Dublin, customary services were limited to suit of court, ploughing at different sowings, hoeing and reaping; on the Co. Dublin manor of Clonkeen during the 1344 harvest, out of a total of 562 days of reaping, 471 days were done by hired labourers and ninety-one by customary tenants.[51]

It is difficult to ascertain whether the plague had any appreciable effect on this changing situation in Ireland. Clearly it helped to worsen the shortage of labour, whether customary or hired. A Statute of Labourers and Artisans was passed in June 1349, and subsequently applied to Ireland, which attempted to order the volatile labour situation:

since a great part of the population, and especially workers and employees, has now died in this pestilence many people, observing the needs of masters and the shortage of employees, are refusing to work.[52]

Parts of Ireland in 1349-51 cannot have differed greatly from the England described by Knighton where

> because of the fear of death everything fetched a low price. For there were very few people who cared for riches, or indeed for anything else. A man could have a horse previously valued at 40s for half a mark, a good fat ox for 4s, a cow for 12d, a bullock for 6d... And sheep and cattle roamed unchecked through the fields and through the standing corn, and there was no one to chase them and round them up. For want of watching animals died in uncountable numbers in the fields and in bye-ways and hedges throughout the whole country; for there was so great a shortage of servants and labourers that there was no one who knew what needed to be done.[53]

The Statute of Labourers attempted to protect the status quo and the interests of the landowners, but it was quite ineffective. In some areas in the wake of the plague, surviving tenants found themselves in a bargaining position and were able to negotiate a reduction in their rents and their customary labour services. Landlords were forced to remit rents and daywork in order to persuade tenants to stay and not leave for other places in pursuit of higher wages and better conditions. Of course, in some areas in England, population pressure was such that labour shortages did not arise in the immediate aftermath of the plague. However, in Ireland labour and tenant shortages were widespread in the years following immediately on the Black Death, especially in manors in Leinster and Munster. Labour services, where still exacted, continued to decline well into the fifteenth century, though even by the sixteenth century they had not yet disappeared altogether. The rents of various manors were also reduced in 1349-52 and, while the reason for the remission is not explicitly mentioned, one may assume, given the timing, that the reasons were the same as elsewhere:

the Black Death's mortality left landowners faced with a shortage of labour and more demanding tenants and workers who could only be induced to stay with the lure of rent reductions or higher wages. There are many such instances: on the manor of Kells, Co. Meath, the rents of certain lands were reduced from sixteen to twelve pence per acre; on the manor of Palmerstown, Co. Kilkenny, in 1351-52, the tenants were pardoned one-third of their rents, and this on a manor whose records do not show any other significant changes in the wake of the plague.[54] Scarcity of labour was widespread in 1349-52 and the manorial accounts extant for these particular years detail many acres of lands lying 'in the lord's [lady's] hands and untilled for lack of tenants'. This scarcity was rendered more acute by the chronic migration of labourers to England and of betaghs to Irish areas. Wages consequently rose and all attempts to fix them at their pre-plague levels proved futile. The overall result was a chronic shortage of labourers and tenants. In many areas, especially on the marches, the great landowners, unable to find English-born tenants for their estates, were forced to accept Gaelic-Irish tenants, a political accommodation that ironically permitted some economic survival.[55]

From the viewpoint of the tenant class, economic conditions improved after the plague and social mobility became more possible. As the labour shortage continued to deteriorate in the post-plague era, the status, conditions and wages of the wage-labourer continued to improve. The result was a social upheaval that struck many elsewhere as unprecedented. Conditions on many Irish manors may have been like those described in the chronicle of the Cathedral Priory of Rochester:

> In Lent, [1349] indeed, there was such a lack of fish that many people who had been accustomed to live daintily had to make do with just pastry, bread and potage. But the threshers, labourers and workmen were so well supplied with cash that they did not need to worry about paying the full price for such foods. And thus, by an inversion of the natural order, those who were accustomed to have plenty and those accustomed to suffer want, fell into need on the one hand and into abundance on the other.[56]

In England, the plagues of the fourteenth century had the effect of opening up possibilities for social mobility and the result was that:

> English society emerged from the medieval period less rigidly stratified than was the case with most of her continental neighbours.[57]

A similar social mobility was evident at all class levels in Ireland, though sources are much scarcer. Continuing population decline throughout the latter decades of the fourteenth century, together with the shortage of tenants, led to a greater availability of land. This in turn helped improve conditions for tenants and lower-class peasants such as betaghs. The position of betaghs had been improving since the late thirteenth century, a process that was furthered with the depopulation caused by plagues and other disasters and the consequent drop in the value of land. As Dr Kevin Down in his survey of the Irish manorial economy points out, the high value now attached to labour meant that once betaghs died out, they were hard to replace and by the end of the fifteenth century betaghry had almost disappeared.[58] Social mobility into the landowner class is also a common feature of post-plague communities in England. In Ireland also, new landowners emerged as subtenants of the great absentee lords; junior branches of Anglo-Irish families, Gaelic entrepreneurs, and others took advantage of the social and political upheaval of the later fourteenth century to acquire larger holdings or take over manors vacated by the absentee lords. From this period dates the emergence of the Tobins in Ossory, the Butlers in Kilkenny and others who by fair means and feuds gradually came to be major landowners in their own areas, mirroring the rise in England of families such as the Pastons.[59]

How widespread this mobility was, however, is not known. Evidence from England indicates that those who most benefited from the new opportunities offered by the shortage of tenants were the richer villagers who enlarged their holdings either through inheritance or through being able to pay entry fines, with the result that the gap between rich and poor widened.[60] Nor may one exaggerate the degree of replacement. The example of Co. Wexford emphasises how difficult it is to make any generalisations about large-scale mobility: the same families held land in 1640 at the time of the Civil Survey as held land in 1247, and generally a similar continuity of tenure is recorded in other places that were not militarily threatened.[61]

The Landowners' Response

The same labour shortage that led to a higher standard of living for peasants led also to changes in the nature of agriculture that directly affected the revenues of landlords. The rising costs of labour in the post-plague era, together with the fall in agricultural prices, the infertility of marginal lands, the dangers involved in cultivating land in areas outside Dublin and growing landlord absenteeism meant that it was more profitable and more secure for some landlords to lease their lands. This policy had already started on some estates including those of monasteries and priories, particularly after the Great Famine of 1315-18, and was well underway by the 1320s, as is evidenced in contemporary monastic registers. But the Black Death, together with its recurrences, accelerated the process. The leasing of demesne lands was actively pursued on the Irish de Burgh estates from the mid-fourteenth century.[62] Studies elsewhere generally point to the Black Death as being the cause of the escalation in the leasing of granges or outlying farms on monastic estates. This happened on the estates of the Archbishop of Armagh where numerous leases were permitted to certain persons, 'as long as they cultivate the said land and do not deliver them to any strange laymen'. In the Priory of Kilmainham in Dublin, holdings were leased to laymen, though this led to complaints that their main interest was in profit and not in the upkeep of the land which, along with buildings, deteriorated. A similar development took place after the Black Death on the estates of the Knights Hospitallers.[63]

In other manors, the disappearance of betaghs in the post-plague era, together with the loss of their labour services and the scarcity and high cost of wage-labour, made it cheaper to raise stock than to plough. Since land became cheaper than labour, the less labour-intensive pasturage became ever more attractive. The plague was then one factor that helped accelerate the shift to pasturage which had been proceeding very gradually since the beginning of the century. The continuation of war made it safer to do so. The result was that over the course of the next fifty years cereal production declined, and by the fifteenth century Ireland, the one-time granary of England, was now importing grain. However, as the pasture economy grew in the course of the fifteenth century, a certain recovery was made, and hides and sheepskins replaced wheat as Ireland's greatest export. Just as the switch from arable to pasture was impelled by the shortage of labour in the fourteenth century, it in turn contributed to further depopulation especially of marcher areas and marginal lands.[64] Throughout Europe, the Black Death played a contributory, though not a causative role in this complex process, as it also did in the development of enclosure. In Ireland, enclosure did not reach any great proportions until the late seventeenth and early eighteenth centuries, but its extent varied and there is evidence of enclosure in Ireland from the fourteenth century and especially the fifteenth century.[65] However, a more common development in Ireland in the post-plague era was that marginal lands, already underpopulated, were abandoned altogether and allowed to revert to scrub or waste.

Clearly, decline in the manorial economy took place on a sliding time-scale, with marcher lands experiencing decline earlier than areas within the colony. The plague helped to level the playing field, as it were, bringing conditions on some manors more in line with those already prevailing on the more marginal lands. Decline affected revenue and this is especially evident in the absence of any significant building activity. From the later thirteenth century, but especially from the 1320s, records of castle and church building become rarer. Though some castles were repaired, few new castles or churches were built and building wasn't to resume to any significant degree until the fifteenth century. However, this again was locally determined: there are references to castles being built in Ulster in 1352, indicating, like the records from the de Burgh estates in Ulster, that the Black Death did not cause any great disruption in that area.[66] Nevertheless, the general pattern elsewhere in the country, as in England, is one of building cessation. The Black Death contributed here, not merely because of its direct effects within Ireland itself, but also in that the large landowning families had to deal with plague-related problems in their home estates in England and had little time or resources to devote to the upkeep of their possessions in Ireland. On the de Burgh estates in England for example, wages doubled after 1349 in response to the labour shortages after the plague and all efforts to curb them failed, clearly making inroads on revenues.[67] Not surprisingly, Ireland's absentee lords allowed their castles in Ireland to fall into disuse and disrepair.

Evidence presently available suggests that many of the more important Anglo-Irish settlements, especially in frontier areas, were no longer permanently occupied after the mid-fourteenth century. Trim Castle is an example: archaeological evidence has shown that the towers, gatehouse and fosse were either partially or fully filled in sometime in the second half of the fourteenth century, and that the castle was not permanently occupied after the mid-fourteenth century. The castle would not be occupied again until the late sixteenth century. Excavations at castles and villages elsewhere reveal a similar absence of occupation in the second half of the century. Motte castles in Ulster and other parts of the country were deserted in the fourteenth century, due to the combination of war and plague. This hiatus in occupation could be explained, suggests Dr T.B. Barry, 'simply by highlighting the degree of population decrease in this period as a direct result of the political and economic disorders', though adding that further investigation is necessary to substantiate such suppositions.[68]

Further, after the Black Death, though again not solely because of it, building patterns in Ireland changed, thanks to new demands and new fashions. From the late fourteenth century, and continuing into the fifteenth and sixteenth centuries, the large seignorial castles typical of the Anglo-Norman settlement were replaced by tower-houses, smaller, stone, fortified houses that were obviously more economical both to build and defend. Estimates of their numbers vary widely from between 3,000 to 7,000. Many were situated in the west and in areas controlled by the Gaelic lords, and reflect both the breakdown of central authority and the rising power of local leaders.[69] Some were built along the Pale frontier, such as that at Kilteel, or to defend harbours, such as the Dalkey tower house or Corr Castle on the Howth peninsula.

Recovery

In the colony in Ireland, recovery was rendered virtually impossible by the dwindling resources, both economic and psychological, of the colonists and by the continuation of warfare which rendered permanent the effects of the plague. Rather than any quick grabbing of holdings widowed in 1348, lands and tenements remained vacant and waste. Nobody had any desire to take up holdings which offered no security and little profit. The increasingly precarious military strength of the colony meant that tenants who before had fled from outlying areas to the 'land of peace', now left even the settled areas of Leinster for England. Moreover, the fact that the plague in England had created an abundance of vacant holdings and opportunities for resourceful men meant that tenants no longer had any reason to go west in search of land. So, lands in Ireland falling tenantless in 1348–50 often remained so until the sixteenth-century colonisation, when land shortages and population pressure in England led many once more to Ireland. The combination of depopulation and emigration was disastrous for the economy of the lordship. The English crown made successive efforts to resettle lands in Ireland. In 1413, a decree was passed that 'for the quiett and peace within the realm of England and for the increase and filling of the realm of Ireland', all the 'wylde' Irish, except those in important positions, were to leave England.[70] All efforts were fruitless. That Ireland was underpopulated in the fifteenth and sixteenth centuries was remarked upon by many contemporary observers, and a population of under half-a-million people has been estimated for the country until after 1600.[71]

Yet, while the thirteenth-century situation was lost, recovery did come, though more slowly and later than elsewhere. In England after the plague, the geographical distribution of taxable wealth spread eastwards and southwards.[72] In Ireland a similar redistribution took place in the fifteenth century, away from the traditional manorial centres. What is most striking is the increase in prosperity evident in fifteenth-century Gaelic Ireland, as is indicated by the great architectural revival in Gaelic areas. Just as the twelfth-century expansion of the colony had been in large measure impelled by demographic expansion in England spilling over into Ireland, perhaps the expansion of four-teenth-century Gaelic Ireland was due to growth, or at least stability in the Gaelic-Irish population and to a demographic decline in the colony. Whatever the cause, the colony retreated to the area around Dublin, the Pale, and to the larger cities. Even though it had become quite prosperous by 1450, the 1300 situation was not reached again until the eighteenth century.

Opinion remains divided as to the long-term effects of the Black Death on the rural economy of Europe, some seeing it as causing only a temporary disruption, others arguing that the plague caused radical and unforeseeable changes.[73] Whether Ireland would without the plague have developed as it did is a moot point. As in other sectors of life in Ireland in the fourteenth century, the Black Death was not the primary cause of change but part of a continuum of disasters that overwhelmed the colony in the later fourteenth century. The fact that economic depression had set in before 1348, that the plague of 1348 was but one of a series of such epidemics in the fourteenth century, and that they fell on a war-torn economy makes it impossible to isolate the effects of the Black Death. However, the decline in the rural economy is clear, and this in turn had far-reaching consequences for the urban economy.

5

The Black Death in the Towns

Pre-plague Conditions

The transmission of bubonic plague in rural areas and its consequences were largely conditioned by the density of surrounding
towns and villages, which acted as plague foci. In general however,
towns suffered far more from plague than did rural areas, due to their
trading connections, their environmental conditions and population
density.

Plague was most likely transmitted from port towns to inland
towns, either in the merchandise of travelling merchants, in river
traffic or by a creeping epizootic. Throughout the east and south there
was an extensive network of market towns and villages which offered
a route along which the plague travelled. In Co. Cork, for example, a
sheriff's list from 1299 names thirty-seven ports and market towns,
and there were approximately forty-four others, all situated largely in
the environs of the city of Cork and in the north and eastern sections
of the county. In the present Co. Tipperary, there were at least thirty-
five chartered boroughs, and many more smaller rural boroughs,
mostly in the southern half of the county and along the River Suir.[1] A
similar density characterised counties such as Wexford, Kildare,
Kilkenny, Dublin and Meath. The distance to most of these markets
would not have been more than thirty miles, easily traversible in a day.
Admittedly, some of these towns were very small, more like agricultural settlements, and consisted of perhaps only a few hundred people.

However, they differed from the scattered homesteads of the rural landscape since settlements, however small, would have been clustered, offering the density necessary for the usual transmission of the plague, either of the bubonic or pneumonic strains. Other towns, particularly market towns, would have been quite substantial population centres. Given, moreover, that many of the larger towns were concentrated within walls, their density would have been quite high; the walls of Cork, for example, enclosed about thirty-six acres and most of the population was concentrated in two narrow streets.[2] In such closed communities, epidemics can spread very rapidly.

Transmission within the towns was further facilitated by environmental conditions that offered congenial quarters for the plague bacillus. Since much of the trade was in grain, hides and cloth, and since many towns and cities would have had stores of grain reserves, towns offered ideal conditions for harbouring rats and fleas. The materials used in construction and furnishing were particularly conducive to the propagation of fleas and rats. Some houses were still timber-framed with clay or mud walls and thatched roofs, though in places these had been replaced with stone houses and slate roofs from the thirteenth century on. Further, the typical brushwood bedding and floors of compacted straw or brushwood, such as were found in excavations in Cork of a typical late thirteenth- or early fourteenth-century house, would have provided an ideal habitat for fleas. People also lived in close quarters and the overcrowding further facilitated transmission. Studies of modern plague outbreaks in India have shown that badly ventilated, crowded buildings as well as cold weather both contributed to the outbreak of the pneumonic form of plague, which is far more virulent and spreads rapidly by direct transmission.[3] The average house in cities such as Cork and Dublin offered little ventilation and, though somewhat larger than a peasant dwelling, was single-storeyed with at most two or three rooms, a living area, kitchen and a communal bedroom.[4]

Public sanitation was a pressing problem. Ireland's larger cities were similar to many other medieval European cities with open sewers, contaminated water supplies and noxious smells. The sewage system in both medieval Dublin and Cork consisted of open drains by the sides of houses which conveyed rainwater and sewage to open areas beyond, which acted as cesspits. Moreover, sanitary facilities in the towns were extremely inadequate, as is suggested by a request around 1300 from the citizens of Dublin that the city be cleansed twice weekly. In 1336, the city was described as being pervaded by 'excessive and noxious stenches' caused by the slaughter of cattle and, as late as the fifteenth century, there were complaints that 'dungheaps, swine, hog-sties and other nuisances in the streets, lanes and suburbs of Dublin infect the air and produce mortality, fevers and pestilence throughout that city'.[5] Nor were other cities more hygienic. Jean Creton, a French visitor travelling with Richard II to Ireland in 1399, described Waterford as a city where 'the wretched and filthy people, some in rags, others girt with a rope, had the one a hole, the other a hut for their dwelling'. Kilkenny was in a similar state in 1337: animals' innards were cleaned in the streets, clothes were washed and pigs roamed as they did in Dublin and Waterford. Water supplies were primitive, often contaminated by sewage and waste, while dumping both in rivers and streets was common.[6]

The reception of the plague bacillus was further facilitated by the poor health of many urban dwellers. The unusually bad weather of the years after 1300, together with the frequent famines and wars, meant that malnutrition was a constant hazard. As has been already discussed, malnutrition in childhood has been tentatively linked to a weakened immune system and therefore to a greater receptivity to the plague bacillus (see pp.21-23). The typical medieval town-dweller was prey to all sorts of other health-risks, which, while not directly linked to plague, undoubtedly contributed to a weakening of immunological health. In excavations of a medieval cemetery in Cork, the individuals there were found to have suffered from an array of ailments including degenerative joint disease, osteoarthritis and dental disease as well as traumas caused by injury; other diseases did not leave any traces. The cause of death could not be ascertained in most cases, but clearly the deaths were premature by modern standards: of the 216 skeletons examined, 24% died before their early twenties, and 36.5% died in the twenty to thirty age group.[7]

Despite such conditions, in the earlier part of the thirteenth century prosperity reigned, with lucrative trade carried on with English and continental cities through ports such as Drogheda, Dublin, Waterford, New Ross, Youghal and Cork. But there were also many thriving towns in the hinterland. Towns such as Kilkenny, Cashel, Ardfert and Kilmallock, for example, were of sufficient commercial importance as to merit notice by Italian mapmakers. Many of these towns were prosperous places with many streets and numerous inhabitants; for example, Kilmallock, Co. Limerick, in 1300 had four streets with twenty burgages on the main street and could afford to pay a large subsidy in that year. Bunratty was a considerable town in 1287 with 226 burgages; Waterford had nearly as many and Youghal, though somewhat smaller, was a wealthy town and in the late thirteenth century accounted for almost 61% of the income of the manor of Inchiquin.[8]

By the end of the fourteenth century a decline had set in, mirroring a similar downturn in the urban economy all over Europe at this time.[9] The decline was local in nature, affecting some towns and ports more than others. At the outset, it must be emphasised that much of the later decline of the smaller towns and villages in Ireland is to be attributed, in the main, to the forced conditions under which they arose and grew. Historians have long argued that most towns in medieval Ireland grew because they were essential to the development of seignorial power. Some had developed in order to meet defence requirements and never became trading centres of any importance. Many had developed solely in response to political needs and were part of the Anglo-Norman effort to attract settlers from an over-populated England to a seriously under-populated Ireland. Some were diminutive, unwalled urban settlements which used burgage tenure to attract small settlers, while others were little more than agricultural villages. And even those that were commercially oriented were nevertheless primarily intended to increase the control and profits of the local lord. As a result, many of these towns did not have a strong economic base and were therefore vulnerable to every crisis. With the demographic decline of the later fourteenth century and the changes in the manorial economy, these villages also declined, some even disappearing in the course of the century. On the other hand, those chartered boroughs that had a strong commercial base, though affected by plague and its consequences, were able to weather the difficulties of the time.[10]

But Irish towns and cities differed in one important respect from towns elsewhere: many of them were situated on marcher lands and were continually vulnerable to attacks both from the Gaelic-Irish and rebel Anglo-Irish lords. This was particularly true in the decades prior to the outbreak of the Black Death, as Gaelic-Irish chieftains began to escalate their raids on the colony. In 1325, writes Friar Clyn, Tadg O Carroll 'scarcely left a house, castle or town in Eli O Carroll among the English and lovers of peace that he did not destroy by fire'.[11] The town of Nenagh in Co. Tipperary, for example, which was to be visited by the plague in 1349, was in 1347 burned by Dómhnall Ó Cinnéide, and elsewhere in Munster, in Gaelic and Anglo-Irish areas alike, the rebellious first Earl of Desmond, Maurice fitz Thomas, between about 1320 and 1346 cut a swathe through the towns and villages of Munster, as well as their hinterlands.[12] The result of such unsettled conditions was widespread economic decline. The Bruce Invasion, in particular, rendered a blow to many cities and towns from which they never recovered. Dublin was especially hard hit. In 1316, the city's fee farm – the fixed annual payment owed to the king by cities – was remitted 'in consideration of the losses entailed on the citizens by the concourse of armed men…, the destruction of the greater part of the suburbs of the city and the decrease of revenue'. In 1334, the poverty-stricken citizens again petitioned for relief of the farm because the houses and suburbs of the city, burned at the time of Bruce, were still waste because of frequent attacks by the Irish.[13] Added to their economic woes was the increasing lawlessness affecting towns in the mid-fourteenth century as the central administration's effectiveness waned. The situation was so fraught that in 1345 a royal decree requested that the Exchequer and common bench be removed from Dublin for security reasons. Even trade between towns was hampered, and in 1340 the Justiciar ordered the arrest of evildoers who waylaid merchants, saying that because of their activities the merchants dared not travel.[14] In sum, the plague hit towns that were already under considerable pressure and ill-equipped to withstand its onslaught. This offers a sharp contrast to the situation in towns in England, where the 1330s and 1340s saw an equilibrium and the beginnings of a recovery from the recession of the earlier part of the century. This was not the case in Ireland and the Black Death ensured even further decline.

Plague Mortality

Most annalists and historians agree that the Black Death hit towns and cities most severely. 'That pestilence,' wrote Friar Clyn,

> deprived of human inhabitants villages and cities and castles and towns, so that there was scarcely found a man to dwell therein.[15]

A range of contemporary and near-contemporary chroniclers further emphasise the severe effects of the plague on Ireland's coastal towns: the contemporary English chronicler, Higden, and the seventeenth-century historian, Barnes, both stressed its effects on the coastal towns of the Irish colony, and Archbishop FitzRalph of Armagh noted the high mortality among coastal dwellers and especially fishermen and sailors.[16] In the walled, crowded enclosures of the medieval town, plague spread rapidly. One could perhaps surmise that the experiences of people living in medieval Dublin or Cork would not have been significantly different to those described by Gilbert Li Muisis in Tournai:

> others, who visited or lived among the sick, either became seriously ill or died; and they died especially in the streets in the market area, and more people died in narrow lanes than in broad streets and open squares.[17]

The numbers dying were high, though those cited by the non-statistically minded medieval chronicler have to be treated with caution. Two hundred people were reported to have been buried in Smithfield cemetery in London between 2 February and 12 April 1349, 57,000 people died in Norwich, and Boccaccio estimated that 100,000 people died in Venice and in Florence.[18] Or, there is the oft-cited instance of Givry, a village in Burgundy, where between August and November 1348, over 615 people died out of a total population of between 1,200 and 1,500.[19] Clyn writes that 14,000 died in Dublin between 8 August and 25 December. It is an unusual figure, lacking the roundness of the figures usually cited by medieval chroniclers, but we don't know how Clyn reached it. The figure does however indicate an average daily mortality of 100, and perhaps Clyn calculated his overall figure on the basis of a daily reckoning. That about 100 people would have died daily in Dublin is not impossible during the early, more virulent stages of the plague. The overall figure of 14,000 is undoubtedly exaggerated, though by how much is an intriguing question. Whatever its mathematical accuracy, it highlights the extent of the mortality in Dublin and since Dublin probably had the highest population of all cities in Ireland, it would have accordingly suffered the greatest death toll.

The historian and bacteriologist, J.F. Shrewsbury, disputed Clyn's estimate on the basis of findings from outbreaks of bubonic plague in India in 1898. He argued that since conditions pertaining to rat infestation in India in 1898 would have been similar to those in late medieval Dublin, absolute mortality rates would therefore have been similar: namely, no higher than 25% of the population. On demographic grounds he also disputed the figure, claiming that 10,000 deaths of women should be added to Clyn's figure, which would result in a mortality rate requiring a population of 96,000, clearly an impossibility.[20] However, Shrewsbury's arguments are not altogether convincing. There is no reason to suppose that Clyn in referring to 'men' is speaking of the male sex only: he uses the generic word *homo* meaning 'human being' and not *vir* or 'man' in distinction from 'woman'. Further, most epidemiologists hold that one cannot compare modern mortality figures with those for the Middle Ages, as the medieval plague would seem to have been far more virulent.

Finally, Shrewsbury did not even allow for the possibility of pneumonic plague, and Clyn's own testimony clearly points to symptoms of pneumonic plague among Dublin's victims. In short, while the figure of 14,000 deaths in Dublin is high, its plausibility is not affected by Shrewsbury's arguments.

A calculation of plague mortality depends of course on what the pre-plague population of Dublin was, another unknown quantity. A comparison with other cities may be helpful in appreciating the possible size of medieval Dublin's population, though there is an extraordinary array of opinions among demographers on the subject. Milan, Venice, Florence and Paris had populations of around 100,000; with populations between 50,000 and 75,000 were Rome, Cologne, Bruges, Brussels and London. Towns such as Avignon, Ghent, Ypres had about 20,000 to 60,000. Bristol's population was between 10,000 and 12,000, perhaps even higher. By far the greatest number of towns had between 500 and 6,000: in Italy, there were over 150 settlements with populations ranging between 2,000 and 10,000, in France there were about fifty towns with a few thousand, and about forty in England had populations just over 2,000.[21] However, recent demographic studies have tended to revise upwards the population of English cities. London, for example, which was estimated to have had around 50,000 inhabitants in 1300, is now estimated at 80–100,000 in 1300; and that of Norwich has been upgraded from 10,000 to 25,000. Most people, however, lived in towns with a population under 10,000.[22]

Dublin's population was more likely in the category of smaller European cities and it would have been far less crowded than a typical European city. But precise calculations are not possible, though many have attempted estimations which, like those for England, keep rising. One estimate put it at 3,500 in the early fourteenth century and the demographer J.C. Russell estimated it at about 10,000. However, the historical demographer T.H. Hollingsworth considered these estimates too low. Using the same evidence of guild membership used by Russell, a household multiplier of four to account for the dependents of each guild member and adding some 6,000 for clergy, soldiers and other non-guild members, he very tentatively guessed its population in 1246 to be closer to 20,000 and in 1280 to be about 25,000, a figure which he considered a reasonable guess in the light of the 50,000 people he estimated for London at the same time.[23] Others, using Clyn's figure of 14,000 mortality and assuming a Black Death mortality of 33%, have contemplated a population figure of about 42,000, while others by favouring the higher mortality rate of 40% have come up with a somewhat lower population figure of 35,000. The permutations seem endless. If Hollingsworth's more cautious figure of around 25,000 is in any way accurate, then Clyn's figures are within the bounds of possibility, and not out of line with mortality figures reported in other European cities of similar size. Bearing in mind that plague is extremely virulent in its initial phases, a case mortality in the region of 50% is quite possible for Dublin.

What is undoubted is that Dublin's population continued to decline, by as much as two-thirds until the middle of the sixteenth century. Using Hollingsworth's methods, Dr Gearóid Mac Niocaill calculated its population would have been about 6,000 in 1476, though acknowledging this figure to be 'the merest guesswork'. By using tithe and various other data to calculate the number of persons Dublin could support, MacNiocaill estimated 8,000 inhabitants for the city in 1540. The fact that the population of Dublin was still in that low region in the mid-sixteenth century must reflect the effect of the crisis mortality engendered by the plague and its subsequent outbreaks in the fourteenth and fifteenth centuries, as well as of declining replacement rates and increasing emigration. It then began to recover, though slowly: even as late as 1650, only 20,000 are estimated as living in Dublin. From that point on, population recovered rapidly and is estimated to have reached 130,000 in the 1750s.[24] On the basis of these estimates, one could then conclude that population did not recover its pre-plague level until the mid-seventeenth century. This too is the demographic pattern that characterised Europe in general between the fourteenth and seventeenth centuries: according to Hollingsworth, among others, the number of people alive in 1444 was about the same as in 1086 and not until the 1600s did the population rise to the level it had reached before the Black Death.[25]

The population of other Irish towns would have been very much smaller, but estimates are difficult because of inadequate data. Based on the custom returns recorded from Irish ports at the beginning of the century, the largest cities were, in order: New Ross, Waterford, Cork, Drogheda, and Dublin. On the basis of the farm paid by different cities in the thirteenth century, which was calculated on house totals, this order would be reversed, with Dublin estimated as the largest and Waterford probably as the second largest city, followed by Cork and Drogheda. New Ross accounted for 26% of the total customs paid by Irish ports at the beginning of the fourteenth century and could also have been equally well populated.[26] From an unusual source we get another idea of its possible size. A poet writing in 1265 about the walling of the town gives the town an adult male population of 3,200; he counted all the different groups helping to build the walls, though coyly admitted to defeat when counting the huge numbers of women. By applying the same household multiplier of four used by Hollingsworth in his estimations of Dublin's population (and most historians today consider this too low) for any dependents of these men, the population would have been just under 12,800.[27] However, an estimate based on the rents paid by burgage holders is far lower and puts the size of New Ross' burgess household population at just over 2,530. On the same basis, the population of the other major cities of Drogheda, Waterford, Cork and Limerick has been estimated at between 1,000 and 2,000, and that of most other towns as under 1,000, and even under 500. A few towns would have had burgess populations of over 1,000 including Bunratty, Nenagh, Thurles, and Galway.[28] However, estimates based on records of burgess rents are not reliable, as they do not include the urban dwellers who were not burgage holders, and there is not a precise correlation between the amount of burgess rents and the number of burgage holdings. Nor is the rate of mortality in these towns known. By analogy with other places, the most commonly accepted estimate of 40-50% may be taken as a general guide for the mortality in the larger towns and ports of the east and south such as Drogheda, Dublin, New Ross, Waterford, Youghal and Cork. However, estimations should perhaps be avoided in view of M.M. Postan's warning against the 'lure of aggregates', speculations about which, he wrote, 'can lead to mistakes on a heroic scale'.[29]

The loss of population, however, was great enough to merit repeated mention by the citizens of many towns. Cork was one of the ports severely affected by plague, and the mortality caused by the plague created problems for the citizenry for years to come. In 1351, the jurors of an inquisition said that

> in the time of the said pestilence the greater part of the citizens of Cork and other faithful men of the King dwelling there all went the way of the flesh.

Though exact figures are not cited, the mortality was so severe that the victims' houses were left uninhabited, indicating that whole families must have died.[30] Archaeological investigations have also offered evidence of Cork's difficulties at this time. Though there is evidence of voluminous pottery imports from many quarters until the mid-fourteenth century, the imports ceased from about 1350 on. The gap in the pottery record between 1350 and 1450 is a silent testimony to the decline in population, decrease in demand and disruption in trade that happened in the wake of the plague. Plagues, as well as emigration and warfare, continued to cause further damage, well into the later sixteenth century. The pre-plague level of pottery imports wasn't reached again until late in the sixteenth century, reflecting the continuing decline of the population which in 1650 was still just 12,000. Only in the eighteenth century, with the disappearance of plague and new waves of colonisation, did the population recover, and by the mid-eighteenth century it had increased to 70,000.[31]

Some forty miles away, the busy port town of Youghal also suffered severe mortality. In an inquisition in 1343, two-thirds of Youghal was said to contain 120 burgesses (how many, if any, were in the other third is not noted). By 1351 this number had fallen to ninety-one. However, an inquisition in 1351 lists the ninety-one burgesses, thirty-nine of whom were represented by their heirs, suggesting severe

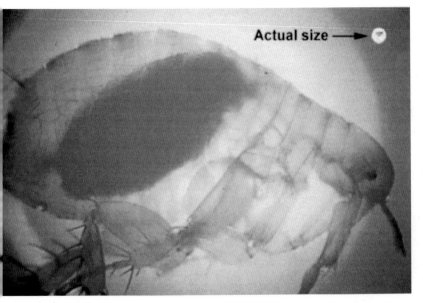

Actual size ⟶

1 *Xenopsylla cheopis*, the plague-carrying flea, here shown engorged with blood.

2 New Ross, a major port in medieval Ireland and one of the commercial hubs of the south-east. Its location at the junction of the Barrow and Nore Rivers gave it access to the great manors of Leinster. Like many medieval towns, its grain stores offered ideal conditions for the propagation of rats and their fleas.

3 Dalkey, the harbour which Friar Clyn names, along with Howth, as the entry point for the plague. In the distance is Dalkey Island with the ruins of St Begnet's Church.

4 Thath Molingis or Teach Moling. Friar Clyn reports thousands of pilgrims coming to this site in 1348 'in dread of the plague'. The pilgrims came to wade in the water along St Moling's watercourse; though now dry, the line of the watercourse is visible to the side of the cemetery and the churches.

5 St Moling's Well. St Moling created this well by diverting water from the Aughavaud River, a tributary of the Barrow River, to this site which became known as one of the 'holy' wells of Ireland.

6 Corbel Figure, St Francis Church, Kilkenny. Dated to *c*.1347, this is one of a number of caryatid figures supporting the vaulting of the bell-tower. The figures represent laymen in various attitudes, supposedly modelled on members of the Confraternity of St Francis charged with supervising the building of the new bell-tower for the church. Many see in the expression of this figure something of the shock and infinite sadness of people confronted with the terror of plague. (Hunt i. 194)

7 *Right* Bambino of Ross. Effigy of a child from a niche in St Mary's Church, New Ross, the largest medieval parish church in Ireland. On either side of the child figure are a male and a female. Dated to the late thirteenth century, its simplicity is in striking contrast to post-plague effigies and tombs. (Hunt, i.238)

8 *Below* Rice Tomb in Christ Church Cathedral, Waterford. Tomb of John Rice, many times Mayor of Waterford, who died in 1482, and of his wife, Catherine Brown. The top slab is covered with the effigy of an emaciated cadaver; the sides feature the apostles and saints, Mary and child at the head, the Trinity at the foot. The inscription is a classic *memento mori*.

9, 10 *Above and below* Detail of fourteenth-century Black Death burial pits from the site of the former Royal Mint at East Smithfield in London. Similar mass graves are most likely to exist in Ireland but are yet to be excavated.

11 *Opposite* Effigy of William Goer and his wife, Margaret, in the churchyard of St Mary's Parish Church, Kilkenny. Dated to *c*.1350, the inscription reads simply '*Hic jacet Wills Goer et Margaret uxor eius*'.

12 Tomb-chest at St Erc's Hermitage, Slane, Co. Meath. A fourteenth-century 'apostle' stone transported here from St Mary's Abbey, Navan. The head end is carved with a crucifixion scene, the sides with the apostles. 'This stone of unusual shape and uncertain use is of particular interest, as it foreshadows the fashion of those tombs with weepers, which commence in the Dublin Pale in the mid-fifteenth century, and became the general fashion in the Ormond Pale in the sixteenth century'. (Hunt, i, 570)

13 The Wicklow Mountains, the territory of the MicMhurchadha. From these lands, high in the mountains and protected by forests, the Gaelic-Irish escaped the worst effects of the plague and were able to take advantage of the colonists in the valleys and villages below.

14 Beaulieu Cadaver. A mid-fifteenth century cadaver tombstone from Beaulieu Churchyard, near Drogheda, one of the more realistic examples of late medieval cadaver tombstones.

15 *Above* St Francis Abbey, Kilkenny, where in 1349, Friar John Clyn wrote his *Annals* which are our main source for the Black Death in Ireland. He died, probably of plague, before he could complete his task. To the rear is the bell-tower which was begun in 1347 and was probably interrupted by the Black Death.

16 *Above* Ennis. In the cemetery of this Franciscan church was buried one of the few named victims of the plague, Matthew Caoch MacConmara.

17 *Opposite* Youghal Town, looking towards the sea. This town was an important port in the fourteenth century, a wealthy trading centre for the surrounding countryside. The Black Death took an estimated 40% of the town's population.

18 *Left* St Peter's Churchyard, Drogheda. A stone-carved cadaver tombstone from *c.*1520, of Sir Edward Golding and his wife, typical of the *memento mori* tombstones of this time.

19 *Below* Rock of Cashel. Seat of the Kings of Munster in the early Christian period and donated to the Church in 1101. Includes the Romanesque Cormac's Chapel and early twelfth-century round tower, with the thirteenth-century cathedral, now in ruins, and at the rear, the fifteenth-century tower-house. In 1351, the Dean and Chapter of the Cathedral pleaded impoverishment because of the mortality amongst the tenants of the episcopal estates.

20 *Right* St Lawrence's Gate, Drogheda. The twin-towered barbican or outer defence gate in the town wall of Drogheda, which was heightened in the fifteenth century. Like many towns, Drogheda was severely affected by the Black Death and other disasters, and was forced to seek royal aid in order to maintain its walls.

21 *Below* Black Abbey, Kilkenny, the Dominican friary where, in only one day (6 March 1349), eight friars died. Though founded in 1225, the present building is not earlier than the fourteenth century.

22 Medieval Kilkenny. A scene that captures the medieval atmosphere of this town: the steps leading to St Canice's Cathedral, most of which dates to the thirteenth century and the adjacent twelfth-century round tower. Kilkenny was struck by the plague in 1348-49 and repeatedly thereafter.

23 Duleek, St Mary's Chapel, Priory of the Augustinian Canons, whose income from tithes was affected by the flight of tenants after the Black Death. From the mid-fourteenth century, its property was leased to laymen. (Gwynn and Hadcock, 173)

24 Thirteenth-century town wall, Youghal. Thanks to the increasing impoverishment of the town's burghers in the later fourteenth century, Youghal was forced to seek royal assistance in maintaining its walls.

25 Tyone Priory, Nenagh, the Augustinian priory where in 1365, after the plagues, only two persons remained.

recent mortality.[32] These numbers indicate a mortality rate of about 45% among the town's burgesses. Such a rate is not an unrealistic figure for a town like Youghal: with its far-flung trading connections, it may well have been one of the first towns affected by the plague. But a rate like this cannot be applied to other towns. In estimating plague mortality, one is always confronted with the uneven incidence of the plague, not only in Ireland, but all across Europe. In Italy for example, cities such as Florence and Siena were severely affected, while Milan escaped lightly.[33] Yet cities escaping one outbreak were often affected by the next one, like Milan which was to be continually visited by the plague over the next 300 years, or cities in Flanders which, though spared the worst effects of the 1348 outbreak, suffered severely in 1361. This pattern highlights once again the fact that the Black Death of 1348 cannot be treated in isolation from later outbreaks of the plague.

Depopulation and Desertion

For the survivors, as elsewhere, economic conditions may have improved in the years after the plague. Thanks to the labour shortage, wages in Dublin and in other towns seem to have spiralled upwards. As elsewhere in Europe and England, the initial response of the authorities was to attempt to check the inflation by freezing wage levels and reimposing labour services. In August 1349, the Justiciar ordered the Mayor and bailiffs of Dublin 'to proclaim publicly at Dublin and cause the observance there of the provisions of the Statute of Labourers and Servants'. This order was repeated for the whole country by the Great Council in Kilkenny in 1351. Clearly this was not successful either, as in 1366 the wages of carpenters, plasterers, tilers, potters and apprentices had to be regulated once more, and the Statutes of Kilkenny in 1366 attempted to freeze wages by threatening judicial sanctions on any labourer who refused to accept a 'reasonable maintenance'.[34]

Such improving economic circumstances elsewhere led to an increase in emigration to the larger towns and cities from the countryside. This phenomenon of the movement of labour was a common one on the continent and in England in the wake of the plague of 1348, as labourers and smaller tenants moved in search of higher wages and the opportunities offered by the shortage of labour in the towns. Some of the larger towns in Ireland benefited from the flight from the countryside, at least for a while, and there is some evidence of Gaelic migration into the towns. This development is already evident from the early thirteenth century, but clearly gained momentum in the troubled conditions of the later fourteenth and fifteenth centuries, though in the absence of records one can only speculate on the effect the Black Death had. There is some evidence of Gaelic-Irish moving into towns and buying property, evincing that same 'upward' mobility that characterised certain English families, like the Pastons. As the historian Kenneth Nicholls has noted, in Cork the earliest example of this was the Ronan or O'Ronayne family.[35] That the Gaelic-Irish had become a threat to the status quo in the colony's towns is suggested by the increasing number of ordinances from the mid-fourteenth century, forbidding the appointment of Gaelic-Irish to the offices of Mayor and bailiffs, or other civic and ecclesiastical offices. However, the presence of the Gaelic-Irish varied from town to town and was still limited in many towns in the later fourteenth century, as is suggested by the predominantly English or Welsh names on a list of burgesses in Youghal in 1351 and on a roll of holdings in Cork dating from some time in the mid-fifteenth century.[36]

Irish towns, in general, were not replenished with rural immigrants, but experienced net emigration and therefore manifested the same problems as were evident in the countryside. This is in contrast to England where continuing emigration from the countryside offset the worst effects of plague depopulation in the towns and allowed for the expansion of cities such as Norwich and Coventry. The populations of continental cities also, especially in the wake of the plague, were continually augmented or at least stabilised by immigration, with immigrants from the countryside constituting at least one-third of the population at any given time.[37] Again, while definite figures for Ireland are not available, the increasing number of references in contemporary documents to the problem after 1348 would seem to suggest that the plague helped intensify the process. In an attempt to stem the flow, measures had already been passed in the 1340s requiring licences for emigration. In 1391-99, official permission was granted to 521 clerks, craftsmen, labourers and artisans. And this figure represents only a small proportion of those who left Ireland at this time. When the licensing requirement proved ineffective, new measures were passed, attempting to penalise those who transported illegal emigrants. In Cork in 1381, Henry Greff, a mariner from Pembroke in Wales, was pardoned for transporting 'certain men from the port of the city of Cork overseas without license'. Clearly, injunctions were not effective as again in 1410 Parliament passed measures ordering that 'any mariner discovered conveying a labourer or servant abroad, without licence from the administration, should forfeit his ship'.[38]

However, the flow of colonists continued, and over the next fifty-odd years, towns all over the colony in their petitions for aid made specific reference to the difficulties caused by emigration. The reasons given are diverse, but the pestilence is almost always mentioned. In 1393 in the town of Carlow, it was alleged that 'the greater part of the commons' were leaving to go to 'divers other parts'.[39] The effects of plague continued to be felt into the beginning of the next century. In 1427, the Mayor, bailiffs and commons of Dublin in their petition for aid specifically point to the plague as one of the causes of their misfortunes:

Owing to pestilence, incursions and divers heavy burthens in the time of the King and his progenitors, the citizens were unable to pay the rent to the Crown without imposing tallage on the commonalty. Many of the commons had subsequently left Dublin and would not return to the city, on which great loss and manifest desolation was thus entailed. The city walls, fortalices and towers in divers parts have become weak and ruinous.[40]

In 1435 the cities of Waterford, Cork and Limerick, as well as the walled towns of Kilkenny, Ross, Wexford, Kinsale, Youghal, Clonmel,

Kilmallock, Thomastown, Carrick, Fethard, Cashel and many others complained that they were 'on the point to be famished' because 'the few liege people left were not sufficient to victual' the cities and towns.[41] Gradually, as the colony's fortunes declined further and as the administration became ever more ineffective, the towns became like colonial outposts attempting to maintain their former status, at great cost to their citizens. Population decline continued as many left for the safer and more attractive conditions of life in English cities. Evidence from England supports the view that the Irish emigrated in significant numbers. In many cases, the influx was noticeable enough to generate hostility, and Irish merchants travelling from Chester to Coventry, Oxford and London were frequently attacked.[42]

The continuous emigration aggravated the population loss already occasioned by the plague. As a result, dwellings were abandoned and occupied areas contracted. Contemporary records create a picture of houses decaying and falling down, empty plots and abandoned areas. Knighton writes that in England after the plague, 'many buildings of all sizes in every city fell into total ruin for want of inhabitants'.[43] Ireland was no different. In Cork after the plague, victims' houses were left empty and by 1351 were reported to be falling into ruin.[44] In Drogheda, Co. Louth, one of Ireland's busiest ports in the earlier part of the fourteenth century, archaeological investigations by Sweetman have shown that part of the medieval quayside fell into disuse at this time and would seem to have remained so into the fifteenth and sixteenth centuries. Sweetman postulated that the depopulation caused by the Black Death and subsequent contraction could explain the gap in activity from the later fourteenth century.[45] Drogheda very likely suffered severe mortality given that seaports in general were heavily affected and that the town was hit by plague in its earliest stages, when it would have been at its most virulent. Similar gaps in the archaeological record were discovered in Dublin. Excavations in Patrick Street encountered an absence of stratified deposits from the later fourteenth and fifteenth centuries, suggestive of severe disruption during the plague years, though investigators acknowledged that the absence could have other causes also.[46] Towns such as Carlow and Trim were left with vacant burgages and houses falling into ruin; this decline together with attacks from the Gaelic-Irish meant that these now became frontier towns.[47]

Smaller inland market towns suffered most, as with the decline of the manorial economy their economic function disappeared. Many would have had far fewer inhabitants than they had earlier in the century. That the decline was widespread is evident from a number of references. The town of Nenagh declined considerably in the early fifteenth century. In Donaghmore, Co. Cork in the mid-fourteenth century, all the burgages were held by one tenant, very likely due to a decline in population in the town.[48] Towns and villages without a commercial base in general suffered most. The three boroughs in the manor of Inchiquin, in Munster, offer a pattern that was perhaps typical. All reported waste tenements in 1351; only Youghal, the seaport survived, Kinsalebeg disappeared and Inchiquin remained seriously waste.[49] By the end of the century, towns were clearly far emptier and more dilapidated than they had been and remained so. Sixteenth-century visitors to Ireland frequently commented on the decay and desertion of the towns they visited. Of Buttevant, Co. Cork, for example, a visitor would write in 1578 that 'in ancient times it was a big town, but is now all but deserted'. Four years earlier another commentator pointing to Ennis, Quin, Clare, Bunratty and other towns in the newly formed county of Clare wrote:

> in old times these were good market towns and had English jurisdiction in them and were governed by portriffes and other officers...; but now they are all wasted and destroyed in a manner, saving the castles and no part of the towns but old houses of stone work, broken gates and ruinous walls.[50]

Overall, only twenty towns of any commercial importance survived in fifteenth-century Ireland. With declining populations and resources, these towns were increasingly vulnerable to attacks from Gaelic-Irish lords. Coleraine, Roscommon, Athlone, Mullingar and Sligo were abandoned by the English, as were all urban settlements north of

Carrickfergus and west of Mallow. None of these towns was to survive under Gaelic lordship, with the possible exception of Sligo which developed trading connections with Spain and Portugal.[51]

In the smaller villages of Ireland, particularly those without any steady commercial base, many burgesses unable to support themselves probably drifted into becoming labourers, taking advantage of the labour shortages in the rural sector. The result was that some of the smaller villages, which had been flourishing in the thirteenth century, had disappeared by the end of the fifteenth century. Knighton writes that after the Black Death in England many small villages and hamlets were completely deserted, 'with no house remaining in them, because everyone who had lived there was dead, and indeed many of these villages were never inhabited again'.[52] M. Beresford in *The Lost Villages of England* calculated that some 1,000 medieval villages disappeared in England. However, the Black Death was not the governing factor in their desertion: some had been deserted in the earlier Middle Ages, generally those that were poorer, smaller and therefore most vulnerable, and most of the depopulation did not take place until the fifteenth century. While there are some authentic cases of Black Death depopulation, the plague's principal though long-term effect was to hasten the disappearance of the weakest settlements and to set others on a path of irrevocable decline.[53]

In Ireland, a similar process developed, though somewhat later. Some nucleated settlements had been deserted during the famine of 1315-18 and this in turn led to an increase in the number of bands of beggars who wandered the countryside in search of alms and food.[54] In the course of the later fourteenth and fifteenth centuries, the process of desertion continued, though most of that desertion would seem to have occurred in the seventeenth century. However, it has been argued that if these villages were deserted as late as the seventeenth century, more remains would be visible today than there are; the hypothetical explanation is that these villages must have been deserted earlier, in the fourteenth and fifteenth centuries.[55] Only one site, Kinsalebeg in the manor of Inchiquin in Co. Waterford, has been positively identified as having been probably deserted due to the

Black Death; in 1351, all the burgages there are recorded as waste, whereas a record of 1338–39 does not describe them so.[56] Some other instances of fourteenth-century desertion have been tentatively identified, including Moyaliff, Athassel (Co. Tipperary), Bunratty (Co. Clare), New Town of Leix (Co. Kildare) and others. Rinndown, Co. Roscommon, was very likely abandoned by the 1350s, though this does not mean necessarily that it was deserted completely as it may have continued as a form of settlement in Gaelic-Irish hands. Most instances of desertion, however, probably followed the pattern to be found at Newtown Jerpoint in Co. Kilkenny. This was a thriving town at the end of the thirteenth century: in 1289 it had twenty-two burgesses and some thirty free tenants with predominantly English names, so that the population must have numbered at least 250, though this number includes only the principal tenants and landowners and their families. In 1595–96 there were only seven tenants, all with what seem to be Irish names, and by 1614 the only six cottiers remaining had Irish names. The town was very likely deserted soon after due, according to local tradition, to plague – possibly the 1650 outbreak of bubonic plague. In Co. Westmeath there are 150 possible deserted villages from the medieval period, but again dating has proved difficult for researchers. Excavations on some moated sites, admittedly more rural than urban in character but which probably functioned as manorial centres, reveal a lack of habitation after the mid-fourteenth century, though the exact timing and causes cannot be ascertained. Excavations on two moated sites in Co. Cork, Rigsdale and Kilmagoura suggest they were both most likely abandoned before the Black Death, probably during the Desmond rebellion in the 1320s. Excavations at Kilferagh, Co. Kilkenny revealed no evidence of any habitation after the mid-fourteenth century, underlining what Dr T. B. Barry calls 'the settlement discontinuity probably caused by the economic and social problems of the age, such as the Black Death and the Bruce Invasion'.[57]

It is difficult to isolate the precise effect of the Black Death on these settlement changes. As elsewhere, the plague's role in the process was to accelerate the decline of those settlements already under pressure and it was one of a number of factors that set many other villages on the course of desertion. A concrete example of the concatenation of all these factors is that of New Town Leys in Co. Laois. In 1283, there were 127 burgesses in the towns; it was attacked by the Irish shortly after the Bruce Invasion and attacks continued, so that by 1324 only forty burgesses are recorded; very likely, it was finally abandoned after the Black Death.[58] In general then, there was a decline in the number of villages in the fourteenth century: thanks to the depopulation caused by plagues, the shift to pastoral farming and the decline of the manorial system, people moved away from the village settlements typical of the earlier Middle Ages, and gradually those settlements disappeared. Most of the villages that disappeared were small rural boroughs whose economic well-being was associated with particular manors, and as the nature of commerce and agriculture changed, such local markets were no longer necessary. It was, to use contemporary terms, a question of restructuring but not necessarily decline. Finally, we cannot rule out the possibility that many of these settlements may not in fact have disappeared, but in being taken over by the Gaelic-Irish, merely disappeared from colonial records.

Financial Decline

The effects of the plague's mortality on the cities and larger towns are however undoubted and are betrayed by the many references to the food shortages, financial difficulties and tax arrears experienced by the towns in the later fourteenth century. After 1348, all the major towns in the colony were forced to petition for assistance because of their impoverishment. Though there was undoubtedly an element of special pleading in many of these petitions, nevertheless there was some core of truth. The impoverishment wasn't of course a recent phenomenon and had already been in evidence before 1348 due in large part to war, but the plague clearly aggravated the situation.

Problems with the food supply in the towns intensified due to the labour shortage and general disruption in the manorial economy. Archbishop FitzRalph of Armagh specifically referred in a sermon to the shortage of foodstuffs in Ireland after the plague.[59] The towns were consequently forced to procure corn in Wales, England and even France for the maintenance of their citizens. In 1352, license was granted to Dublin's civic authorities to buy wheat in England and trade with it in Ireland because they were 'so impoverished as well by the late pestilence in their land as by other misfortunes'. Similar licenses were granted to Cork and Youghal in 1375 and periodically thereafter.[60] Nevertheless, difficulties continued and by 1394 the food supply had become such a problem that the export of provisions from all corporate towns in Ireland was forbidden. The problem was finally alleviated by granting licenses to those living in border areas to trade with the Gaelic-Irish.[61] Implied in all of this were rising prices for grain and its products as well as food shortages which caused immense hardship for urban dwellers.

The decline in population also meant that the tax base was no longer adequate to support the expenses of towns and cities. With fewer citizens to contribute to the fee-farm or to the costs of maintaining walls, many towns fell into arrears in their payments, and in ever-increasing numbers petitioned for tax relief and for grants to rebuild walls and bridges. Dublin, New Ross and Clonmel all petitioned for aid in 1351 because of their impoverishment due to the pestilence. In 1355, a grant of murage and pontage was made to the town of Clonmel for eight years, on account of 'the poverty of the town from the pestilence and depredations'.[62] In Youghal, as Dr A. F. O'Brien has shown, revenue from rents and court fees declined by 21% between 1288 and 1348. Just after the plague in 1351, four holdings in the town, which until recently had returned rent, were reported as waste. With continuing warfare and later outbreaks of plague, revenue continued to decline, at least until the later fifteenth century. And at the other end of the country, in the town of Antrim, revenues also declined and by 1358-59 the rent for burgages had fallen to 2d, approximately a sixth of what it normally should have been, clearly reflecting a shortage of burgesses and low demand.[63]

The effects of the plague in Cork were severe enough to cause the city's already severe financial difficulties to become particularly pressing as early as 1351. Thanks to raids by the Gaelic-Irish, rents could not be collected in 1342 and the city pleaded for relief. The effects of the plague were therefore felt all the more quickly and led to appeals for relief couched in terms that evoke all the difficulties of the time. An account from July 1351 may be indicative of what happened in many of the larger towns in the wake of the plague:

> The citizens of the said city of Cork and others faithful to the King living there at the time of the pestilence for the most part went the way of all flesh. As a result, their dwellings in that city are going to ruin because of lack of habitation and they cannot be repaired because of the impoverishment of the said citizens. Moreover, the lands of certain merchants…near the city and villages in the vicinity have been so destroyed and plundered by Irish thieves and enemies of the King, that the said citizens and villages have been impoverished and to this day they have not been able to get any profit from their lands.

The jurors go on to relate that a quarter of the city had been burnt, their merchants killed and their ships destroyed by Irish enemies, and that they are so impoverished they cannot repay their debts to the king 'without depression of their state'. Three years later in 1354 another appeal is couched in equally pressing terms, and the king remitted £50 arrears because 'the city, by the late pestilence as well as by dangers of wars in those parts has so much deteriorated'.[64]

Though the citizens of Cork were granted their petition, the combined effects of war and of plague were felt for many years to come. Some towns would have been able to weather the difficulties caused by the plague, but the persistence of plague outbreaks, together with chronic warfare, meant that few cities and towns could survive without aid. The farm of Cork continued to fall into arrears and frequent petitions by its citizens for tax remission are recorded during the later years of the fourteenth century: in 1376, 1388, 1391, 1400 and later. In the petition of 1388, for example, the citizens referred to their:

almost complete destruction by frequent invasions of Irish rebels, the burning of the suburbs of the city, the capture in war and impoverishement of many citizens loyal to the royal house and the withdrawal of many to other places of abode.[65]

Cork's burgesses, an ever-dwindling number, were increasingly forced to pay for the city's defences and eventually started trading with the Gaelic-Irish in an attempt to bolster their declining revenues.

Numerous other cities made similar petitions for aid to the crown, and while they no doubt exaggerated the degree of impoverishment in order to strengthen their case, nevertheless their pleas bear witness to continuing economic, and by implication demographic, decline. New Ross pleaded for aid, naming the plague as the cause of its difficulties. Waterford made frequent petitions for aid 'on account of recent calamities'; in 1388 the Mayor and citizens complained of their being 'greatly impoverished' and a decade later its citizens declared that they were still 'so impoverished that they cannot any longer support the charge of defending and repairing its ancient walls', while formerly fertile lands within the city lay waste.[66] Numerous grants were made to the city of Dublin in the second half of the fourteenth and the early fifteenth centuries: its rent was remitted in 1355-56; in 1363 a grant was made to enable the citizens 'to carry on their commerce'; and again in 1423 rent remission was granted, 'in consideration of the great burthens sustained by the Mayor, bailiffs and commonalty of Dublin, both in war and peace'.[67] Government subsidies became increasingly necessary for the walling of towns, expenses which hitherto had been borne by the citizens themselves. Subsidies were granted to Drogheda and to numerous other towns such as Youghal well into the 1400s.[68] In this decline, the Black Death was clearly seen by contemporaries as instrumental and there is no reason to doubt their perceptions.

A temporary decline also set in the volume of trade at this time, a decline that may be attributed largely to the effects of war, the general economic contraction in Europe and the administrative difficulties of the Irish administration. Some ports were already declining at the beginning of the fourteenth century, such as Wexford which in an inquisition of 1326 recorded 221½ waste burgages. Competition from Waterford and New Ross as well as the silting up of Wexford's harbour help explain its decline. Other towns in the south-east were similarly declining at the beginning of the fourteenth century, again for a variety of reasons, some due to war, others to competition from neighbouring towns.[69] What effect the Black Death had is difficult to ascertain. Elsewhere, the plague brought about a slump in trade which proved, in general, to be of short duration. Ireland seems to have experienced a similar slump, not surprising given the often-noted heavy mortality among Irish mariners and coastal dwellers and the delays of up to two months in crossing the Irish Sea in the summer of 1349.[70] As a result of the disruption both in Ireland and in England, trading was curtailed, and in 1354 Irish merchants were given special license to trade in English ports because 'alien merchants do not commonly come to Ireland to buy merchandise as they had heretofore'. In the later fourteenth century, ports (especially those on the east coast such as Drogheda), reported declining revenues from trade. Many factors contributed to this development, particularly the opening up of the Spanish and Portuguese wine trade which favoured ports on the west coast. However, the severe effects of the plague on the ports of the eastern and southern coasts undoubtedly played a part. The fact that Galway seems to have escaped the plague must have played a part in its becoming the foremost trading centre in Ireland in the fifteenth century. In Waterford, for example, the decline in trade further aggravated the emigration of citizens and the progressively weakening position of the traditional merchant class. The result was that when recovery took place in the wool and hide trade in the fifteenth century, exports were shipped by continental and English companies and were handled not by Irish, but by Dutch and English merchants. Trade in ports on the eastern coast continued to decline and was reflected in the customs returns. In 1369 the customs of Dublin and Drogheda yielded respectively £59 8s 1d and £18 5s 5d, by contrast with Galway's return of £118 5s 10d in 1393-94.[71] The financial difficulties of these ports on the eastern coast were to continue into the next century.

Recovery

In England and Europe the larger towns recovered quickly from the difficulties of the later fourteenth century. Though they remained demographically depressed, they took an increasingly important role in the economy and gradually helped to make European society increasingly urban. In Ireland also some measure of recovery became evident, though not until late in the fifteenth century. Until then, many towns had to weather food shortages, Irish attacks, continuing population decline and a host of other troubles. An account of life in Waterford and Dublin in 1399 by the Frenchman Jean Creton, who came to Ireland with Richard II's second expedition, paints a dismal picture of living conditions in Irish cities. He commented on the food shortages even in Dublin, where he saw four to six soldiers having to share a loaf, some going hungry for five days and concluded that

> I should have been heartily glad to have been penniless in Poitiers or Paris, because here [in Dublin] there was no amusement or mirth, only trouble, toil and danger.[72]

Recovery did come, though not till later in the fifteenth century. It is indicated in the numbers of fortified town houses that were built, for example in Dalkey, Co. Dublin among other places. Like the tower-houses in the rural landscape, they spoke of the towns' recovering prosperity and at the same time of their increasingly beleaguered state as colonial outposts. Towns in well-settled areas in the east and south survived. In the fifteenth century many of these towns such as Ardee, Cashel, New Ross and Kilkenny recovered and prospered, with Kilkenny in the fifteenth century being described as 'well-walled and well replenished of people and wealthy'. Port towns also recovered, such as Waterford which re-established its mint and embarked on building projects that revealed the town's increasing wealth.[73] However, as in the rural sector, much of this new wealth was concentrated in the hands of a few, and the business of the large towns and cities became increasingly the preserve of new patriciates; the extent to which the recovered prosperity filtered down through the social ranks was limited.

Urban recovery may be variously explained. Changing political conditions and the fragmentation of political authority meant that from the early fifteenth century towns, particularly in the south and west, were increasingly independent of the Dublin administration and free to chart their own affairs. Their growing independence mirrors the independence of the Gaelic-Irish and Anglo-Irish lordships as each became increasingly responsible for the execution of their own affairs. Many towns started trading with the Irish and made whatever other adjustments were necessary to recoup their losses of the previous decades: 'the profits of trade, like those of warfare, had an attraction that surmounted the ethnic divide.'[74] By the later fourteenth century, the Irish were already deeply involved in commercial activity. In 1394, one Felim O'Toole wrote, 'without buying and selling, I can in no way live', and the Irish were so involved in trade that in 1390, an ordinance was deemed necessary forbidding the furnishing to Irishmen not resident among the English of corn, malt, bread, wine, ale salt and other necessities.[75] This trading with the Gaelic-Irish hinterland accounted for much of the recovery in towns in the south and west, such as New Ross, Waterford, Cork, Limerick and Galway.[76]

Much of the recovery was occasioned by a pick-up in trade in the fifteenth century which made Irish ports in the fifteenth century among the busiest in Europe.[77] That these were not the same ports that dominated the commercial map in the earlier years of the century is a reflection of trends and developments taking place all across Europe. Cities such as Lincoln, Winchester, Florence and Bruges all declined in the fourteenth century and others such as Venice, Antwerp, Amsterdam, Coventry and Bristol came to the fore.[78] This type of regional redistribution was also evident in Ireland, and the later fourteenth century saw ports on the southern and western coasts dominating. Ports on the southern coast such as Youghal, and on the western coast such as Galway, Limerick, Sligo and Dingle all experienced increasing prosperity in the fifteenth century. The reasons for this are complex. The decline and obvious financial difficulties of the eastern ports undoubtedly played a part, and in this the Black Death was instrumental. The fact that it affected the colony more severely than the Gaelic sector is of considerable significance in view of the changing balance of power, whether political, military or economic.

Yet, while the urban economy may have recovered, a country's well-being can and should also be measured in other ways. Population recovery was to take much longer and demographic stagnation, if not decline, was to continue well into the sixteenth century. As a result, settlement in Ireland remained predominantly rural for the next few centuries. Demographically depressed, Irish towns outside the Pale became embattled enclaves of colonial settlement. The decline in the medieval town therefore mirrors the changes in the political structure and the decline of the colony which had fostered the growth of towns in Ireland in the first place.

6

The Church and the Black Death

The decline characterising manors and towns in Ireland on the eve of the Black Death was also evident in the life of the Church. Before the plague ever struck, bad times had come. The earlier Middle Ages had been a burgeoning period: a vast programme of church building was under way and religious houses were founded in all parts of the country. But the promise of the thirteenth century was not realised and rivalries and recession beset the Church in the fourteenth century. The abuses, social tensions and poverty that characterised the Church in Ireland at this time mirrored the general European situation. However, this period is also one of change as old patterns of settlement and power structures gave way to new. In this flux, the Black Death was an important factor. It presented the Church in Ireland with difficulties and problems that, while not new *per se*, were of unprecedented proportions. In order to evaluate these problems, it is first necessary to examine the state of the Church in Ireland in pre-plague Ireland.

The Church Before 1348: Decline

The reasons for the decline are complex. The close relationship between Church and State consequent on the Norman Conquest brought in its wake a tide of abuses: the conquerors attempted to use the Church as a weapon of political advancement and as a source of revenue and reward. In consequence, Irish-born ecclesiastics were relegated to minor benefices and the poorer bishoprics. Absenteeism was widespread, as English clergy already resident in benefices in England were promoted to Irish benefices. In the course of the fourteenth century, as the authority of the crown and the Dublin administration waned, and as the Gaelic chieftains reasserted control particularly in marcher areas, priories and abbeys came increasingly under the control of local families, and in the process more secular.[1]

Above all, the history of the Church in fourteenth-century Ireland is dominated by rivalries and tensions between the differing political groupings, which the historian J. Watt traces back to the Norman Conquest and the consequent split into a Church '*inter Hibernicos*' and a Church '*inter Anglicos*'. Within the ranks of the secular clergy, these divisions were often not so much between Gaelic-Irish and English as between Anglo-Irish and English-born, or between two competing Gaelic-Irish rivals for ecclesiastical office.[2] The divisions were most sharp within religious houses and especially within the Franciscans. By 1325, Clyn could write that

> there was discord, as it were universally amongst all the poor religious
> of Ireland, some of them upholding, promoting and cherishing the part
> of their own nation and blood and tongue; others of them canvassing
> for offices of prelates and superiors.[3]

The Irish complained of the English as oppressive and responded in kind. By 1331, the situation had reached such a pitch that the Justiciar and the Council of Ireland called on the Pope to authorise a crusade against the Gaelic-Irish and their supporters.[4] The consequences of this hostility were far-reaching. Divided dioceses and parishes made it especially difficult for bishops to maintain proper standards among the clergy and to minister to the pastoral needs of the people.

Allied to this was the growing poverty of the Church, due in the main to the endemic warfare in the country from the early fourteenth century onwards. Initially, the threat of war forced the Church to spend its revenues on defence and reconstruction. This drain on resources worsened through the fourteenth century as attacks on Church property became more frequent. In the Diocese of Dublin alone, poverty was not an uncommon complaint by many abbeys and benefices in the early fourteenth century. St Mary's Abbey, the Hospital of St John the Baptist outside Newgate and the Hospital of St John of Jerusalem (among others) all pleaded poverty at this time because of attacks by the Irish, and this despite the vast holdings of these houses. A similar situation existed among the secular clergy: in August 1307 the Archbishop-elect of Dublin was permitted to retain all his benefices, 'the debts of the see being heavy on account of its frequent violence and the wars in which it has suffered', while in the 1302-06 Papal taxation list many boundary churches of the diocese were returned as waste due to war.[5] A similar poverty pervaded other dioceses: even in the closing decades of the thirteenth century, the Dioceses of Armagh, Derry, Kildare and Emly were complaining of poverty and debt. In 1302-06 and 1327-30, the income of the See of Cork decreased by almost a fifth, that of Cashel by a quarter, while that of Cloyne fell to a sum that was insufficient to support a bishop.[6] Abbeys and priories as far apart as Selskar in Co. Wexford and St Mary's Kells in Co. Kilkenny, were similarly impoverished: in 1334 the priory of Selskar alleged that its lands and rents were destroyed by war, with the monks about to abandon their house and dwell in the countryside with their friends. Three years later it was claimed that the revenues of St Mary's Kells were not sufficient to maintain hospitality because of war and other disasters.[7]

A host of other factors completed the conditions of decline. Escalating taxation exacerbated the fall in revenue. The Irish Church was particularly oppressed by the heavy taxation imposed to fund the campaigns of the king in France in 1335, 1338, 1346 and subsequently. Other burdensome demands included local taxation to meet the needs of defence and Papal taxation. Absenteeism among benefice holders worsened as the fourteenth century progressed. Much of the revenue from benefices went to absentee ecclesiastics, while the care of benefices was administered by chaplains for labourers' wages. Parish clergy relied principally on tithes, a precarious source of income since it was affected by famines, bad harvests, storms, the fluctuations of the market, warfare and, increasingly, by the reluctance of the laity to pay it. Whatever were the difficulties faced by beneficed clergy, unsalaried parish clergy were even more destitute, without access to the resources claimed by the holders of benefices. The poverty of many of the benefices, moreover, encouraged the practice of holding in plurality. Abuses and indiscretions of all kinds gained ground as may be seen from the Synod of Ossory in 1317 which passed decrees on absenteeism, pluralism, the ignorance of the clergy, clerical marriage, the leasing of ecclesiastical property and the harming of ecclesiastical persons or goods.[8]

Thus, when the Black Death struck, the Church was already declining from its thirteenth-century position. As with the urban and rural sectors, the Black Death exacerbated and hastened trends already begun. Above all, the mortality it caused led to profound difficulties for the Church.

Mortality among the Secular Clergy

There are no well-documented sources, such as are to be found for England and the continent, from which one could estimate the mortality among the Irish secular clergy. Unlike England, Ireland doesn't have complete episcopal registers, which might offer records of institutions to benefices at this time. Our only continuous sources are the Papal registers which, though not comprehensive, nevertheless indicate some of the general changes engendered by the plague. The surviving evidence again bears out the general pattern of the Black Death's effect: some areas, especially along the east and south, were badly affected, a few communities in particular were devastated.

Of the twelve clerical deaths recorded in the *Calendar of Papal Letters* in 1348-50, nine were of bishops from all parts of the country – Leighlin, Meath, Waterford, Derry, Dublin, Ferns, Clonmacnoise, Achonry and Tuam.[9] This seems an unusually high figure, though evidence from other sources indicates that not all these were plague deaths. The death of the Bishop of Tuam in August 1348 cannot confidently be accounted a plague death as the plague would not have reached the west by August (though the possibility exists that he could have contracted it elsewhere).[10] The appointment in October 1348 in Achonry arose not because of a death, but after a long hiatus since 1344. And in Clonmacnoise the vacancy arose because of the translation of its incumbent to the See of Derry, which had been vacated by the death of its bishop in December 1349. If these three – Tuam, Achonry and Clonmacnoise – are eliminated, we are left with six episcopal deaths during the plague years. Of the other deaths recorded, the dates are consistent with the plague's progress: the Bishop of Ferns died in October 1348, that of Leighlin before April 1349, the Bishops of Meath and Dublin in July 1349 and the Bishop of Waterford in 1349, all dates being consistent with the plague in Leinster and Munster. The Bishop of Derry died sometime before December 1349. Calculating the rate of mortality is not straightforward, however, as the number of bishoprics in Ireland at this time was in a state of flux. The official number of dioceses was thirty-five, in which case episcopal mortality was 17%. By including only those bishoprics that had an occupant during the 1330s and 1340s, we are left with a total of thirty-three. The mortality rate would then be 18.2%. In any case these figures indicate a mortality almost the same as the 18% mortality recorded among the bishops of England.[11] However, the *Calendar of Papal Letters* is not complete and other sources indicate further episcopal deaths in these years. From an annals we know that William Ó Dubhda, the Bishop of Killala, died of plague in 1350. In Waterford, not only did Bishop Robert (Richard) Fraunceys die in 1349, but so did his successor within one year, in 1350.[12] Obviously, given all the assumptions, calculations of aggregate mortality are more in the nature of guesswork but are useful in giving a rough estimate of mortality.

Benefices falling vacant in 1348-50 were often not recorded in the Papal registers, again rendering difficult any estimate of clerical mortality. From other sources we know that the Archdeacon of Lismore and the Treasurer of Waterford Diocese both died in 1349.[13] Some vacancies were not officially filled for many years. For example, in 1355 John Gate requested Papal confirmation for his appointment in 1349 to the treasurership of St Patrick's Cathedral Dublin; a Papal letter of 1358 provided for David to the Augustinian Priory of St Catherine's Waterford which 'became void in the time of the pestilence, that is in June 1349 by the death of Prior Philip'; in 1359 the Archdeacon of Cloyne requested Papal approval for his appointment nine years earlier 'on the death of the previous incumbent'.[14] Moreover, gaps and disruptions were common in these years. The See of Meath remained vacant for a year until May 1350, and then its new incumbent died in 1352; Killala remained vacant until June 1351 and Clonmacnoise from 1349 until 1369. Clearly, such disruption would help explain the many gaps in the record-keeping at the time.

Still, using only the *Calendar of Papal Letters* as source and without making any allowances for non-plague deaths – which presumably would have remained the same both before and after the plague – a comparison of the number of vacancies recorded in this period with the corresponding figures available for the years prior to and following on the plague indicates that the number of vacancies rose considerably in the period 1348-54 (see Appendix, Fig. 4).

The mortality among the lower ranks of the clergy, however, must have been on a corresponding if not an even higher scale, since they had greater contact with the public than had the more privileged members of the hierarchy. Contemporary chronicles on the continent indicate that the clergy suffered particularly badly. Friar Clyn, writing of Ireland, bears this out:

> This pestilence was so contagious that those touching the dead or those sick of it were at once infected and died and both the penitent and the confessor were together borne to the grave.[15]

That many clerics died is suggested by the high number of extraordinary appointments made in the post-plague years, with special dispensations being given to irregular candidates because of the shortage of priests in Ireland. This occurred in the Dioceses of Armagh, Elphin and Emly, to name but a few. These dispensations cannot all be attributed to vacancies arising from Black Death mortality, as warfare and the decline in the colony had already begun to affect the personnel of the Church in Ireland. Nor had such dispensations been unusual in prior times, especially given that the sharp differences between canon law and Irish law – which allowed divorce and remarriage – often accounted for the label of illegitimacy, which was not recognised in Irish law.[16] Still, the numbers dispensed were unusually high and this can only have been a response to an increasing number of vacancies due to the Black Death. Moreover, the combined effects of the pestilences of 1348, together with its recurrences in 1357 and 1361 further exacerbated the shortage.

What evidence we have indicates that mortality was greatest in the Leinster region, in towns and along the coast. Waterford was clearly badly affected, with two bishops, a prior and two chapter officials dying in these years. On the other hand, there is not any break in the succession of bishops in nearby Lismore and Cork, nor in Limerick or Killaloe.[17] The deanery of St Patrick's Cathedral Dublin seems to have experienced a heavy mortality: Roger de Moclowe, appointed in 1348, died before he got possession; his successor, appointed in the same year, died before entering office; in February 1349 Matthew de Brissells was provided, but he too died before the end of the year. Among the other offices in the cathedral, the Treasurer died in 1349 as did the Archbishop, though there is an unbroken line of precentors and archdeacons. In 1349-50, appointments were made to the prebends of Castleknock, Rathmichael, Stagonil and five unnamed prebends; two of these vacancies were due to the promotion of the previous incumbent to the Archbishopric, the remainder to death, though the cause of death is not mentioned.[18] The presence of the Black Death is sufficient explanation for this unprecedented mortality and disruption.

The total mortality for the Diocese of Dublin eludes calculation. Perhaps inferences could be drawn on the basis of mortality in English dioceses. Gwynn in his study, 'The Black Death in Ireland' compared the Dioceses of Dublin and Exeter, which offered similarities in their coastal location, their size, and the fact that both were among the first places visited by the plague in their respective countries. In the Diocese of Exeter, the average number of inductions to livings in normal times was three per month, and in autumn 1348 no significant changes were recorded. Change came in January 1349, when thirty-one inductions to benefices were recorded, rising steadily in the succeeding months: thirty-five in February, sixty in March, forty-three in April, forty-eight in May, forty-six in June, thirty-seven in July, seventeen in August and a gradual return to the average of three by the end of 1350. Gwynn inferred a somewhat similar mortality in the Diocese of Dublin. Definite figures, however, are impossible; perhaps all that may safely be said is that 'the loss of life during the Black Death in 1348-49, followed by four pestilences between 1362 and 1391, reduced the number of religious of both races in Ireland considerably'.[19]

Global figures for deaths among the clergy are difficult to reach not only in Ireland. There is little agreement among historians of the plague elsewhere as to whether the clergy in particular suffered more than any other section of the population. Their pastoral duties would have exposed them more than other classes to infection, but their far superior living conditions, both in terms of housing and nutrition, would also have protected them against plague. The historian of the plague, J.F. Shrewsbury, contended that the numbers cited for plague deaths among the clergy were exaggerated and that many vacancies arose from resignation or flight. Recent studies, however, indicate otherwise: studies of the episcopal registers of Bath and Wells, Exeter, Lichfield, York, Lincoln and others all indicate a death rate of approximately 40% to 50% for 1348.[20]

Mortality Among the Regular Clergy

Abbeys, friaries, priories and convents fared particularly badly everywhere in Europe, largely because they offered the necessary conditions for the propagation of the plague bacillus. As has already been noted, many abbeys were particularly vulnerable to the inroads of the black rat, since flour mills and breweries in which rats burrowed were generally located near the monks' living quarters. In Ireland, many Cistercian abbeys were heavily involved in the wool trade – such as

Duiske Abbey in Co. Kilkenny and other abbeys particularly in Wexford and Kilkenny – and so were situated on trading routes along which rats and fleas travelled. Archaeological excavations at Tintern Abbey, Co. Wexford not coincidentally revealed evidence of many rats. Housing conditions were similarly conducive to the spread of plague, as people lived in close quarters in buildings that often were constructed of soft materials with thatched roofs. Admittedly, the monks' quarters in most Irish abbeys were often built in stone, affording them some protection, but it may be significant to note that the lay brothers' quarters in the Cistercian abbeys, which all but disappeared in the later fourteenth century, were often not as solidly constructed, as revealed by excavations at the Cistercian abbey at Dunbrody, Co. Wexford.[21] Mendicants' friaries were more exposed and vulnerable since most were situated in towns, especially along the more densely populated east coast. Of the sixty-nine friaries established by 1300, sixty-one were in the larger towns and many of these towns had more than one mendicant friary – all four mendicant orders, the Franciscans, Dominicans, Carmelites and Augustinians had houses in both Dublin and Drogheda, while three were represented in Cork. And of the thirty-one Franciscan monasteries in Ireland in 1348, all but four were situated in towns or seaports and all but eight were in large towns in constant communication with other areas.[22]

The effects of the Black Death on European and English monasteries have been well recorded. The Black Death is estimated to have taken three-fifths of all the Cistercians in Northern Europe and in Egypt, of 100 monasteries in the desert in 1346, only seven remained in 1450. In the Cistercian abbey of Meaux in Yorkshire, in the month of August 1349 alone, the abbot, twenty-two monks and six lay brothers died, so that by the end of the plague only ten monks and no lay brothers survived out of a pre-plague population of fifty. Walsingham in his *Historia Anglicana* writes that in some religious houses, barely two out of twenty survived. The mendicant orders were particularly hard-hit, not surprising given their urban apostolate. Knighton in his *Chronicon* notes this in detail, though without any sympathy for the mendicants whom he despised:

358 of the Dominicans in Provence died during Lent. At Montpellier only seven friars survived out of 140. At Magdalen seven survived out of 160, which is quite enough. From 140 Minorites at Marseilles not one remained to carry the news to the rest – and a good job too. Of the Carmelites of Avignon, 66 had died before the citizens realised what was causing the deaths; they thought that the brothers had been killing each other. Not one of the English Augustinians survived in Avignon – not that anyone will be upset by that.[23]

Friar Clyn writes of the devastation wrought by the plague in Ireland where, 'scarcely one alone ever died in a house but… all went the way of the Lord'. The only details he gives, however, are for the mendicant orders, and above all for his own order, the Franciscans. He records that by Christmas 1348, twenty-five Franciscans had died in Drogheda and twenty-three in Dublin; these numbers would have represented at least half of the total number of friars in these houses. In one day alone, 6 March, 1349, eight Friars Preachers died in Kilkenny.[24] How many more died we don't know, as Friar Clyn himself died shortly after. Clyn's figures are quite credible, given that the popularity of the Franciscans, especially as confessors, would have exposed them to contagion. Moreover, since he also described symptoms indicative of the pneumonic form of plague, which has a high rate of contagion and kills within two to three days, many more friars probably died than are recorded.

The surviving evidence for other places is suggestive, though sketchy. The path of these reported deaths is generally along the lines of densest population, in the east and south. The Prior of Kilmainham in Dublin, John Larcher, died (probably of plague) in November 1349, and his successor John Fitzrichard, appointed in the same year, died within a few months; no other deaths in the priory have been recorded.[25] Two friars died in the Franciscan monastery at Nenagh in August 1349 and one in the house at Limerick in the following November. Whether these houses experienced further mortality or not is not known, though we do know that in 1361, after successive outbreaks of plague, only two friars remained in the house at Nenagh.

The neighbouring Tyone Priory of St John (a Cruciferi house belonging to the Hospital of St John the Baptist in Dublin) was severely affected by the succession of plagues. In 1365, in a petition to the Pope, two of the monks, John Whyte and William Cantwell, stated that hardly two persons remained in their house due to the great mortality during the recent pestilence. Moreover, since there was no suitable candidate for prior among their own order, they asked that an Augustinian canon be appointed.[26] What other houses may have been affected has not been recorded. But it is quite likely that some religious houses which may have escaped in 1348-50 were visited in later outbreaks, as happened for example in Christ Church Canterbury where only four deaths are recorded during the Black Death, while twenty-five died in 1361.[27]

The plague and its later visitations may have left many monasteries stricken like the Priory of Augustinian nuns at Lismullin (Lysmolyn) in Co. Meath. In 1367, it was stated that

> the premises are worth £68 yearly, wherewith at different times there have been sustained in the priory before the time of the great pestilences in Ireland, a prioress, thirteen nuns and a household of forty...; but since the pestilences there are maintained there a prioress, seven nuns and five young girls... with other servants to the number of thirty-two persons.[28]

This record indicates a mortality of 42.6% in that convent in the period of 1348-67, a figure that is close to the 45% average death rate calculated for monasteries in England.[29] Again, variables such as location, communications and housing conditions preclude applying such a rate generally. But it could be taken as a rough guide to the average rate of mortality among the regular clergy in the east and south of Ireland in this period. Among the friars, the number may have been even higher, given the location of their monasteries in towns and cities.

Such evidence may suggest that Irish religious houses suffered more than the extant sources allow us to verify. Many of the sources are highly selective and many of the monastic records include only the deaths of abbots. There isn't any reference to the plague in the charters of the Cistercian abbey of Duiske in Co. Kilkenny, and this despite its extensive trading links and the known ravages of the plague in Kilkenny. There is not any break in the succession of abbots in St Mary's Abbey Dublin, nor in the Hospital of St John the Baptist in Dublin. However, this does not signify that the plague did not affect these monasteries, particularly given its devastation of the Franciscan house in Dublin.[30] In St Catherine's Waterford, only the death of the prior is recorded, but given the contagious nature of the plague, some of his fellow monks must have died also.

All the available evidence, and especially archaeological evidence, points to a decline in the population of the older established orders, such as the Cistercians and the Canons Regular of St Augustine throughout the latter half of the fourteenth century and into the fifteenth. Some even closed, such as Burriscarra Abbey in Co. Mayo, which was abandoned in 1383 and remained unoccupied until taken over in around 1413 by the Augustinian friars. Of course, one must not exaggerate: thirty-three houses of the Cistercian order survived until the sixteenth century. Still, they survived in a contracted form. In one of the more far-reaching developments, the lay brothers or *conversi* of the Cistercian order, who had farmed the land and done all the manual labour, became almost non-existent in the later fourteenth century and were not replaced; their quarters in the west ranges of the abbeys fell into disuse and Cistercian lands were increasingly leased to lay men. The number of monks had also significantly decreased by the fifteenth century, since parts of church buildings were in that century converted into dwelling apartments. Excavations in Tintern Abbey in Co. Wexford unearthed drains that fell into disuse and were backfilled in the late fourteenth century, again signalling a declining population in the abbey. Churches were curtailed because of shrinking communities, as for example at Tintern and in the Abbey of Inch, Co. Down. In other places, expansion was halted until the sixteenth century, as happened at the Kells Priory of the Augustinian canons in Co. Kilkenny, where excavations have shown that while considerable building was carried on in the twelfth, and again in the late thirteenth and early fourteenth centuries, there is a lull thereafter in construction until the sixteenth century. Finally, the effect of the Black Death is most evident in that the decline in church building already in progress gained momentum in the post-plague years. This is reflected in the fact that not a single new monastery of monks or of canons regular was founded in Ireland in the period 1349-1539.[31]

Shortage of Clergy

The primary task facing the survivors was that of filling the depleted ecclesiastical ranks, and just as landowners had to prove flexible with their tenants, so too the ecclesiastical authorities were forced to bend traditional requirements. There does not seem to have been any shortage of candidates for vacancies, but many of these were illiterate in the medieval sense of not knowing Latin, or were in some other way unsuitable for the office. Knighton's account of what happened in England is typical of what happened in many places:

> At that time there was such a great shortage of priests everywhere that many churches were widowed and lacked the divine offices, masses, matins, vespers, and the sacraments and sacramentals. A man could scarcely get a chaplain for less than £10 or 10 marks to minister to any church, and whereas before the pestilence there had been a glut of priests, and a man could get a chaplain for 4 or 5 marks, or for 3m with board and lodging, in this time there was scarcely anyone who would accept a vicarage at £20 or 20m. But within a short time a great crowd of men whose wives had died in the pestilence rushed into priestly orders. Many of them were illiterate, no better than laymen – for even if they could read, they did not understand what they read.[32]

In France, the contemporary chronicler Jean de Venette attributed the ignorance that flourished in the wake of the Black Death to the fact that 'few men could be found in houses, towns or castles who were able or willing to instruct boys in the rudiments of Latin'.[33] The problem of ensuring a literate, educated clergy had already been a major concern of the hierarchy in pre-plague Ireland, and the Papal registers are strewn with references to the lack of literate candidates. A university in Dublin had been planned in 1321 to remedy the situation, but nothing came of it.[34] Warfare and financial difficulties rendered the situation critical. After the Black Death and subsequent outbreaks, the pool of educated clergy shrank noticeably and in the post-plague years many 'illiterate' candidates were appointed. Archbishop FitzRalph of Armagh considered the ignorance of the clergy to be so serious that in the first sermon he preached after the plague, in March 1349 in the Carmelite church in Drogheda, he put it on a par with the pestilence as a reason to pray for the intercession of Mary. Nor was this problem restricted to Armagh. In November 1363 a group of clerks petitioned for prebends in Ireland where 'by reason of pestilence and wars…there is a great lack of clerks, and the value of benefices is small' and they warned the Pope that 'he must not be surprised that the persons have no scholastic degrees, in as much as in all Ireland there is no university or place of study'. These men came from all parts of Ireland: Meath, Dublin, Kilfenora, Limerick, Down, Cork, Cashel, Ardfert and Cloyne.[35]

In Ireland, as in England and the rest of Europe, the Church was also forced to relax its rules regarding the parentage and age of its priests. Canon law forbade ordination to the priesthood to those under the age of twenty-four and to illegitimate candidates, defined as the offspring of unmarried parents or of clergy. This requirement was gradually relaxed throughout Europe from the later fourteenth century. One of the reasons for this increase was that the Avignon Papacy deliberately pursued a dispensations-for-fees policy as a revenue-raising measure. Still, this policy was also a response to demand and clearly there was a shortage of priests that had to be met in some way. Requirements were being relaxed in Ireland from the late 1330s and early 1340s, but the number of instances increased after 1348. The Papal registers offer a litany of these. In January 1351, Archbishop FitzRalph of Armagh was given permission to dispense sixty persons with impediments – forty of illegitimate birth and twenty who were either married men or under age – to hold a benefice apiece. The fact that FitzRalph, a man of seemingly unbending principle, would seek such dispensations, testifies to unusual circumstances. Similar concessions were granted in 1363 to the Bishops of Dublin, Emly and Iniscathaigh. In 1352, the Pope was petitioned for a benefice for one 'not withstanding that he is over twelve and under fourteen years of age'.[36] The increase in such petitions in the post-plague era underlines the shortage that increasingly led the Papal curia to overlook impediments such as wives, children and lack of education in filling clerical ranks.

The shortage of clergy after the plague also had administrative repercussions. Together with the declining value of benefices, it encouraged the practice of pluralism in benefices and monasteries. The *Calendar of Papal Petitions* notes that, 'on account of the slender value of benefices and the scarcity of fit persons, it is hardly possible to subsist on two benefices'. Again, this was not a new phenomenon and was well established in Ireland by the early fourteenth century, yet it seems to have become even more widespread in the latter half of the century, particularly in the Leinster area where the wealthier benefices were held by ambitious ecclesiastics living elsewhere. Many entries specifically mention the plague as one of the causes. In March 1352, Dublin's Archbishop John of St Paul was given Papal permission to hold three or more benefices because of his see's poverty 'due to Irish attacks and high mortality'. Clearly the practice was widespread, as in 1364 the Pope ordered the bishops of Ireland 'to make a return within eight months of benefices and offices held or expected by Papal authority, their qualities and taxations, so that a stop may be put to pluralities and other scandals'. Such efforts had little effect. In 1378-84, a group of twelve canons attached to St Patrick's Cathedral in Dublin, but resident in England, complained of the exorbitant charges being levied on non-resident officeholders. John Swayne, later Archbishop of Armagh, typifies the pluralists of this time: in 1404 he was rector of of Galtrim in Meath, Treasurer of Dublin Cathedral, canon and prebendary of Newcastle Lyons, Dublin and of Taghmon in Ferns. The increasing incidence of pluralism also meant an intensification of the problem of absenteeism. Even Richard FitzRalph, who in his sermons railed so often against abuses, lived in Ireland for only six of the fourteen years he was Archbishop of Armagh.[37]

Clerical shortage as well as the general disruption of these years also led to increasing disorganisation in the parish system, especially in those areas affected by both plague and warfare. In England, the Black Death had similarly affected the organisation of parishes and population decline led to the closure of many parish churches, especially in towns. A similar process is evident in those areas in Ireland for which there are records. Tipperary is an example. There a well-organised parish structure had been in place since the thirteenth century, but under the impact of plague and warfare, the system gradually fell apart, churches were not maintained and the clergy became more corrupt. How widespread the closure of parish churches was is difficult to say. Parishes in the Diocese of Ardagh in the early fifteenth century were said to be 'without churches owing to wars and other calamities' and there is ample evidence of churches all over the country falling into ruin due to lack of funds. [38]

Abbeys and friaries faced similar shortages of unqualified candidates and had to make similar compromises in order to gain new recruits. That some novices were attracted to the better living conditions offered in religious houses is suggested by the Papal decree of October 1348 granting leave to the Friars Preachers in Ireland

> to eat flesh meat on lawful days when they go out to preach the word of God..., the disturbances and consequent lack of food in Ireland making it impossible for friars to obtain the prescribed kinds of meat outside their houses, which causes a diminution of the persons entering the said order.[39]

The Franciscans everywhere suffered severe shortages and tried to resolve the problem by attracting very young candidates. The statutory age to enter the priesthood was lowered to fourteen, but the Franciscans in Ireland allegedly recruited candidates even under the age of thirteen, or at least so Archbishop FitzRalph of Armagh, no friend of the Franciscans, contended. Other orders relaxed their literacy and legitimacy requirements. In 1363, Alan Omolchonarius was given dispensation to be promoted to any dignity in the order of the Augustinian canons, despite being the son of a priest, 'seeing that by reason of the mortality in Ireland there are few and literate persons'. The Cluniac priory of Elphin made similar accommodations.[40] The Augustinian canons in particular were badly affected. In 1354 they were granted dispensation for three years to appoint 'good and qualified brethern' as priors in local priories, 'notwithstanding the fact that they do not know how to speak Latin'. That this problem was not peculiar to the Irish province of the order is made evident by the entry immediately following recording similar petitions from other communities in Italy. Moreover, this development was clearly a recent one among the Irish Augustinians who had until then sent novices abroad for study: just prior to the Black Death in May and July 1348, they had petitioned Edward III for help in paying for the education in England of six Irishmen which the Irish congregations had hitherto subsidised, but could no longer afford.[41]

However, while the mendicant orders weathered these recruitment difficulties, the older monastic orders, and especially the Cistercians, continued to experience shortages into the next century, a pattern that is echoed elsewhere in Europe and England as these orders gave way to the mendicant orders.[42] The older orders were too exclusive and didn't address the changing realities of Ireland in the later four-teenth and fifteenth centuries. Young men joined the mendicants, not the Cistercians. The Cistercians particularly suffered with the disappearance of the lay brothers whose ranks were not replenished by new recruits. Perhaps the lowly status of a lay brother could no longer match the more attractive alternatives offered by the friars. Moreover, one might note that while the contemporary monastic registers have voluminous entries in the thirteenth century recording grants of land to abbeys and priories by pious laymen, there is a clear dwindling in the number of such entries for the fourteenth century, testament not only to the more straitened economic circumstances of the post-plague era, but also perhaps due to dwindling respect for the older abbeys and monasteries.

Financial Difficulties

In contemporary accounts, war and pestilence are mentioned together as the inseparable agents of the decline in ecclesiastical revenue which gained momentum in the later fourteenth century. The process affected the whole of Ireland and no one particular region escaped, though there were some notable exceptions. Again, the east and south suffered most. Shortly after the plague, the income of the Archbishop of Dublin was reported to have been severely affected by the 'invasion of enemies and the mortality'. In Ossory, many churches were reported waste in November 1351 and unable to pay the procurations they owed to the bishop. The See of Emly was impoverished in 1363 and the poverty of Armagh was such that Archbishop FitzRalph in January 1351 requested permission to appropriate a number of churches in England and Ireland.[43] Even dioceses in predominantly Gaelic areas were affected. By 1414, the See of Clonfert was so poor it couldn't pay for necessary repairs to the Cathedral; in the same year, the Bishop of Annaghdown alleged that because of wars and other calamities he had received nothing, nor was he even able to reside in his church; the sees of Derry and Dromore were also reported as destitute.[44] The poverty of diocesan churches in Ireland was to last well into the later fifteenth century .

The declining fortunes of the Diocese of Cashel may be cited as an instance. In 1351, the Dean and Chapter of Cashel petitioned Edward III to remit their taxes because of the loss of revenues due to attacks from the Irish and the mortality among their tenants from the pestilence. Twenty-five years later, in 1377-80, the economic situation there had clearly not improved, as is evident in a petition by the Archbishop, Philip Torinton, to Richard II concerning the advowson of the church of Dungarvan and its annexed chapels. This advowson had been granted to the See of Cashel by the king in 1334, but had been later the subject of much dispute. Since then, Torinton explained, 'as much due to pestilence as to war all the chapels of the said cathedral church, except for three or four, were destroyed in the time of my predecessor, Ralph [Ralph Kelly, 1346-61]'. To help alleviate the poverty of the diocese, Torinton now asks that the advowson be once again returned to him.[45]

Not all religious houses suffered and there are some notable and puzzling exceptions to this general trend. The possible reasons are various: some were not affected at all by plague; with smaller numbers, some houses became wealthier; others through good management recovered quickly and within a few decades were prospering, much as some towns were to weather the Black Death. Llanthony Secunda Priory in Duleek, Co. Meath, for example, in 1381 reported falling tithe revenue due to plague, yet was still able to send £80 in profits to its motherhouse in England.[46] In general, however, priories and abbeys did not easily recover from the accumulated effects of war and plague. The Priory of the Hospital of St John in Drogheda in 1359 alleged that its lands were not yielding any revenues. Even in the Dublin area, the centre of the colony, numerous abbeys and priories experienced continuing decline. Holy Trinity Priory was so impoverished 'by war and pestilence' that its diocesan taxes were reduced by half in 1390 and by a further half in 1426. By 1410, the Priory of Kilmainham was so stricken 'by mortality and other disasters' that its revenues were not sufficient for defence.[47] Similar conditions are reported elsewhere in the country. The Cistercian Tintern Abbey in Co. Wexford was so poor by 1378 that its abbot was relieved of attendance at parliament. Priories were too destitute in many instances to maintain their inmates, as happened in the Priory of Gilabbey in Cork.[48]

Worst hit by the combination of declining revenue and declining numbers were monasteries and abbeys in marcher areas. Many of these priories were situated in the east and south of the country, in areas where the Black Death struck hardest. The Augustinian priory of St Mary's in Toomeveara, near Nenagh, was reported as destitute in 1363 and its fortunes clearly did not recover as in 1403 the warden, John O'Meara, pleaded that his house was impoverished because of the 'wars and pestilence which have long afflicted those parts', a complaint repeated yet again in 1450.[49] Many monasteries were reported to have reached the point where the monks were forced to become wandering beggars. This happened in the Augustinian Priory of Monaincha, near Roscrea, in 1397 when 'eight canons were obliged to go forth and seek their necessities through the courts of temporal princes to the diminution of divine worship therein'. A similar fate befell the Augustinian priory in Fertagh in Ossory which by 1421 was said to be 'so destroyed and desolated and exposed to ruin by the wars and calamities which have afflicted those parts that its religious cannot remain therein, but must wander about and beg their daily bread'. In 1445, the Franciscan church in Meelick in the Diocese of Clonfert pleaded that

> on account of wars, pestilences, and divers other sinister events which have affected and continue to affect those parts ... [it] is threatened with the ruin of its church, dormitory, cloister and other offices, and is utterly destitute of ornaments, books, chalices and ecclesiastical paraments.[50]

There is an ever-increasing record of indulgences being granted to all those who give bequests to such destitute churches, including Askeaton, Co. Limerick in 1400, Goleen in Co. Cork in 1442, Clare, Galway in 1433 and Trim in 1430.[51] A similar tale of ruined buildings, lost revenues and diminished tithes is told of priories, churches and cathedrals throughout the country: the Augustinian priories of Kells, Navan, Derry, Galynn, Inisygad and Athlone; the cathedral church of Clonfert, the Dominican church in Carlingford, the church of St John the Baptist in Ballinrobe, and churches in Meath, Dublin, Ardagh, Kildare, Emly, Lismore, Kilkenny and many more.[52]

The poverty of the diocesan churches was due largely to a decline in revenue from tithes, caused partly by a declining population either through death or flight. This happened in the priory of Llanthony Secunda in Duleek, County Meath, for example, where the tithes of its churches had dropped by 1381: those of its Chapel of St Kenan [Cianán] declined only slightly from £13 6s 8d to £12, but in the chapel of Platyn, tithes that formerly had amounted to £9 dropped to £6 13s 4d, since the land annexed to the chapel was not occupied 'because of the flight of tenants'.[53] In the case of monasteries with property, the shortage of labourers after the plague also meant that revenues from rents declined and land could not be cultivated. The chronicler of the Cistercian abbey of Meaux in Yorkshire carefully explained what happened in the aftermath of plague:

> From this time the rents and goods of the monastery began to dwindle, largely because the majority of our tenants had died, and because after the abbot, prior, cellarer, bursar and other experienced men and officials had died, the survivors made misguided grants of the goods and possessions of the monastery.[54]

A similar chain of events no doubt happened elsewhere. In other places, tithes declined due to friction between clergy and laity. Such disputes were not unfamiliar occurrences even before the plague. In 1345, for example, licence was granted to the Archbishop of Cashel to create notaries public 'there being suits and quarrels among the clergy and people of that land'. However, the instances become much more frequent in later decades of the century, a familiar development also in post-plague continental countries. From 1350 onwards, Archbishop FitzRalph in his sermons frequently refers to the laity's reluctance to pay tithes. He particularly chastised the merchants of Drogheda with whom he had a running battle on the subject, he claiming they should pay tithes on each sale, they wishing to pay tithes only on the end-of-year profits. But the battle continued after his death. A provincial synod in Armagh in around 1383-89 decreed that 'all traders and merchants [are] to pay tithes faithfully to the rectors or vicars of their churches' and in 1411 the Archbishop of Armagh threatened excommunication to 'all who hinder the collection of tithes, first fruits or any other obventions belonging to the Church'.[55] All over the country, an increasing number of bishops sought licence to create notaries public whose main function was to settle disputes between clergy and laity.[56]

Declining Moral Standards

Widespread mortality and the consequent despair have been cited as the cause of a general decline in moral standards among the clergy everywhere in the post-plague era. What sources there are seem to warrant the conclusion that the clergy in Ireland evinced the same behaviour as their European counterparts. While the Black Death did not create such practices, increasing lay criticism of the moral habits of the clergy after 1348 would seem to suggest that the plague intensified clerical abuses, or at least made the public less willing to tolerate them. Some of these complaints emerge in the sermons of Archbishop FitzRalph. In a sermon in 1352, he accused the clergy of fornication, adultery, marriage, nepotism, gluttony, drunkenness, hypocrisy, greed and in sermon after sermon inveighed against their lack of spiritual motivation.[57] The decrees of the provincial synod of Armagh in 1383 bear ample testimony to a Church riddled with abuse, at least by official Vatican standards: decrees against the oppression of the Church, the sale of ecclesiastical offices to lay persons, the irresponsibility of the clergy, the keeping of harlots and concubines by priests and more. We can only guess how many were like the pleasure-loving Dean of Armagh, who in 1427 was found guilty of 'carrying arms, going to dice and other unlawful games, keeping a concubine, entering taverns, gardens, vineyards, cornmeads, etc'. The author of the fifteenth-century Irish tract, *Salus populi*, bewailing the times, wrote, 'persons of ye church covet more to plough with ye plough rusticall than with ye plough apostiall' and goes on to complain that

> the prelates of the Church and the clergy is much the cause of all the
> disorder of the land; for there is no archbishop, no bishop, no abbot, no
> prior, parson, no vicar, nor any other person of the Church, high or
> low, great or small, English or Irish that useth to preach the word of
> God, saving the poor friars beggars.[58]

However, another writer from the Kildare area didn't share this admiration of the monks, and in a poem given the title 'Satire (on the people of Kildare)', speaks of

> ye holy monks with your corrin,
> Late and early filled with ale and wine!
> Deep can ye booze, that is all your care

But he does not spare the priests:

> … ye priests with your broad books
> Though your crowns be shaven, fair be your crooks.

He goes on to smile devastatingly on the nuns of St Mary's who wear shoes, the brazenly beggaring Franciscans and the proud and arrogant Dominicans.[59] Such sentiments echo those of Langland and other contemporary English writers, albeit expressed more ironically.

The Franciscans, in particular, were everywhere accused of greed and worldliness in the wake of the plague. These charges arose particularly after a Papal order of 1350 granting them special privileges with regard to preaching, hearing confession and burial rights, all of which threatened the position of the secular clergy and were seen by some bishops, FitzRalph of Armagh in particular, as interfering with the running of their dioceses. Intense friction developed between them and various bishops, including FitzRalph and the Bishops of Limerick in 1376 and of Meath in 1385.[60] These feuds usually centered on confession, tithes and testamentary bequests, though the cause according to the contemporary English chronicler, John of Reading, was directly connected to the plague:

> The mammon of iniquity wounded the regular clergy very much, but wounded the mendicants fatally. The superfluous wealth poured their way, through confessions and bequests, in such quantities that they scarcely condescended to accept oblations. Forgetful of their profession and rule, which imposed total poverty and mendicancy, they lusted after things of the world and of the flesh, not of heaven.[61]

The Franciscans had long been popular confessors, and the reason for their popularity, according to Archbishop FitzRalph, was that they gave light penances and easy absolution without demanding restitution as required by canon law. The payment of tithes was a particular bone of contention. FitzRalph accused the Franciscans of releasing penitents from their duty to pay tithes, a move that would have directly affected the revenue of the diocese, particularly at a time when a falling population and high mortality had reduced the number of possible tithe-payers. From 1350 on, he also accused them of deliberately encouraging lay people to leave testamentary bequests to the order. His charges cannot be taken at face value completely. Many of the Franciscans in Armagh at this time were Gaelic-Irish and this may explain some of the tension here, a tension which FitzRalph himself embodied and aggravated. Nevertheless, his complaints echo those of churchmen and lay people all over Europe. They are memorably echoed in 'Poem on the Council of London' of 1382 in which the writer says that if a rich man dies, the friars come immediately, but if a poor man dies and his family come looking for burial, they say, 'I'm afraid the guardian's out at the moment'.[62] Such comments reflect either the Franciscans' loss of their original ideals or the envy of the secular clergy who were not profiting from the charitable bequests of the laity – or perhaps even both. In the context of this criticism must be seen the growing popularity of the Observant Franciscans, particularly in Gaelic Ireland, that became such a distinct feature of the Irish Church in the fifteenth century.

Recovery

Clearly, the Black Death was not solely responsible for the changes in the medieval Church. War and pestilence worked in tandem: the effects of war rendered the Church even more vulnerable to plague, continuing war rendered recovery from plague a virtual impossibility. Yet, despite the widespread disruption and poverty of the latter half of the fourteenth century, continuity was the dominant theme in the fifteenth. Recovery seemed impossible, but a certain recovery was made, reflecting the general economic recovery in the country at large. With fewer inhabitants, some abbeys and priories now had the resources to devote to rebuilding and repair; they were also the recipients of generous aid from both Gaelic and Anglo-Irish families. In the fifteenth century, at least seven of the Irish Cistercian houses embarked on the construction of towers, usually for reasons of prestige or defence, and as early as the 1430s the Cistercian abbeys in Holy Cross and Kilcooly in Co. Tipperary were extensively repaired and refurbished. The Augustinians in some areas also recovered. Their priory at Clontuskert in Co. Galway was rebuilt after a fire in 1404 and was flourishing in the fifteenth century under the patronage of the O'Kellys. The Augustinian Priory of Kells in Co. Kilkenny, which in the mid-fourteenth century had been reported as destitute, in the mid-fifteenth century began a programme of rebuilding. Parish churches were extended or new churches constructed, not only in Gaelic areas, but also within the Pale and in other areas of the colony, though in response to the insecurities of the time, they were often accompanied by a fortified tower.[63] One should add that while all this rebuilding and building clearly evinces economic recovery, it does not necessarily betoken a spiritual recovery. As C.A. Empey in his study of the Priory of Kells argues, the heads of these monastic houses were inspired not by spiritual concerns, but by a desire to match the building activities of local secular lords to whom they were often related: 'the rash of late medieval monastic building activity would seem to have been the consequence, not of a modest renaissance, but of a continuous slide into the secular abyss'.[64]

Recovery is most evident among the mendicant orders. Where the churches in abbeys shrank, those in the friaries were enlarged as extra altars were added and extra space created by adding aisles or lengthening the choir.[65] New friaries were founded everywhere. Some ninety new mendicant houses were built in the period 1400–1508, and these mostly in predominantly Gaelic areas: forty in the ecclesiastical province of Tuam, twenty-eight in Armagh, eighteen in Cashel and only four in the Dublin province. Most of these friaries were established in rural areas, near small towns, thus changing the pattern of religious settlement. The biggest gain was by the Franciscans, who founded sixty-seven new houses in this period, in comparison to thirty-one in the period 1224–1300 and eight in the period 1300–1402. In a development whose popularity in Ireland was exceptional, some forty-four houses of the Franciscan Third Order Regular or Tertiaries were also founded. This was an outgrowth of the Third

Order Secular, the confraternities of lay people that had first appeared in Italy in 1221. The Third Order Regular consisted of small, loosely-knit communities of priests and lay brothers who were concerned mainly with teaching and pastoral work. Most of the houses were founded in the fifteenth century and mostly in the west though there is a record of one having been founded in Kilshane, Co Limerick, in 1399.[66]

The causes of this upsurge in the mendicant friaries are many, reflecting new political realities as well as more purely ecclesiastical reasons. Part of the reason was no doubt occasioned by various ordinances culminating in the Statutes of Kilkenny in 1366, which prohibited any religious house or benefice '*inter Anglos*' on pain of confiscation from accepting any Irishman 'of the nation of the Irish'.[67] Such statutes, if enforced, would clearly create a need for foundations in Gaelic areas. The increase must also have been a response to an increase in the number of postulants in Gaelic areas, an increase accentuated by the Black Death's more severe effects on friaries in towns in the colony. The phenomenon also reflects the growing independence of local lords, both Gaelic- and Anglo-Irish. Their motivation in founding monasteries was surely ambiguous and complex: at once an undoubted piety, a desire to provide pastoral care for their territories and a desire for status, part of which traditionally involved establishing monasteries under their own patronage. In opting for the mendicant friars, Ireland mirrored the European-wide cult and patronage of religious poverty among the wealthier classes which everywhere was reinforced by the Black Death. In Ireland, the mendicant orders provided what in England was offered by the Carthusians, 'an economical form of personal remembrance'.[68] The foundation of a Franciscan friary required less outlay than would, for example a Cistercian abbey. Clearly too for young men in the straitened financial environment of late medieval Ireland, the Franciscans would have provided a ready career path. But economic factors do not preclude more religiously-inspired motives. Clearly in Ireland, as elsewhere, the Franciscans in particular seem to have captured the religious imagination. They had always been particularly popular in Ireland, especially in Gaelic areas, and especially in the post-plague era, as the older monastic orders lost their appeal. Particularly unique to Ireland was the popularity of the Observant movement. Most of the newly established Franciscan friaries were Observant, and as early as the 1420s, the movement took hold among the Dominicans and the Augustinians and continued throughout the fifteenth century.[69] The popularity in Ireland of the Tertiaries or Third Order Regular was not paralleled elsewhere in Europe and certainly suggests a spiritual renaissance in late medieval Ireland. Rae sums up the phenomenon:

> The meaning for history of the late medieval Irish friary seems clear. As Gaelic and Anglo-Irish self-assurance found full voice, these little establishments sprang up, often the primary concern of one family or group, spurred on by a genuine spiritual reform, as seen in the institution of the strict observance and a sometimes quite remarkable social involvement.[70]

The later fourteenth century was a time of disruption but also continuity, as the Church in Ireland adapted to changing circumstances. The mortality caused by the Black Death and ensuing consequences led to changes that were common all over Europe at the time. Perhaps the most obvious change was in the political complexion of the Church. As the Gaelic-Irish began to push back the frontiers of the colony, so Gaelic ecclesiastics came to acquire high offices and wealthier benefices and by 1381, the process had already reached such a pitch that the Pope was asked not to provide anyone to a benefice who could not speak English.[71] The Black Death, by dealing comparatively lightly with Gaelic Ireland, helped forward this shifting balance. The changes are perhaps best symbolised by the Franciscan friary at Quin in Co. Clare, the first house of strict observance of the Franciscans in Ireland. It was constructed soon after 1433 by the Mac Namaras on the site of a thirteenth-century de Clare castle, which they had captured in the early fourteenth century. The stones of the castle were used to build the friary, its walls becoming the friary's supports.[72]

7

The Effects on the Governance of Ireland

The theme of expansion and contraction is played out once more in the political history of late medieval Ireland. Openness and expansion were evident in the rapidly developing colonisation of thirteenth-century Ireland. Demographic growth, a booming agriculture, a thriving commerce, the mushrooming of boroughs and the growth of manorial settlements promised much for the colony in Ireland. By the end of the next century, a change had come over Europe, with widespread recession, demographic decline and lawlessness. By 1400 too, the Anglo-Irish colony was generally fragmented and war-ridden. The colony had shrunk territorially, politically, economically and culturally. This contraction was due to a multitude of interrelated factors. Some were peculiar to the Irish situation, more were an integral part of the vicissitudes of English government, and yet more were prevalent in Europe generally in the later Middle Ages. At the same time, from the point of view of Gaelic Ireland, the collapse of the colony and the retreat of the central administration could be seen as evidence of the hibernicisation of the colony, as colonisers began to adopt the political organisation and culture characteristic of Gaelic-Irish society, and the country returned to the conditions that prevailed before the Norman Conquest. The growing military strength of many Gaelic-Irish lords in the fourteenth century also suggests a growing strength in economic and demographic areas. In this interplay of contraction and resurgence, the Black Death had a supporting role to play. Its short-term impact was temporarily disruptive, but in the long term it contributed to profound changes in the political complexion of late medieval Ireland. Moreover, the plague's profound effects on England had wide repercussions, albeit indirect, for the colony in Ireland, and help explain its increasingly marginal role in English politics in the later fourteenth century.

Administrative Disruption

In the immediate aftermath of the plague, the administration would seem to have experienced some setbacks in the day-to-day execution of government business. The Black Death came at a time of general disruption in the administration, and the extent to which it undoubtedly aggravated this situation is difficult to estimate precisely. The plague was no respecter of status, though inevitably its incidence was greater among the more populous poor who lived in crowded and inferior housing than among the wealthier classes who lived in stone dwellings. On the other hand, mortality among public officials was high in many instances on the European mainland, since they were not free to flee the towns and cities as so many wealthier citizens could. Evidence for mortality among government officials in Ireland is scarce and what evidence exists indicates some difficulties, though no major hiatus. There is an unprecedented alteration of Justiciars or Chief Governors in the years 1348 and 1349 – the period when the Black Death raged in Dublin. The average duration of the office of Justiciar at this time was two and a half years. Admittedly, tenure of a few months had been common in earlier times, but with the appointment of Ralph d'Ufford as Justiciar in July 1344, some continuity had been established. The terms of offices for Justiciars in the period 1347-52 were as follows:

PERIOD	JUSTICIAR/CHIEF GOVERNOR
June 1346 – Nov. 1347	Walter de Bermingham (appointed May 1346)
Nov. 1347 – Apr. 1348	John Larcher (Deputy Justiciar)
Apr. 1348 – Oct. 1349	Walter de Bermingham
Oct. 1349 – Dec. 1349	John de Carew (Deputy Justiciar)

Dec. 1349 – Mar. 1352	Thomas de Rokeby (appointed July 1349)
Mar. 1352 – June 1352	Maurice Rochfort (Deputy Justiciar)

Walter de Bermingham was summoned to parliament in Westminster in November 1347 and left Ireland some time later. His successor, John Larcher, who was also Prior of Kilmainham, was dismissed for his involvement in altercations between the Archbishops of Dublin and Armagh regarding the primacy of the Church in Ireland, and he died later in the year, very probably of plague. His successor as Deputy Justiciar, John de Carew, remained in office for only three months and does not again appear on the administrative lists, unusual in medieval Ireland since the same men held office many times. [1]

In the records concerning other administrative officers, there is clear evidence of disruption, though that for mortality is sketchy. [2] In the available lists of Chancellors and Keepers of the Seal, John Larcher served as Chancellor until March 1348, while he was also acting Justiciar. There isn't any Chancellor recorded from then until April 1349 when John Darcy was appointed Keeper; he remained in office until January 1350 and then disappears from the lists, even though his successor William of Bromley reappears later as Treasurer. While plague deaths cannot be assumed, the possibility exists. Moreover, the gap between March 1348 and April 1349, while the plague was prevalent in Dublin, indicates that the business of the chancery was disrupted.

In the treasury some dislocation is also evident, as there seems to have been an unusual alteration of officials at this period:

PERIOD	TREASURER	DEPUTY TREASURER
Aug. 1321– Hilary 1343	8 Treasurers appointed	7 Deputy Treasurers appointed
May 1343 – Sept.1349	John of Burnham	Robert Power (appears as Baron of the Exchequer in Trinity 1349)
Hilary 1348		Nicholas Allen (appears as Treasurer after 1350)

Trinity 1348 – Michaelmas 1349		Robert of Embleton (appears as Baron of the Exchequer after 1350)
Sept. 1349 – Jan. 1350	Robert of Embleton (arrested in Feb. 1350 and sent to England)	
Sept. 1350 – June 1360	8 Treasurers and Deputy Treasurers appointed	

Neither John of Burnham, Treasurer until September 1349, nor Robert Powell, Deputy Treasurer, appears again on the administrative lists. This is the only such instance recorded for the treasury. On the other hand, the Barons of the Exchequer seem to have been spared: only one, Robert Power, Baron of the Exchequer in Trinity 1349, does not again appear on the lists, even though others such as Hugh de Burgh, John de Troyes and Nicholas Snitterby, Barons of the Exchequer in 1347 and 1348 were reappointed in 1350 and in subsequent years. Of the other administrative offices, only the Escheator and Chamberlain of the Exchequer, John of Carrow, finally disappeared from the administrative lists in August 1349. Death by plague may have been the reason for these non re-appearances, though there are no doubt innumerable other causes.

Within the City of Dublin itself, evidence suggests the city's administrative officials may not have completely escaped. There seems to have been considerable dislocation in the administration, as is evident from the list of Mayors and bailiffs for Dublin in 1343-52:[3]

PERIOD	MAYORS	BAILIFFS
1339-40	Kenewrek Scherman	John Callan, Adam de Louestoc
1340-41	Kenewrek Scherman	William Walshe, John Crek
1341-43	John Le Seriaunt	John Crek, Walter de Castleknock
1345-46	John Le Seriaunt	William Walshe, Thomas Dod
1346-47	John Le Seriaunt	Walter Lusk, Rogert Grauntcourt

1347–48	Geoffrey Crompe	Walter Lusk, William Walshe
1348–49	Kenewrek Scherman	John Callan, John Dent
1349–50	Geoffrey Crompe	Roger Grauntcourt, Walter Lusk
1349–50	John Le Seriaunt	John Dent, John Bek
1350–51	John Bathe	Robert Burnell, Richard Heygrewe
1351–52	Roger de Moenes	John Dent, Peter Morville

The fact that Mayors and bailiffs were appointed yearly makes it difficult to see whether there was any exceptional mortality in 1348–50. Three Mayors were appointed in 1348–50. The first, Kenewrek Sherman, died later in the Dominican priory in Dublin in February 1351. His successor Geoffrey Crompe was Mayor from 1349–50 and then disappears from the list, but it is not likely, though not impossible, that the plague would still be claiming victims in Dublin as late as 1350. The bailiffs for the period 1348–49, John Callan and John Dent, were again appointed in 1349, 1351 and 1352, though the bailiffs for the first period in 1349–50, Roger Grauntcourt and Walter Lusk, do not again appear at any later time. The reasons for these non-reappearances are not given. However, as with government officials, the same men held civic offices on more than one occasion, and their disappearance from the lists in 1348–50 would seem unusual. Moreover, the fact that there are two entries for the year 1349–50, the only instance of such between 1300 and 1447, points to at least a temporary dislocation of business during the plague years.

Little is known of plague mortality among officials outside Dublin. However, the fact that bishops and members of the upper ranks of the clergy in many areas of the country died makes it highly unlikely that members of the lay upper class should have escaped, though they would have had less contact with sources of infection than others. The extant lists of county sheriffs indicate a certain disruption in the years 1348–50, undoubtedly caused by plague. In Co. Cork, William de Rupe, sheriff in 1343–44, and again in 1346–48, does not again appear as sheriff. There is a gap in the lists of sheriffs in the County of the Cross in Tipperary from 1347–55, even though the records for the preceding years are complete. Whether or not the shrievalty in fact remained vacant during the plague years is not known, but the hiatus is significant. Similarly, there is an unprecedented gap in the lists of the sheriffs of the liberty of Tipperary in 1344-58. Finally, the exact dates of office of the seneschals of Tipperary in the period 1330-58 are not known, a confusion no doubt the legacy of the dislocation caused certainly by war and perhaps aggravated by plague. There is no break, however, in the succession of sheriffs in Co. Dublin, as Adam Talbot held the office throughout the period 1336-56.[4]

The higher echelons of Gaelic-Irish society in certain areas were also affected by the plague, though for this sector, sources are even more scarce. Among those explicitly named as having died of plague in 1349-50 were the following: Matthew, son of Cathal Ó Ruairc; the Earl of Ulster's grandchild; Richard Ó Raighilligh, King of East Breifne; Maurice Mac Donnchadha; Cucoicuche Mór Mac Eochagain, Cathal Boygh Ó Flathartaigh.[5] Given the contagious nature of plague, many other lesser persons, ignored by the annalists, probably also died of plague at this time. However, as contemporary commentators remarked, the Gaelic-Irish may have escaped lightly on this occasion. Later outbreaks carried off many leading men – in 1361, eight prominent Irishmen and one king are mentioned as having died of plague. An outbreak in 1363, known as *cluiche an ríogh* or 'the king's game' is recorded as having caused 'great mortality in Ireland and especially in Connacht, Thomond, Kerry and Desmond'.[6]

Though there is little information regarding the possible short-term effects of the plague on the execution of day-to-day business, the deaths of officials undoubtedly caused some disruption. We do know that during later outbreaks of the plague in Ireland, the administration was temporarily suspended, as in 1382 when all 'pleas and proceedings (were) adjourned till fifteen days after St Michael on account of plague or pestilence'. One hundred years and many outbreaks later, people were still so afraid of plague that in 1489 parliament in Dublin was prorogued because 'the fear of pestilence prevents the coming thither of lords, ecclesiastics and lawyers'.[7] There are no such explicit references extant indicating any dislocation of parliamentary business in 1348-50, but the absence of evidence in itself indicates a hiatus.

Between 1341 and 1348, parliament was held in November 1341, April 1345, June 1345, October 1346 and May 1348. The next parliament was not held until 25 June 1350 and two sessions were then held in 1351, on 17 October and again on 31 October. Though parliamentary sessions were held irregularly in the period 1340-50, nevertheless the complete gap between May 1348 and June 1350 suggests that the outbreak of the plague caused the temporary suspension of parliament, as well as of many other public functions. This is borne out by a survey of parliamentary sessions held in these decades. In the period 1340-50, only five parliaments were convened, in comparison to nine in 1330-40 and eleven in the decade 1350-60.[8]

A similar disruption during the plague years is evident in the administration of justice. In the list of sessions of the Justiciar's court – that is, pleas held before Chief Governor – for this period, the impact of the Black Death is intimated.[9] In the year 1345, sixty-one sessions of the court were held; in 1346 this dropped to seventeen without any sessions being recorded for the period April to September. In the following year, 112 sessions of the court were held, admittedly an unusually high number. Then in 1348 the number dropped again, with seventeen sessions being held throughout the whole year: no sessions are recorded for the period January to October 1348; eight are then recorded for October 1348, the time when the Black Death was spreading throughout Dublin and surrounding areas; only two sessions were held in November and two in December. Disruption becomes most obvious in 1349, presumably when the mortality and upheaval in the wake of the plague had made an impact. Only two sessions are recorded for the whole year, on 12 January and 20 January. Nor are any sessions recorded for the year 1350. Business was resumed in January 1351 and sixty-seven sessions are recorded for that year, no doubt to catch up on the backlog caused by the break from January 1349 to January 1351. Moreover, of the sessions held in 1348 and 1349, all were held in the south of the country, in Tralee, Co. Kerry, Cork, Buttevant, Co. Cork and Kilmallock, Co. Limerick. All these towns, with the possible exception of Cork, were in areas where the plague would not yet have penetrated to any significant degree. When sessions resumed in 1351, they were held not only in

Buttevant and Kilmallock, but also in those Leinster towns which formerly had featured prominently in the lists: Dublin, Naas, Kilkenny, Wexford, Trim, Drogheda, Carlow and Wexford. The sources do not permit a definitive explanation for these lacunae and changes of locale, but it cannot be merely a coincidence that such disruptions should have taken place in the years when the plague was spreading throughout the country and wreaking havoc, especially in the towns of Leinster, the administrative centres of the Anglo-Irish colony. The declining population also resulted in a decline in business for the Justiciar's court, as was suggested by an order on 25 March 1351 that there were to be only two justices in the future, for there was not enough work for three.[10]

The execution of other justiciary business, such as military campaigns, seems not to have been affected during these years.[11] The justiciarship of Bermingham in 1346-47 and again in 1348-49 was a busy one, and he had considerable success in campaigns against both Anglo-Irish and Gaelic-Irish lords. But the plague's effects on the colony were such as to undermine his efforts. The justiciarship of Sir Thomas de Rokeby, in the years immediately following the plague, was to be the most energetic for a long time. In fact, in the winter of 1350, when the plague was still active in the west, de Rokeby conducted a campaign in Thomond to re-establish central power, rebuilt Bunratty Castle and even introduced settlers into lands recaptured from the Irish. The Black Death would not seem to have dampened his energy, even if his efforts, like those of Bermingham, did not have any long-term success. It might be said then that in the short-term the plague caused only a very temporary administrative dislocation. But in the long-term, in contributing to the contraction of the colony and to the decline in revenue, the plague helped aggravate existing administrative and defence problems.

The Contraction of the Colony

The contraction of the colony was a long-term development and did not even originate in the fourteenth century. Many historians have commented on the incomplete nature of the conquest of 1169 as being the fundamental cause for much of the decline of the later Middle Ages. The frontiers of the settlement had been extended in a piecemeal fashion, and not enough English settlers were introduced to ensure lasting success. While parts of Connacht were extensively colonised, settlement there did not have a strong economic base. Leinster, south Munster and Ulster, east of the river Bann, were effectively colonised and settled, but many other areas remained untouched by the Normans and by the feudal system.[12] Even in terms of a purely political conquest, the Irish were never defeated. Many retained their ancestral lands in Connacht, western Ulster, North Munster and parts of Leinster. Within the predominantly Anglo-Norman manorial structure, the Irish returned as betaghs, labourers, and occasionally as free tenants while in the more outlying, march areas, the Irish would have formed a majority. The result was that 'ecologically, there were generally too few settlers to withstand eventual overcrowding and displacement by more vigorous native elements'.[13] This displacement became increasingly evident from the end of the thirteenth century and even more so as the fourteenth century progressed. Thanks to increasing depopulation in feudalised areas, the absenteeism of landowners and improvements in Irish military organisation, the inherent weaknesses in the Anglo-Norman settlement were aggravated and the colonists became ever more vulnerable to the rising Gaelic-Irish population.

However, no one fatal flaw can explain the colony's depopulation. Excepting certain of the larger towns and manorial centres, the colony had never been over-populated. Its effectiveness had from the beginning depended on the influx of new settlers and officials from England, though outside of the more settled areas of Leinster, Munster and eastern Ulster, there was very little immigration. Immigration continued at least up to the end of the thirteenth century and ensured the Anglo-Irish dominated at least in the east and south. But this had ceased by the first half of the fourteenth century. Thanks in the main to the escalation of warfare, the colony no longer offered English people the attractions it had a century earlier. The plague of 1348 intensified this process. Because of the huge mortality it exacted in both urban and rural areas of England, and the consequent labour shortages and spiralling wages, the ambitions of survivors in search of opportunities could be met within England itself. Above all, the rural depopulation caused by the Black Death in England meant that after 1348, there was more land available per head of the population. So, the pressure on land, which in the twelfth century had brought to Ireland a colony of English and Welsh peasants and artisans, could now be satisfied within the bounds of England itself. Even outright grants of land no longer provided an inducement to settle in Ireland, as Janico Artoye admitted in a letter to the Bishop of Salisbury in 1394-95:

> Our Lord, the King, has granted me a parcel of land in the country of
> the Irish rebels, which if it were in the parts of London would be worth
> by the year fifty thousand marks, but by my faith I have so much
> trouble holding on to it that I would not like to lead such a life for long
> even for a quarter of the land.

And nobody answered the Duke of Surrey's call in 1398 for a man and his wife from every parish or two in England to come to Ireland and 'inhabit the said land where it was wasted on the marches'.[14]

The same reluctance and waning colonising fervour is evident among administrators and colonists already resident in Ireland. When in 1355 a local council at Naas selected guards to defend the marches of Kildare, many of those summoned failed to turn out, country people refused their assistance and magnates such as the Earl of Kildare and Thomas Wogan refused to participate until ordered to do so.[15] Finding suitable administrative officials increasingly becomes a problem, and the government looked to English officials for personnel. But there was a great reluctance on the part of Englishmen to live in Ireland and few were willing to take up posts there. Nobody wanted the offices of Serjeant and Sheriff, for example, and even the office of Justiciar became increasingly difficult to fill: Richard of Pembridge flatly refused the job in 1371 and William of Windsor accepted it only under pressure in 1374.[16] Nor were local candidates any more willing to become involved. In Waterford and in Kilkenny there are records of wealthier people buying immunity to protect themselves even against the possibility of being elected to public office. Part of the reluctance arose because of the financial burdens imposed on public officials, which ever fewer were willing to assume. The insecurity and the scarcer resources in the post-plague era explain what may be called the risk-avoidance behaviour of wealthier men. Further, argues Dr Gearóid MacNiocaill, with a declining urban population in the later fourteenth and fifteenth centuries, the pool of eligible candidates shrank and this was rendered even smaller by the exclusion of non-citizens and the Gaelic-Irish from public office.[17] However, the difficulty of finding willing candidates for public office was not peculiar to Ireland. The larger English cities, such as Bristol and Coventry, experienced similar problems in the fifteenth century, as citizens refused to shoulder the financial and other burdens of public service.[18] In Ireland this trend was further reinforced by the weakening support for towns forthcoming from the administration, as well as by the growing threat posed by the Gaelic-Irish.

The ending of the immigration of colonists and officials was compounded by an increase in emigration and absenteeism of office-holders and landowners. Again, even before the advent of plague, the colony's population had been declining through emigration, first from the march areas to more secure land and thence to England. The result was economic instability for the colony's towns and large manors, which in turn had political repercussions. The problem was further compounded by the chronic absenteeism of landowners, on whom the government relied for governance and law enforcement. The return to England of officeholders and landowners had been progressing even before the advent of the plague. As their holdings in Ireland became ever less remunerative in the course of the fourteenth century, the large landowners were even less inclined to live in the country. This was particularly true of the absentee landlords who had taken over the large holdings of some of the original settling Anglo-Norman families. These families – the families of de Burgh in Ulster, de Clare in Thomond and Leinster, Bigod in Carlow, de Valence in Wexford and de Verdon in Louth – died out in the male line and their lands were subdivided among the female heirs. The great lordships were then split up into smaller holdings that were to prove less profitable and less effective in maintaining law and order. The historian A. J. Otway-Ruthven particularly emphasises the importance of this development:

> the passing of so much authority all over Ireland into the hands of absentee lords in this century, and the fragmentation of lordships by division among coheiresses, was to bring about the decline of the colony.[19]

Since the new owners were based in England, their Irish holdings formed but a minor part of their revenues and by 1330 almost half of the colony's land was owned by absentees.[20] As political instability increased in the fourteenth century, they were increasingly accused of neglecting their lands and castles and failing to provide for the defence of their estates. The Black Death contributed to this trend. In severely affecting the English holdings of some of these magnates, it further weakened their interest in their Irish holdings and in its effects on the Irish manorial economy, it made their Irish holdings even more unprofitable than was already the case. This had immediate repercussions for the defences of the colony. The Great Council of Kilkenny explicitly acknowledged the connection in a 1360 petition to the king: complaining of absentee lords who failed to defend the marches, the Council said that there was a lack of great lords due to the plague which had severely affected the English community and not the Gaelic-Irish. Faced with penalties for absenteeism and neglect, some absentee lords resolved the issue by selling their lands in Ireland at this time.[21]

Contemporaries saw this problem of absenteeism – and not any antagonism to the English crown – as being the main cause for the success of the Gaelic-Irish. Numerous ordinances dealing with the problem were issued throughout the fourteenth century, all repeating the ordinance of November 1311, which had decreed that all those with lands in Ireland should either reside on them, or provide for their defence. In the 1340s and 1350s an increase is evident in the number of petitions and ordinances dealing with the issue. In 1351, the Great

Council in Kilkenny ordained that absentee landlords were to defend their property or face forfeiture. In 1365, the king ordered that all the rents and profits of absentee landlords and officeholders be seized for a year to pay for the defence of the country. Again in 1368 parliament in Dublin complained about absentee landlords neglecting their Irish properties and stressed that the only remedy for the ills of Ireland was the residence of absentee lords, or their strongmen, on their Irish territories. These measures were repeated in the Statute of Absentees of 1380, again in 1394 when Richard II ordered all Irish-born living in England to return to Ireland, and in numerous other royal decrees throughout the fifteenth century.[22] Enforcement, however, was impossible, contributing even further to the ineffectiveness of the central administration.

The Interplay of War and Plague

Warfare was ultimately the major factor in the political and military decline of the colony – warfare not only with the Gaelic-Irish who rarely presented a unified front anyway, but also between the settlers themselves. Many historians agree with A. J. Otway-Ruthven that 'the constant state of warfare among themselves into which certain of the settlers had fallen' irreparably damaged the colony. The Gaelic-Irish partook in these skirmishes, as is evidenced in the struggle in Connacht in the 1330s between rival de Burgh families, in which the O'Connors and other clans took part, changing sides as opportunities arose. The central administration's efforts to control these feuds between those it called the 'rebel English' proved futile. The Bruce Invasion of 1315 served only to exacerbate the general ineffectiveness of the administration. All of this played into the hands of Gaelic chieftains ready to take advantage of the colony's difficulties. From the early fourteenth century, the Gaelic resurgence gathered pace thanks to the weakness of the central administration, improved military tactics and leadership and perhaps also to land pressure due to a growth in the population of Gaelic Ireland.[23]

Gradually, the 'land of peace' began to contract as 'the land of war' was enlarged. By 1342, royal castles along the Shannon in Roscommon,

Randown, Athlone and Bunratty were in Gaelic-Irish hands; in one evening alone, the annalist Clyn reports, Laoighseach Ó Mórdha burned eight castles and destroyed the fortress of Dunamase in Offaly.[24] The Dublin administration's control in Munster was, by the 1330s and 1340s, dependent on the co-operation of the Earls of Ormond and Desmond, and during their frequent quarrels the Irish made inroads and regained the northern parts of the province. Most of Connacht and Ulster east of the Bann were entirely outside the control of the Dublin government. Writing some centuries later, the poet Edmund Spenser lamented that after the Bruce Invasion:

> all that goodly country (Ulster) was utterly wasted and left desolate and as yet remaineth to this day… For that part of the North sometimes was as populous and plentiful as any part in England.[25]

Small towns, generally centres of colonial influence, were contracting thanks to the recession in the manorial economy on which they depended; on many manors, Irish tenants who formerly paid rent and rendered military service because of war rendered nothing. One may not exaggerate the lack of governance in the colony, as records indicate that revenues were still coming in regularly from Leinster and from some towns such as Cork, Waterford and Limerick. However, those areas remaining loyal to the crown were scattered and isolated from one another, and the colonists felt themselves to be under siege by an enemy that was becoming increasingly powerful. By 1341, the colonists felt so vulnerable that they sent a petition to Edward III, complaining that:

> the third part and more of your land of Ireland which was conquered in the time of your progenitors is now come into the hand of your Irish enemies and your English lieges are so impoverished that they can hardly live.[26]

So, even before the plague struck, the typical late medieval economic recession in the colony was exacerbated by a decided military shift in favour of the Gaelic-Irish chieftains. The Black Death's effect on changing power relations cannot be underestimated, even if it cannot be precisely quantified. Because the plague severely affected the colony's manorial settlements, towns and villages, it contributed to the demographic decline of the colony, thereby further weakening the colony's defences. At the same time it left non-urbanised, Gaelic Ireland virtually unscathed. Many contemporary observers remarked on this anomaly: Archbishop FitzRalph of Armagh noted that the plague killed about two-thirds of the English nation in Ireland, but hadn't killed many in Gaelic Ireland. This observation was borne out in a petition in 1360 from the Great Council in Kilkenny, which spoke of the plague 'which was so great and so hideous among the English lieges and not among the Irish' and by the observations of the English chronicler, Geoffrey Le Baker, among others.[27] Whether or not population growth among the Gaelic-Irish is responsible for their resurgence at this time is a matter of speculation. All the available evidence suggests that purely Gaelic areas remained under-populated for centuries to come. However, what is more likely is that the Gaelic-Irish population remained stable while that of the colony declined, thereby contributing to the shifting balance of power in their favour in many areas and to the territorial expansion of the Gaelic-Irish chieftains.

That the plague affected the changing military situation is highlighted by the fact that the administration had experienced a modest recovery against the Gaelic-Irish in the 1320s, which might have continued but for the advent of the Black Death. In 1348, the Irish in Munster and Leinster were quiet, officials were being appointed regularly and revenue was being collected. 'It might have seemed', writes Dr Otway-Ruthven, 'that the position had been stabilised, that further recovery would be possible'.[28] But the plague's effects on the colony were such as to undo all that had been gained. The vulnerability of the plague-stricken colony presented an opportunity for expansionist-minded Gaelic-Irish lords. A similar development occurred in Egypt which, in the fourteenth century, had also seen chronic warfare between the central Mamluk administration and the Bedouins. There too, the Black Death severely affected the settled population, while scarcely affecting the nomadic Bedouins. Some individual Bedouin chieftains in outlying regions took advantage of the situation to attack and raid rural communities in Upper Egypt which had been left depopulated and even deserted.[29]

Similarly, some Gaelic chieftains also took advantage of the disruption in the colony to mount raids, particularly on exposed manors in the richer Anglo-Irish areas. This happened particularly in Leinster, where throughout the first half of the fourteenth century, the MicMhurchadha had proved to be a continuing security risk. Though often fighting on behalf of the crown against other Irish chieftains and rebel Anglo-Irish magnates, the head of the clan toyed with the ambition of becoming 'King of Leinster'. But the years following the plague saw the MicMhurchadha stepping up the pressure, and the plague itself would seem to have provided the occasion for this. Dr Robin Frame stresses this point:

> The 1350s saw, from the crown's viewpoint, a further deterioration of security in Leinster, which seems to have been produced by the disproportionate impact of the Black Death upon the towns and nucleated settlements of the seaboard and river valleys.[30]

Further, since the MicMhurchadha territory lay high in the Wicklow hills, it was probably protected from the inroads of the plague. In the years after the plague, they gained even more power in Wicklow and particularly in the area controlling the route from Dublin to the south, and succeeded in making travel to Dublin so hazardous that in 1361 the decision was made to shift the seat of the Exchequer to Carlow. Throughout the 1350s they made alliances in an opportunistic fashion with other Irish chieftains, Anglo-Irish lords and with the administration. By the end of the century, Art MacMurchadha Caomhánach was claiming the kingship of Leinster, while at the same time maintaining links with the Dublin administration, alternately raiding and negotiating. In short, by severely affecting the towns and villages of Leinster, the plague helped to give the advantage to the MicMhurchadha. Again, the plague did not initiate this development, but it added to the momentum that it had been gathering in the course of the fourteenth century.

In a similar fashion, Gaelic-Irish lords in other areas took advantage of the increasing vulnerability of the colonists, and the general upheaval of the post-plague era to continue their expansionist activities: the O'Briens in Thomond, the McCarthys in Desmond and the O'Cahans and McQuillans in Ulster were among the many.[31] Nor was the expansion of Gaelic Ireland merely a political and military one. In marcher areas, as mortality left landowners with a shortage of tenants, vacant lands were taken by Gaelic-Irish who pushed their boundaries forward into formerly feudalised areas. This did not happen everywhere: more solidly established Anglo-Irish communities, such as those in south Tipperary and Kilkenny, were to survive all these vicissitudes and remain largely unchanged.[32] But in general, the colony contracted in north Tipperary and other parts of Munster, in Connacht, Ulster and even parts of Leinster.

Continuing military failure further exacerbated the ineffectiveness of the central administration and contributed to the decentralisation of power. Since the administration did not have the resources to govern, the business of defence and administration was gradually ceded to towns, local magnates and chieftains, both Anglo- and Gaelic-Irish.[33] This devolution of government was symbolised by the tower-houses erected in towns or by individual lords on their own territories to provide for their own defence. It was also evident in the activities of lords such as the First Earl of Desmond, Maurice fitz Thomas, who maintained a huge private army which had to be supported by the local people. The post-plague political situation in Ireland, then, was in direct contrast to the situation that developed in other countries where similar political conditions prevailed. In Egypt, the Bedouin attacks, which had strengthened in the wake of the Black Death, were in the longer term countered by a revitalised central administration which re-established central authority. This pattern was repeated elsewhere, particularly in the wake of succeeding outbreaks of plague. With the recession in the agricultural sector, which was the base of baronial power, countries with strong central governments succeeded in broadening their tax base to include a larger portion of the growing revenue from trade. In Ireland, to the contrary, the administration continued to be decentralised as the power of the Gaelic-Irish and Anglo-Irish magnates and of the larger towns continued to grow. Ireland's decentralisation was, as Professor Kenneth Nicholls argues, rooted in Gaelic not English practice and reflects the growing hibernicisation of the country.[34] But it also mirrors what happened in other countries in the years after the plague. The historian L. Genicot writes that the political changes wrought by the Black Death varied from one country to the next:

> Where the State still lacked firm structure and doctrinal justification they merely provoked fragmentation. This is how events turned out in Russia and most other countries in Eastern Europe. Civil wars and foreign attacks had so weakened the princes that they were constrained to cede much of their power to the nobles on whose support they depended…. In the West, the development was precisely opposite: by revealing the evil effects of a breakdown of authority, the troubled times established a case for centralisation.[35]

The need for centralisation was also clear in Ireland, but the resources were lacking. While the colony never reached the political nadir of late medieval Russia, nevertheless the administration was forced to rely increasingly on local magnates, such as the Earls of Ormond and Desmond, and on compromises with Gaelic chieftains for law-enforcement and governance. As the century progressed, Irish chieftains as well as Anglo-Irish lords were drawn increasingly by the Dublin administration into what Dr Robin Frame calls 'a web of practical lordship spun over and beyond the increasingly fragmented scheme of English law and government it was trying to manage'.[36] It would take another century and more for the English government in Ireland to establish the kind of bureaucracy and centralisation that had earlier come to characterise the administrations of other European countries.

The colonists themselves acknowledged that both plague and warfare were the causes of the crisis that they faced in the later decades of the fourteenth century. In 1360, the Great Council in Kilkenny in an urgent plea to the king for help, complained that partly due to the plague's effects on the English in Ireland, and partly to the incompetence of the lords,

> the lieges are so enfeebled that they can no longer defend themselves; the lieges are impoverished by oppressions without payment, tallages and bad government; the treasury is empty because the justiciar is too preoccupied with wars to attend to holding pleas or making profits.[37]

Five years later, in 1365, Ireland is again described as being 'sunk in the greatest wretchedness through the poverty and feebleness of his (the king's) people there.'[38] Admittedly, in subsequent years efforts were made to reassert central control, but gains made were quickly lost. In 1393, it was asserted that

> the Irish enemies are strong and arrogant and of great power, and there is neither rule nor power to resist them, for the English marchers are not able, nor are they willing to rule them without stronger paramount power.[39]

By the later fourteenth century, the need for royal intervention was pressing, and between 1361 and 1376, five military expeditions were sent to Ireland. But Richard II's expeditions by their very extent were an admission of defeat. He did not intend to conquer the land in Gaelic hands or to reconquer those parts of the colony that had been seized by the Irish; his sole aim was to make Leinster safe and otherwise to maintain the status quo as it existed in 1390. The only effective answer now was withdrawal, abandoning the marcher areas altogether, and creating a heavily-fortified nucleus within the lordship, the Pale. In this way the colony was to survive, though in an attenuated form. At the same time, Gaelic Ireland remained underpopulated and this, together with the political fragmentation characteristic of Gaelic political life, meant that Gaelic Ireland failed to conquer the colony absolutely.

Declining Revenues

It is finally in the context of financial resources and the attitude of the crown that the failure of the Anglo-Irish colony and the increasing strength of Gaelic Ireland must be viewed. From early in the thirteenth century, it had become clear that the English kings did not always have the resources to rule a colony in which the conquered continually impinged on the conquerors, and in which the conquerors themselves often proved more troublesome than the conquered. Neither had they any serious interest in Ireland, with Scotland and France presenting more attractive prizes and later imposing more demands on royal resources. Up to the mid-fourteenth century, Ireland was regarded as a good recruiting ground for soldiers and an important source of revenue. However, the colony's wealth and manpower were drained to support the kings' wars in England, France and Scotland. In the reign of Edward I, more than three-quarters of the revenue accruing to the Irish treasury went on the king's purposes outside Ireland. For example, between 1294 and 1299, Ireland yielded a total revenue of over £26,000; of this £4,000 went to the king's wardrobe and £3,700 into the Westminster treasury; £750 went on the Welsh wars, £11,300 on the Scottish wars and an inconsiderable amount on Ireland. Throughout the thirteenth century, there were numerous royal requests for loans and subsidies from Ireland to pay the king's debts, while the lordship was also expected to provide soldiers and military supplies. Up until 1311, at least £90,000 was sent to the king and even this does not represent the full amount sent from Ireland.[40] Stripped of its resources, the colony was left unable to meet the extraordinary demands imposed by the increasing costs of the latter half of the century and the administration was left without the financial means necessary for good government. The result was chronic financial embarrassment and increasing lawlessness.

Nevertheless, Ireland continued to yield considerable sums to the English treasury throughout the plague years, at least until the 1360s, but each year saw a dwindling in this amount. The annual average revenue in 1278-99 had been £6,300; after 1315 and the Bruce Invasion, this fell to about £2,300 and in 1339-40 the lowest point was reached with £1,243. But by the time the plague struck, a recovery had been made. Higher revenues are recorded for the period of 1344-49, when the annual average reached £2,500 and for the period of 1349-50, when £2,724 was collected. Accordingly, in the year of the plague, a slight recovery was noticeable and this increase was maintained until 1350. The increase has been attributed to the more thorough collection of taxes by the central administration in these years and to the sequestration of Kildare in 1345. After 1350 however, a change is noticeable. By 1350, royal income had begun to suffer the full effects of the Black Death for numerous reasons: vacant holdings and lowered rents on the royal demesnes; arrears in the farms from towns and lower customs revenues and difficulties with revenue collection consequent on the Black Death. Whatever the reason, in the period September 1350-April 1352, the revenue amounted only to £2,617, an annual average of £1,570 which was but a little over half of the yield in 1349-50. This decrease cannot be explained simply by reference to an already declining economy, given the slight recovery evident in the preceding years. The Black Death is the only reasonable explanation for the drop in the period 1350-52.[41]

The plague contributed then to the decline in royal income. The area in which taxes could be raised had already been contracting, thanks to the inroads of Gaelic chiefs. With the plague, this contraction gathered pace, especially as cities experienced difficulties with paying their farm. Though a slight recovery was made, the pre-plague situation was never again repeated. Revenue continued to fall and in the period 1368-84 the average annual revenue was only £2,512. The higher costs of defence forced the Justiciars to collect on all debts, raise rents, enforce custom duties and impose extraordinary taxation. Their efforts were to no avail, other than angering the colonists and further alienating them from the administration. In brief, after the mid-fourteenth century, Ireland was no longer self-sufficient; it became a drain on the English Exchequer and was to remain a financial liability for the rest of the century. A nadir was reached in 1361 when the treasury was reported to be empty.[42]

Recovery?

Though the plague was not as immediately devastating in Ireland as it had been on the continent and did not cause the major administrative problems it caused elsewhere, in the long-term its principal effect in Ireland, as throughout the rest of Europe, was to intensify processes already underway. In contributing to the depopulation, declining revenue and contraction of the colony, it indirectly affected the history of the Irish parliament in later times. While elsewhere in England and Europe, by the fifteenth century, the depredations of the previous century were overcome, the colony in Ireland remained stricken. Recovery was impossible in the context of general warfare and the fifteenth-century colony in Ireland suffered from a lack of governance. On the other hand, Gaelic Ireland experienced a resurgence. A concrete reminder of this reversal was the falling into disuse of the old centres of Anglo-Norman power, such as Trim Castle in Co. Meath, and the erection of stone tower-houses all over the country, particularly in Gaelic areas and along the boundaries of the Pale. Kilteel in Co. Kildare was one such place: next to a thirteenth-century preceptory of the Knights Hospitallers was erected in the late fourteenth or early fifteenth century a tower house that functioned as a stronghold on the Pale boundary in the later Middle Ages. Such structures are witness, on the one hand, to the fact that the economic resources existed for their construction, but on the other to the fact that their construction was in itself a testament to the failure of the colony and the resurgence of the Gaelic sector. The themes of contraction and expansion, then, which mark the history of late medieval Europe, existed simultaneously in late medieval Ireland. The expansion of the Anglo-Normans and the contraction of Gaelic Ireland are the leitmotifs of the late twelfth and early thirteenth centuries. These roles were gradually reversed as poverty and impotence came to characterise the late medieval English colony, while the Gaelic sector of the population profited from its difficulties.

Or perhaps one should speak of what the historian Robin Frame calls the 'middle ground' that developed between Anglo-Irish and Irish, where, unfettered by categories such as foreigners and enemies or rebels, 'powerful men protected their interests and pursued their ambitions'. A new pragmatism took hold as towns and magnates increasingly dealt directly with Irish chieftains in a policy of rapprochement; the result was that 'the boundary between Anglo-Irish and Gaelic became increasingly blurred in a society where "the frontier" is to be understood as a process of interaction.'[43]

This rapprochement and interaction was further quickened by the demographic decline of the colony. The plague's ravages on the towns and manors of the colony meant that the colonists were even more a minority than they had ever been. Nor were their numbers replenished by new colonists, as English people, thanks to the Black Death, now had more extensive opportunities for work and land in England itself. A new movement for the colonisation of Ireland was impossible in the context of post-plague England with its easy availability of land and its financially embarrassed crown. Gradually, the cultural character of the colonists changed. As contact with England slowed, there was more interaction between the colonists and the Gaelic-Irish. Increasingly, many Anglo-Irish colonists intermarried with the Gaelic-Irish and were drawn within the reach of the Irish language and culture. As a result, much of Ireland was dominated for over a century by Irish-born lords, ruling their own territories, speaking the Irish language and pursuing their own cultural path. It is the phenomenon that has characterised many colonial settlements over time, as they are gradually subsumed by those they intended to dominate. Interaction worked also in reverse order, as the Gaelic-Irish were also brought within the sphere of Anglo-Irish influence, particularly evident in their increasing participation in trade and in their construction of stone tower-houses. Yet, assimilation was never total. The colony, contracted though it was, never disappeared completely, though it wasn't until the later sixteenth century, when England was again overpopulated, that another attempt was made to colonise Ireland fully. By that time, the threat of plague had passed and with it the crisis mortality that had so undermined the medieval Anglo-Irish colony.

Aftermath

For those alive in 1348, the Black Death seemed to signal the end of history. Friar Clyn in his annals recounted a vision current at the time:

> The lofty cedar of Lebanon shall be set ablaze, and Tripoli destroyed and Acre taken and Saturn will ambush Jove and the bat will put the duke of the bees to flight. Within fifteen years there will be one faith and one God, and the others will vanish away, the sons of Jerusalem will be delivered from captivity, a race will arise without a head. ...There will be many battles and great slaughter, fierce hunger and mortality, and political upheaval; ...the eastern beast and the western lion will subjugate the whole world by their power; and for fifteen years there will be peace throughtout the whole earth and an abundance of crops. Then all the faithful will pass to the Holy Land over the parted waters and the city of Jerusalem will be glorified and the Holy Sepulchre honoured by all. In this tranquillity there will be heard news of the Antichrist. Be watchful.[1]

Contrary to expectations, however, the Black Death was overcome and human history continued. Clearly, the plague had a profound impact. But that impact was far less dramatic than Clyn thought. Clyn's words do speak to the despair that the Black Death could inspire in Ireland in 1348, and in a certain way, what he says was true. It brought not the end of the world, but hastened the passing away of many features of the medieval world in Ireland. Changes that had been occurring for many years prior to 1348 received a significant impetus from the outbreaks of plague. Yet one must always remember that these developments occurred over generations and that the plague was one factor among many: it was not a world-shattering cataclysm. There was no complete break with the past, but rather a large measure of continuity, readjustment and realignment – most conspicuous perhaps in the construction of new friaries and tower-houses throughout Ireland.

People also had to adjust to the continual recurrence of this new disease that was to reappear throughout the rest of the fourteenth century and even into the next century, with varying degrees of virulence. Thanks to the greater availability of sources, the details of these later outbreaks have been more fully described and we can, by analogy, gain a further perspective on what may have happened in those hidden years of 1348-50. To cite some random examples: in 1439, a plague raged in Dublin and 3,000 people died between the beginning of spring and the end of May. Another outbreak in 1489 was so great that people did not even bury the dead. In an echo of the effects of the plague of 1348, a report on the outbreak of 1515 empha-sises the fact that the plague had destroyed the English, but not the Irish:

> the pestylens hathe devowred the Englysche folke, bycause they flee not therfro; and bycause the Irysche folke abyde not ther wyth, hyt do them noo hurt.

An outbreak in 1519 lasted until 1525. The *Annals of Loch Cé* report that it killed 'a great number of the Foreigners of Dublin' and the Earl of Surrey described it as being 'so sore that all the people be fled out of their houses into the fields and woods, where they likewise die wonderfully, so that their bodies be dead like swine unburied'.

In 1535, towns and especially Dublin were devastated. As the century progressed, greater efforts were made to contain plague by instituting quarantine measures and providing public health facilities. During the outbreak of 1574-76 in Dublin, 'three thousand men at least' died. The wealthy and powerful fled and the city's authorities provided a doctor to care for the victims, as well as temporary houses to isolate them from the rest of the population. In 1604-05, Dublin was again visited and, in an effort to control the spread of the disease, only those coming from a plague-free area were allowed into the city. The plague of 1650-51 was the last major outbreak and one of the most destructive. It started in Galway, brought probably by ships from Spain, and within nine months 'many thousand soules died of the said sickness'. It spread throughout the country and caused 'immense mortality' in Kilkenny, reducing its garrison from 1,200 to 300 men. In terms reminiscent of the effects of the plague of 1348, the plague of 1650 was reported to have 'exceedingly depopulated' the city of Dublin, leaving half its houses destroyed, the rest 'very much decayed and ruined'. A petition from the citizens of Dublin in 1657 blamed the plague on public immorality:

> there is very much of sweareinge, curseinge and blasphemie used and practised (as in the English tongue too much soe also in the Irish tongue), which as it is a breach of the good lawes of the land, soe it is a high provokeinge of God which may justly cause the plague and other judgements to sease uppon this cittie.[2]

From the mid-seventeenth century, as was the case all over Europe, outbreaks of the plague in Ireland became increasingly rare, though they recurred periodically in Europe until 1894 and a case of plague was officially reported in Ireland as late as 1920.[3]

The disappearance of the plague is still a subject of some discussion. Some have suggested that the reason may lie in the increasing domestication of rats, that with improved housing and food storage in western countries, rats did not migrate as they used and so the plague remained restricted.[4] Others point to the growing acceptance and understanding of the notion of contagion which led public authorities to set up pesthouses, impose quarantine procedures on ships, merchants and even entire towns and to burn the belongings and even the houses of plague victims. Others dismiss all this in favour of more biological causes, speculating that there is a tide in the affairs of disease over which human beings have no control. McNeill in his history of epidemics argued that 'there are natural rhythms at work that limit and define the demographic consequences of sudden exposure to initially very lethal infections', and that after five or six human generations, the disease had played itself out.[5] It is a view echoed by Hans Zinsser in his ground-breaking work on the subject, *Rats, Lice and History*:

> Nothing in the world of living things is permanently fixed... on purely biological grounds, therefore, it is entirely logical to suppose that infectious diseases are constantly changing; new ones are in the process of developing, and old ones being modified or disappearing.[6]

Livi-Bacci also concurs:

> For reasons not entirely clear the plague underwent a process of mutual adaptation between pathogen (*yersinia*), carrier (flea) and host-victim (human).[7]

Plague also came into competition with newer, more virulent diseases such as typhus. Other research has focused on the hypothesis that populations exposed to plague acquired immunity to it.[8] The possible reasons for its eclipse are many, but most agree that improved public health and sanitation, better nutrition and housing, a changing climate and advances in medical knowledge were most instrumental in bringing about the effective end of bubonic plague. Whatever the cause, plague had all but disappeared by the early eighteenth century, and with it the crisis mortality that had kept population levels so low throughout the medieval period.

Yet plague has not disappeared from the human landscape. Human plague cases were reported in 1992 in Brazil, the United States, China, Madagascar, Mongolia and Congo, and India experienced outbreaks as late as 1994. In the United States, ten to twenty cases are reported on average per year and the World Health Organisation reckons about two to three thousand cases appear annually. These latter-day outbreaks are different to the medieval plague in that they occur mostly in rural areas and small rural villages and case fatality is about 14%.[9] Fatality, however, was much higher when it was used as a weapon of biological warfare, as for example by Japan in 1935, and both the bubonic and pneumonic strains of plague remain in the arsenal of biological weaponry. Plague has also entered our lives in other ways. It helped develop the science of medicine, originated the notion that public authorities should take responsibility for public health and sanitation. The perfume industry owes much to the scents developed to combat the stench of plague, and the diamond industry profited from the custom of a young man offering his fiancée a solitaire as a protection against plague. And it has continued to inspire artists and writers.[10]

Many questions remain about the Black Death, and historians and epidemiologists still debate the causes of its appearance, its uneven incidence and its eventual eclipse. Demographic questions in particular are hotly debated, and there is very little consensus about the extent of the mortality caused by plague and the long-term demographic trends it initiated. Moreover, much about the plague can be explained not by reference to human factors, but to bacilli, fleas and rats, and here many questions remain unanswered. These issues are in Ireland aggravated by the problem of negative evidence, particularly for the years around the time of the Black Death. However, what is clear is that Ireland's response to this event must be seen in the context of responses in England and on the continent, and that the changes taking place in Ireland were of a part with Europe-wide changes. Human societies everywhere evince similar responses when dealing with the threat of a disease as lethal and terrifying as the Black Death. Ireland's story during the plague years is similar to that elsewhere, though all the details of that story may never be fully known. Friar Clyn's prophesy of the Anti-Christ may not have been fulfilled, but extreme terror and death there was, and also, albeit in altered form, continuing life.

Appendix

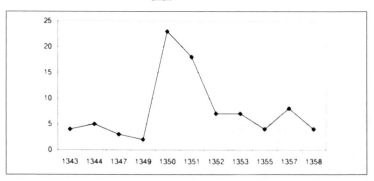

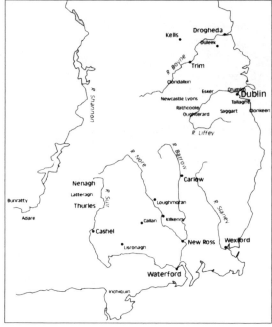

Fig. 1 above Graph of Petitions for Permission to Choose a Personal Confessor, 1343–1358.

Fig 2. right Manors of Leinster and Munster (based on Down, 455).

Fig. 3 left The Dioceses in Ireland in the later Middle Ages.

Fig 4. below Graph showing vacancies in benefices, 1338–56.

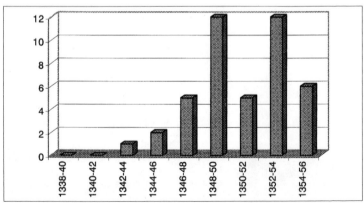

𝒩otes

CHAPTER 1: THE BLACK DEATH

1. Cited Ziegler, *The Black Death*, 240.
2. Preface to Hecker, *The Black Death*; Gasquet, *The Great Pestilence*, xvi; Trevalyan, *English Social History*, xi.
3. *Waning of the Middle Ages*, 25.
4. Shrewsbury, *History,* 29, 36, 123; McNeill, *Plagues and Peoples*.
5. Biraben, *Les hommes et la peste*, i; Carmichael, *Plague and the Poor*, 18-26; Hatcher, *Plague,* especially 16-24; Lamb, *Climate, History and the Modern World*; Cohn, S.K., *The Black Death Transformed*; Scott, S. and Duncan, C.J., *The Biology of Plagues: Evidence from Historical Populations*; Twigg, *The Black Death: A Biological Reappraisal*; Raoult *et al.*, 'Suicide PCR/Yersinia pestis* as cause of the Black Death', 12800-12803; Paterson, R., '*Yersinia* seeks pardon for the Black Death', 323; Herlihy, *The Black Death*, 25-31, 51, 81; Gottfried, *The Black Death and 'The Black Death'*, 266.
6. Ryan, M. (ed.), *Illustrated Archaeology of Ireland,* 17.
7. MacLeod, 'Late medieval wood sculptures', 53-5; Rae, 'Architecture and sculpture', 759ff.; Hunt, *Irish Medieval Figure Sculpture*, i. 4.
8. In the following discussion, I have relied on: Biraben, *La peste*, i. 7-21, 333-7; Dols, *The Black Death in the Middle East,* 68-83; Herlihy, *The Black Death*, 17-38; Hirst, *The Conquest of Plague*; Hollingsworth, *Historical Demography*, 355-75; Horrox, *The Black Death*, 3-13; Morris, 'The plague in Britain'; Shrewsbury, *History*, 1-6; Twigg, *The Black Death*; Watts, *Epidemics and History*, 1-6.
9. Though see M. Dols, 'Al-Manbiji's "Report of the Plague"', 71 which notes one instance in Arab literature that connects rats and plague; cf. Gottfried, *The Black Death*, 110. Because rats are not mentioned in connection with the

human illness in 1348, Twigg argues that the disease could not have been bubonic plague, adding the further argument that that there wasn't any significant rat population in medieval England or Ireland and that the brown rat did not colonise Europe until the eighteenth century. *The Black Death*, 52-3, 75-6, 80-85.

10. Hirst, *Conquest of Plague*, 33-5, 222; Biraben, *La peste*, i. 12; Zinnser, *Rats*, 50ff.; Shrewsbury, *History* 5; Crawfurd, *Plague*, 120.
11. McNeill, *Plagues and Peoples*, 155, 158.
12. Horrox, 41; on portents of the plague, cf. Nohl, *The Black Death*, 34ff. Cf. Biraben, *La peste*, i.133-4, 154; ii. 9-11; Twigg, *The Black Death*, 78ff.
13. Cf. Morris, 'The plague in Britain', 205-224; McNeill, *Plagues*, 168; Shrewsbury, *History*, 6ff.; 14. Twigg, *The Black Death*, 113ff.
14. Shrewsbury, *History*, 17, 21.
15. Twigg, *The Black Death*, 52-3, 80-85; Houston, *Population History*, 167.
16. Hirst, *Conquest of Plague*, 308.
17. Hatcher, *Plague*, 28; Nicholas, *Medieval Flanders*, 266; Gottfried, *The Black Death*, 60.
18. Lamb, *Climate, History and the Modern World*; Bailey, M., '*Per impetum maris*', 186-206; Biraben, *La peste*, i. 134-9; Twigg, *The Black Death*, 113ff.; Gottfried, *The Black Death*, 9. Horrox, 54, 160-161.
19. Livi-Bacci, *A Concise History*, 53. Cf. Campbell, B., 'Population pressure', 127; Herlihy, *The Black Death*, 39; Gottfried, *The Black Death*, 4.
20. Schofield, *et al.* (ed.), *The Decline of Mortality*, 9, 14-17.
21. Van Bath, *Agrarian History,* 84; cf. Duby, *Rural Economy*, 286.
22. Schofield, *et al.* (ed.), *Decline of Mortality*, 10-11; Perrenoud, A. 'The attenuation of mortality crises', 20; Rotberg & Rabb, *Hunger and History*, 308; cf. Bernard, J. *Le sang et l'histoire* .
23. Jordan, *The Great Famine*, 186-7.

24. Razi, *A Medieval Parish*, 107-9, 129-134.

25. Lunn, 'Nutrition', 137; Walter & Schofield, 'Famine', 18-21; Herlihy, *The Black Death*, 4.

26. Houston, *Population History*, 167; Dols, *The Black Death in the Middle East*, 38n.8.

27. Fossier, 'The great trial', 53.

28. Fossier, *ibid.*, 55; Bernard, *Le sang et l'histoire*.

29. Biraben, *La peste*, i. 12, 15; 130-1; Morris, 'The plague in Britain', 212-3; Gottfried, *The Black Death*, 4; Livi-Bacci, *A Concise History*, 49.

30. Biraben, *La peste*, i.125ff; Duby, *Rural Economy*, 308-10; Gottfried, *The Black Death*, 4; 129ff.

31. Schofield, *et al.*, *Decline of Mortality*, 7.

CHAPTER 2: THE COMING OF THE BLACK DEATH TO IRELAND

1. J.F. Shrewsbury maintains that since there is no evidence that the black rat had colonised Ireland or England at this stage, no pestilence in the British Isles before the fourteenth century can be identified as bubonic plague. He suggests that that most of the earlier epidemics were of confluent smallpox whose symptoms are similar to those of bubonic plague. *History*, 20-21. However, not all agree with Shrewsbury's theories. For an opposite viewpoint, see MacArthur, 'Identification of some pestilences recorded in the Irish annals', 174-81; Biraben, *La peste*, i. 32; Simpson, *A Treatise*, 17ff.

2. *AU*, i. 49; *Ann. Clon.*, 95, 106 n.2, 109, 186; *AU*, ii.55; *AFM*, ii. 949-50; Clyn, *Annals*, 9; 'The Book of Howth' in *Cal. Carew MSS*, v. 142.

3. On the plague's progress, see Dols, *The Black Death in the Middle East*, 35-55; Biraben, *La peste*, i. 48-55, 71-85.

4. On the plague in England, see Ziegler, *The Black Death*, 123-53; Horrox, 10-11.

5. O'Brien, 'Politics, economy and society', 97ff; McEneaney, 'Mayors and merchants', 154-5

6. Barry, *Archaeology*, 96-9; Twohig, 'Archaeological heritage'.

7. *Annals*, 35.

8. Ó Lochlainn, 'Roadways', 465-74; *Cal. Ormond Deeds*, 180, 296.

9. *Black Book of Limerick*, 12-13; Sayles, 'Legal proceedings', 10; *Hist. & Mun. Docs. Ire.*, 64, 111;

10. Curtis, *Richard II*, 207; *Cal. Docs. Ire.* 1252-80, nos. 1693, 2303, 2304; Harris, 'Collectanea', 446; 'Cal. of Liber Ruber', 164-5; Graham, 'The high Middle Ages', 87.

10. Coulton, cited Shrewsbury, *History*, 28.

11. Ministers' Accounts, SC6/1237/23; Falkiner, 'The Hospital of St John of Jerusalem'.

12. Otway-Ruthven, 'The med. county of Kildare', 184; Mitchell, *The Irish Landscape*, 184-5.

13. *Cal. Pat. Rolls 1330-34*, 43; *Liber primus Kilkenniensis*, 11, 12; *Cal. Close Rolls 1343-6*, 672.

14. Shrewsbury, *History*, 21-4; Twigg, *The Black Death*, 98; Hatcher, *Plague*, 28.

15. O'Conor, *Med. Rural Settlement*, Chap. 3 and 4; Graham, *Med. Irish Settlement*.

16. Nicholls, *Gaelic and Gaelicised Ireland*, 122 and 'Gaelic society', 396-9.

17. *Froissart's Chronicles*, 369.

18. Curtis, *History of Med. Ireland*, 134.

19. McNeill, *Anglo-Norman Ulster*, 84-8.

20. Edwards, *et al.*, 'The med. settlement of Newcastle Lyons', 351-76; Simms, A., 'Core and periphery', 33-5; Otway-Ruthven, 'Organisation of Anglo-Irish agriculture', 3; Graham, *Med. Irish Settlement*, 24-5; Down, 'Colonial economy', 468.

21. O'Riordain & Hunt, 'Med. dwellings at Caherguillamore', 38-9, 43-4.

22. Graham, 'Definition and classification of med. Irish towns', 20-32 , 'The high Middle Ages', 82-3; 87-8; and 'Towns of med. Ireland', 35.

23. Colfer, 'Anglo-Norman settlement in Co. Wexford', 82-3; Otway-Ruthven, *History of Med. Ireland*, 115ff, and 'The med. county of Kildare', 183, 196; Curtis, *Richard II*, 28; *Cal. Justic. Rolls 1305-7*, i. 265; O'Brien, 'Politics, economy and society', 92-95; Bradley, 'The med. towns of Tipperary', 35; O'Conor, *Med. Rural Settlement*, 44ff.

24. Reprinted in Heuser, *Kildare-Gedichte*, 146, ll. 36-38, and in Seymour, *Anglo-Irish Literature*, 105.

25. Quinn, *Elizabethans and the Irish*, 54; G. Cambrensis, *Topography*, 44; Maxwell, *Irish History*, 316-21.

26. *Scotichronicon*, in Horrox, 84-5; Shrewsbury, *History*, 4, 34-6.

27. O'Riordain & Hunt, 'Med. dwellings at Caherguillamore', 44-9; *Cal. Justic. Rolls 1305-7*, i. 346; 28. *Account Roll of Holy Trinity*, 60-61; Nicholls, 'Gaelic society', 403-4; Twohig, 'Archaeological heritage'; Barry, *Archaeology*, 7, 73-4, 81, 91, 121-2; O'Conor, *Med. Rural Settlement*, 50-7.

28. Shrewsbury, *History*, 36.

29. *The Tour of the French Traveller M. de la Boullaye le Gouz*, cited Harbison, *Guide*, 28.

30. Horrox, 62, 66, 74; cf. Lamb, *Climate*, 181, 186-7; Bailey, *'Per impetum maris'*, 184-208.

31. Cf. Lyons, 'Weather', 31-74.

32. Cf. 18-19 above.

33. Cited Gwynn, 'The Black Death in Ireland', 34; Van Bath, *Agrarian History*, 89.

34. Potts, 'History and blood groups', 239ff.

35. Nicholls, K., 'Anglo-French Ireland and after', 370-40, 'Gaelic society', 403, 413-4, and *Land, Law and Society*', 9; Simms, K. 'Nomadry in med. Ireland', 379-91.

36. Watts, *Epidemics*, 27-8.

37. Ryan, M. (ed.), *Illustrated Archaeology of Ireland*, 17.

38. Clyn, *Annals*, 36ff; 'Annals of Nenagh', 160-61.

39. Gwynn, 'The Black Death', 30; Walsh, K., *Richard FitzRalph*, 282-3.

40. Biraben, *La Peste*, i. 86-7; Robo, *Med. Farnham*. 208-27.

41. *CPP*, i. 331; *CPL*, iii. 290; *Cal. Close Rolls 1349-54*, 376; *Cal. Pat. Rolls 1350-54*, 117; *ibid., 1354-8*, 91; Gen. Office, Dublin, MSS 192, 193; 'Annals of Nenagh', 160-1.

42. *Polychronicon* in Horrox, 62; Gwynn, 'The Black Death', 34 and Walsh, K., *Richard FitzRalph*, 292; Barnes, *History*, 440; Marlborough, *Chronicle*, ii.12.

43. *AU*, ii.491; *AFM*, i.595; *Ann. Clon.*, 297; *AC*, 303; 'Frag.Annals', 153; *ALC*, ii.7.

44. *Chronicon*, Horrox, 82; Gwynn, 'The Black Death', 32; *Parliaments and Councils*, i. 20;

45. Barnes, *History*, 440.

46. See below 78 ff, 118, 122, 124.

47. Titow, *English Rural Society*, 69-71; Hatcher, *Plague*, 26-7.

48. Van Werveke, 'De Zwarte Dood in de Zuidelijke Nederlanden', 22; Nicholas, *Med. Flanders*, 266.

49. *Chronicon*, in Horrox, 82.

50. Watt, *Epidemics*, 1; Hollingsworth, T.H., and M.F., 'Plague mortality rates by age and sex'.

51. *Annals of St Mary's*, 397; *Historia Anglicana*, in Horrox, 91.

52. Razi, *Med. Parish*, 107-9, 129-134, 150-151; cf. Russell, *British Med. Population*, 230-1, 260-70; Hatcher, *Plague*, 57-62.

53. Marlborough, *Chronicle*, 13; *Ann. Clon.*, 301; Fitzmaurice & Little, *Materials*, 160; *Annals by*

Clyn and Dowling, 39; *CPP*, i. 461-2; *Annals of St Mary's*, 395, 397; *ALC* Hatcher, 'Mortality in the fifteenth century', 29. Cf. Lyons, 'Weather', 67-73.

54. For a summary of these views, see Hatcher, *Plague*, 19-22.

55. Shrewsbury, *History*, 49.

56. Gwynn, 'The Black Death', 32; Walsh, K., *Richard FitzRalph*, 294.

57. Otway-Ruthven, *Med. Ireland*, 115; Russell, 'Late thirteenth century Ireland', 502.

58. Miller & Hatcher, *Med. England*, 29; Hatcher, *Plague*, 18; Smith, 'Demographic developments', 49-50; Jordan, *The Great Famine*, 12 and n. 29.

59. *Gaelic and Gaelicised Ireland*, 7.

60. Razi, *Med. Parish*, 100.

61. Hatcher, J., Plague, 29; Ziegler, *The Black Death*, 235-9; Platt, *King Death*, 9; Horrox, 3; Bolton, *The Black Death*, 6; Razi, *Med. Parish*, 103.

62. Nicholas, *Med. Flanders*, 266; Gottfried, 'The Black Death', 261.

63. Postan, 'Some evidence of declining population'; Hatcher, *Plague*, 36; Hollingsworth, *Historical Demography*, 385; Livi-Bacci, *A Concise History*, 31, 53.

64. Nicholls, 'Gaelic society', 408-9.

CHAPTER 3: PLAGUE: THE HUMAN RESPONSE

1. Power, C., 'A med. demographic sample', 66-7.

2. Ottaway, *Archaeology in British Towns*, 207; cf. Miller & Hatcher, *Med. England*, viii; Smith, 'Demographic developments in rural England', 57-60.

3. Lydon, *Lordship*, 140.

4. Lydon, 'The impact of the Bruce Invasion', 278; cited Gwynn, 'The Black Death', 32.

5. *Annals of Innisfallen*, 371.

6. 'Annals of St Mary's', ii. 372-3; Clyn, *Annals*, 12ff; Lyons, 'Weather', 31-74.

7. *Chart. St Mary's*, ii.392.

8. Cited Watts, *Epidemics*, 1.

9. Horrox 14, 130; Crawfurd, *Plague*, 4-7, 9.

10. Chester Beatty Library, Dublin: MS 3676/6, cited Barkai, 'Jewish treatises on the Black Death', 21. In this discussion I have relied on the following: Barkai, 'Jewish treatises', 6-25; Biraben, *Les hommes*, ii. 7-27; A. Campbell, *The Black Death and Men of Learning* ; Dols, *The*

Black Death in the Middle East, 84-94; Horrox, *The Black Death*, 101-6; Watts, *Epidemics*, 12-14; Ziegler, *The Black Death*, 67-78; French, *et al.*, *Practical Medicine*, 237-288; Nutton, 'The seeds of disease', 1-34.

11. BL Sloane MS 965, cited Ibeji, 'Black Death: the blame'.

12. Shaw, 'Medieval medico-philosophical treatises', 144ff. and 'Medicine in Ireland'; McGrath, *Education in Ancient and Med. Ireland* , 211

13. Cited Dunlevy, 'The medical families of med. Ireland', 19-20.

14. *Cal. Anc. Rec. Dublin*, ii. 139.

15. Bliss & Long, 'Literature in Norman French and English', 735; Nohl, *The Black Death*, chapter 4; Lydgate, 'A Doctrine for Pestilence', ll. 1-3, cited Wenzel, 'Pestilence', 150; Colledge (ed.), *Poems of Richard Ledrede*, 71-3; 137.

16. Cited Ziegler, *The Black Death*, 197.

17. *Seanchas Mór*, T.C.D., MS. H. 2.15, 36.

18. Clyn, *Annals*, 37

19. *Med. Ireland: The Enduring Tradition*, 68.

20. Clyn, *Annals*, 36; John of Reading in Horrox, 74; cited Lerner, R., 'The Black Death', 90.

21. Cited Nohl, *The Black Death*, 58.

22. Hunt, *Irish Med. Figure Sculpture*, i. 10-9, 125.

23. *Annals*, 35.

24. Plummer, 'Vita Sancti Moling', 190-205; MacNeill, *The Festival of Lughnasa*, 263-268; Logan, *The Holy Wells of Ireland*, 52, 87; Pochin Mould, *Irish Pilgrimage*, 36-8, 127.

25. 'Cal. of liber niger and liber albus'; Mac Leod, 'Some late med. wood sculptures ', 54-5.

26. Walsh, K., *FitzRalph*, 291.

27. Horrox, 30, 85; di Tura in Bowsky (ed.), *The Black Death*, 14.

28. Cited Platt, *King Death*, 4.

29. Cited Crawfurd, *Plague*, 30; Horrox, 29, 61.

30. *CPL*, iv. 106.

31. Jean de Venette in Horrox, 57.

32. Colledge (ed.), *Poems of Richard Ledrede*, No. XXXVII, 91; Heuser (ed.), *Kildare-Gedichte*, 133-9, 154-8.

33. Walsh, K., *FitzRalph*, 232-8, 284-8, 314, 320, 323-5, 337, 343-7; Gwynn, 'Richard FitzRalph', part vi, 86.

34. *AC*, 31; *Cal. Justic. Rolls 1308-14*, 162, 150, 210, 230, 254-6; Lucas, H.S., 'The Great European Famine', cited Jordan, *The Great Famine*, 232, n.42.

35. Cited Moorman, *History*, 343.

36. *CPL*, iii. 606.

37. Lucas, A. 'The plundering and burning of churches in Ireland, 7th-16th centuries'.

38. Gwynn, 'The Black Death', 36-7; Walsh, K., *FitzRalph*, 288, 285-90; cf. similar complaints by the bishops of Ossory in 'Cal. of Liber Ruber', Nos. 14, 17, 18, 166-9, 170-174, 174-5.

39. Keen, *English Society*, 35. Lydon, *Lordship*, 114-5.

40. Dols, *The Black Death in the Middle East*, 240 n.40, 294, 298-301.

41. *CPL*, iii. 311; Walsh, K., *FitzRalph*, 340 n.71

42. Horrox, 44, 60.

43. 'Some unpublished texts from the Black Book of Christ Church', 301-3; Seymour, *Irish Witchcraft*, 25-51; Carrigan, *History of the Diocese of Ossory*, i. 45; Lydon, *Lordship*, 115-6. 'Cal. of Liber Ruber', 167; Gleeson, 'A fourteenth-century Clare heresy trial', 36-42; CPP, i. 216; Fitzmaurice & Little, *Materials*, 144.

44. Grenfell Morton, *Elizabethan Ireland*, 17.

45. Walsh, K., *FitzRalph*, 287-8; Leff, *Med. Thought*, 296-9; Du Boulay, *An Age of Ambition*, 168-71.

46. Duffy, *The Stripping of the Altars*, 344

47. Horrox, 271-2.

48. *The Catholic Encyclopedia*, Volume VII. Online Edition © 1999 by Kevin Knight; see also, Swanson, *Church and Society in Later Med. England*, 291-4.

49. Walsh, K., *FitzRalph*, 188, 289

50. *CPL*, iii. vi.

51. *CPP*, i. 15-16, 206, 461-2.

52. *Ann. Clon.*, 186.

53. See below 127ff.

54. Gwynn & Hadcock, *Med. Religious Houses*, 263ff; Moorman, *History*, 417-428, 560ff.; 355; Fitzmaurice & Little, *Materials*, xxx, 163.

55. Clyn, *Annals*, 34; *Annals of Nenagh*, 160-1.

56. Cf. Nohl, *The Black Death*, 145-150; Heer, *Med. World*, Plates 74, 75; Huizinga, *Waning of the Middle Ages*, 134-46.

57. Duffy, 305.

58. Wenzel, 'Pestilence', 132-46.

59. Polzer, J., 'Aspects of the fourteenth-century iconography', 111 and note 5.

60. Colledge (ed.), *Poems of Richard Ledrede*, xlvi-xlvii.; cf. Heuser (ed.), *Kildare-Gedichte*, 141ff; Seymour, *Anglo-Irish Literature*, 52-117; MacKenna, 'Some Irish Bardic Poems'; Murphy, J.E., 'The religious mind of the Irish bards', 82ff.; Bliss & Long, 'Literature in

Norman French and English', 72off.

61. Heuser (ed.), *Kildare-Gedichte*, 81-5 and Seymour, *Anglo-Irish Literature*, 53-4.

62. Colledge, (ed.), *Poems of Richard Ledrede*, No. XXXI, 75.

63. Cf. Bliss, 'Language and Literature', 34.

64. Carney, 'Literature in Irish', 688-9; Watt, *The Church in Med. Ireland*, 213; Ó Rathile, *Dánta Grádha: An Anthology of Irish Love Poetry*.

65. Ó Háinle, C., 'Congaibh Ort, A Mhacaoimh Mná: content and form', 57 and *passim*.

66. *Waning of the Middle Ages*, 134.

67. Heuser, (ed.), *Kildare-Gedichte*, 89-96.

68. Mac Leod, 'Some late med. wood sculptures', 57-62; Leask, *Irish Churches*, iii. 174-5; Rae, 'Architecture and sculpture', 771; Stalley, *Cistercian Monasteries*, 215-6; Crawfurd, *Plague*, 134.

69. Rae, 'Architecture and sculpture', 760-1, 774.

70. Horrox, 245, and note 36; cf. Platt, *King Death*, 139ff.

71. Hunt, *Irish Med. Figure Sculpture*, i. 57; also, i.100, 114-6, 214.

72. Cf. Platt, *King Death*, 137ff.; Leask, *Irish Churches*, ii. 134.

73. Cf. Duby, G., *The Age of Cathedrals*, 195-220.

74. Hunt, *Irish Med. Figure Sculpture*, i. 53; also, 114ff; Bradley, 'The med. tombs of St Canice's Cathedral', 49.

75. Stalley, 'Irish Gothic and English fashion', 79 and 'Gothic art and architecture', 172ff; Hunt, *Irish Med. Figure Sculpture*, 9.

76. Seanchas Mór, TCD, MS H.2.15.

CHAPTER 4: THE BLACK DEATH AND THE COUNTRYSIDE

1. Otway-Ruthven, *Med. Ireland*, 113-116, 122, and 'The character of Anglo-Norman settlement', 78-9.

2. Postan, *Med. Economy and Society*, 33-38; Titow, *English Rural Society*, 73-96; Russell, 'The pre-plague population of England', 1-21; Smith, 'Demographic developments', 38-50.

3. Postan, 'Some economic evidence of declining population', 246; cf. Postan, *Med. Economy*, 40-44; Titow, *English Rural Society*, 36-7; Van Bath, *Agrarian History*, 89; Gottfried, *The Black Death*, 24-26; Miller & Hatcher, *Med. England*, 241.

4. Empey, 'The Norman period', 88-9; *Cal. Doc. Ire.1302-7*, 189, 195-196. Cf. Otway-Ruthven, 'The character of Anglo-Norman settlement'.

5. Kosminsky, *Studies*, 62-3; Van Bath, *Agrarian History*, 134; Mate, 'The agrarian economy', 105-8; Miller & Hatcher, *Med. England*, 30, 241; Jordan, *The Great Famine*, 89ff.

6. Down, 'Colonial society', 458; Cullen, *Life in Ireland*, 32; Titow, *English Rural Society*, 78ff; Keen, *English Society*, 66.

7. Mills, 'Earl of Norfolk's estates', i. 57; *Account Roll of Holy Trinity*, xxiii, 50, 52.

8. Lydon, *Lordship*, 88-89; Otway-Ruthven, 'The organisation of Anglo-Irish agriculture', 1-13; Mills, 'Tenants and agriculture', 61ff; *Cal. Doc. Ire. 1302-7*, 188-196.

9. Livi-Bacci, *A Short History*, 48; cf. Harvey, 'Introduction', 19.

10. Lamb, *Climate*, 186-7; Bailey, '*Per impetum maris*', 187ff; Jordan, *The Great Famine*, 16-18; Lyons, 'Weather', 40-44; Mitchell, *The Irish Landscape*, 184-5.

11. Miller & Hatcher, *Med. England*, 245; Hatcher, 'Plague', 76-8; Harvey, 'Introduction', 21-22.

12. See Frame, 'The Bruces in Ireland', 3-37; Otway-Ruthven, *Med. Ireland*, 242-3.

13. *Cal. Justic. Rolls* 1305-7, part ii, 6.

14. Mills, 'Tenants and agriculture', 56 and 'Notices of the manor of St Sepulchre', 37-41.

15. *Cal. Pat. Rolls 1330-1334*, 551; *Cal. Fine Rolls 1327-37*, 363.

16. *Red Book of the Earls of Kildare*, 119, 122-5.

17. *Cal. Doc. Ire. 1302-7*, 73

18. 'Cal. of liber niger and liber albus', 43-5; cf. Sayles, 'Legal Proceedings', 45.

19. Otway-Ruthven, *Med. Ireland*, 214-6.

20. Razi, *A Medieval Parish*, 99-101, 103; Hatcher, *Plague*, 21-6; Titow, *English Rural Society*, 69-72; Robo, *Medieval Farnham*, 212, 224-5; Ballard, 'The Black Death', 196, 213; Campbell, B., 'Population pressure', 95-7, 107, 127.

21. *Cal. Pat. Rolls 1354-8*, 91; PROI, *Mem. Rolls*, Vol. 26, 17-19; *Cal. Close Rolls*, ix. 376; *Roll of Proceedings of King's Council*, 138-9.

22. Cf. Edwards, *et al.*, 'The medieval settlement of Newcastle Lyons', 351-76.

23. Cited Duby, *Rural Economy*, 298; cf. Saltmarsh, 'Plague and economic decline', 36.

24. Levett, 'The Black Death', 81, 142; Titow, *English Rural Society*, 69-72; Razi, *Medieval Parish*, 105-6.

25. Cited Keen, *English Society*, 31.

26. Mitchell, *The Irish Landscape*, 186, 188-9;

O'Conor, *Med. Rural Settlement*, 98.

27. Hatcher, *Plague*, 28.

28. Nicholas, *Med. Flanders*, 266; Gottfried, 'The Black Death', 261.

29. Shrewsbury, *History*, 23, 123; Russell, *British Med. Population*, 221, 226-7; Levett, 'The Black Death', 10; Titow, *English Rural Society*, 69-71; Hatcher, *Plague*, 28-9, 74; Miller & Hatcher, *Med. England*, 31.

30. Levett, *Studies*, 235ff.; Bridbury, 'The Black Death', 591, 581-9; Hatcher, *Plague*, 42-50, 74-80; Razi, *A Medieval Parish*, 110ff.; Robo, *Medieval Farnham*, 253, 224-6.

31. Ministers' Accounts, SC 6/1237/8-11, 23-6, 29-31; SC 6/1238/10-16, 21-22; SC 6/1239/13-33. Cf. Down, 'Colonial society' 440ff; Lyons, 'Manorial Administration and the Manorial Economy'.

32. Lyons, 'Weather', 45 and 'Manorial Administration', i. 137.

33. Latthedran: SC 6/1238/12, SC 6/1239/20, m.8; Loughmoran: SC 6/1238/15; Callan: SC 6/1239/20 m.3; SC6/1237/8, 10, 11; Palmerstown: SC 6/1238/21, 22.

34. SC 6/1237/29, 30, 31; SC 6/1239/20, m.11, 6/1237/23, 24; SC 6/1238/10.

35. SC 6/1238/13, 14; Curtis, 'Rental of the manor of Lisronagh', 48.

36. Holmes, *The Estates of the Higher Nobility*, chap. 4; Hatcher, *Plague*, 37-8.

37. Lyons, 'Weather', 45; 'Manorial Administration', i.153-6, ii.53-7.

38. Mem. Rolls, vol. 26, 17-19; Lyons, 'Weather', 46.

39. SC 6/1237/25, 1238/32, 15, 1239/20 m.9; SC 6/1237/23, 29, 30.

40. Watts, *Epidemics*, 26ff.

41. *Cal. Close Rolls 1349-54*, 195, 587-8; *Statutes John-Henry V*, 374-396, 476-500; *Cal. Close Rolls 1354-60*, 575-8; *Parliaments and Councils*, i. 19-22.

42. *Cal. Dowdall Deeds*, x; Otway-Ruthven, 'The partition of the de Verdon lands', 417.

43. *Statutes John-Henry V*, 516-8; *Irish Historical Documents*, 58.

44. *Cal. Pat. Rolls 1420-36*, 64; Down, 'Colonial society', 449.

45. Cited Cosgrove, 'The emergence of the Pale', 552-3; Lydon, *Lordship*, 206.

46. 'Nomadry', 379-391; Nicholls, 'Gaelic society', 403, 413-4, and *Gaelic and Gaelicised Ireland*, 117ff.

47. Curtis, 'Rental of the manor of Lisronagh', 41-76.

48. Saltmarsh, 'Plague', 23-41; Bean, 'Plague', 423-437; Harvey, 'Introduction', 12-19.

49. Cf. Curtis, 'Rental', 41-76; *Red Book of Ormond*, 123, 157 and *passim*; *Account Roll of Holy Trinity*, 189-191, 191-4, 195-6; Lydon, *Lordship*, 90-91; Otway-Ruthven, 'The organisation of Anglo-Irish agriculture', 9-12; Frame, *Colonial Ireland*, 78. *Cal. Doc. Ire. 1293-1301*, 259.

50. *Statutes John-Henry V*, 215.

51. Mills, 'Tenants and agriculture', 54-6; *Account Roll of Holy Trinity*, 64-7, 189-191; Otway-Ruthven, *Med. Ireland*, 118.

52. Statute of Labourers and Artisans, 18 June 1349 in Horrox, 287; *Cal. Anc. Rec.*, ii.132-5.

53. *Chronicon*, Horrox, 78.

54. Ministers' Accounts, SC6/1238/10, 21, 22.

55. Cosgrove, 'The emergence of the Pale', 551-2; *Red Book of Ormond*, 20, 30.

56. Horrox, 73.

57. Keen, *English Society*, 44.

58. Down, 'Colonial society', 458-9.

59. Platt, *King Death*, 50ff; Empey, 'The sacred and the secular', 143.

60. Cf. Postan, *Med. Economy*, 139ff; Hatcher, *Plague*, 49ff; Razi, *A Medieval Parish*, 131, 147-150.

61. Colfer, 'Anglo-Norman settlement in Co. Wexford', 74.

62. Ministers' Accounts: SC 6/1238/16; 6/1239/14, 16; cf. Down, 'Colonial society', 459-463.

63. *Reg. Swayne*, 65, 68, 82, 89; *Reg. de Kilmainham*, vii; Gwynn & Hadcock, *Med. Religious Houses*, 333; Stalley, *Cistercian Monasteries*, 21.

64. Lydon, *Lordship*, 90-91; Nicholls, 'Anglo-French Ireland', 392-3.

65. Down, 'Colonial society', 477; Aalen, 'The origin of enclosures', 211.

66. Leask, *Irish Castles*, 25 and *Irish Churches*, iii. 124; Barry, *Archaeology*, 69, 186-8.

67. Holmes, *The Estates of the Higher Nobility*, 90-91.

68. O'Conor, *Med. Rural Settlement*, 39; Barry, *Archaeology*, 57, 69-70, 180.

69. See Leask, *Irish Castles*, 75ff; Barry, 'The last frontier', 217-228, 'The people of the country', 113 and 'Late medieval Ireland', 108; O'Conor, *Med. Rural Settlement*, 102-6.

70. *Roll of Proceedings of the King's Council*, 221; *Cal. Pat. Rolls 1413-16*, 122.

71. Nicholls, 'Gaelic society', 408-9.
72. Du Boulay, *An Age of Ambition*, 411-3; Schofield, 'The geographical distribution', 483-510.
73. Harvey, 'Introduction', 22-4.

CHAPTER 5: THE BLACK DEATH IN THE TOWNS

1. O'Brien, 'Politics, economy and society', 93-4; Bradley, 'Med. towns of Tipperary', 35.
2. Rynne, *Archaeology of Cork City*, 45.
3. Dols, *The Black Death in the Middle East*, 74
4. Barry, *Archaeology*, 91, 121-2; Hurley, 'Excavations in med. Cork: St Peter's Market'.
5. Rynne, *Archaeology of Cork City*, 49ff; *Hist. and Mun. Doc. Ire.*, 365, No. 82; *Cal. Anc. Rec.*, i. 145, 298, 306, 327; ii. 92, 96, 101, 139, 370, 382.
6. Gransden, *Historical Writing*, ii.172; *Liber Primus Kilkenniensis*, 5, 6, 13; *Cal. Anc. Rec.* ii. 370, 382.
7. Power, 'A med. demographic sample', 66-7.
8. Westropp, 'Early Italian maps of Ireland'; *Cal. Justic. Rolls*, i.304; *Cal. Doc. Ire. 1285-92*, 202; Westropp, 'The manor of Bunratty', 14-15; O'Brien, 'Med. Youghal', 355.
9. See A. Simms, 'Core and periphery in med. Europe', 22-40.
10. Otway-Ruthven, 'The character of the Anglo-Norman settlement', 79, *Med. Ireland*, 112-3, 117 and 'The med. county of Kildare', 183; Glasscock, 'Moated sites', 171; Graham, 'Economy and town', 241-260 and 'The high Middle Ages', 82ff; Empey, 'Conquest and settlement', 10.
11. *Annals*, 9, 10.
12. Sayles, 'The rebellious First Earl', and 'Legal proceedings', 7; Otway-Ruthven, *Med. Ireland*, 279ff.
13. *Cal. Anc. Rec.*, i.11; *Cal. Pat. Rolls*, vii. 20 June 1334; *Hist. and Mun. Docs.*, No. 59.
14. *Cal. Close Rolls 1343-6*, 672; *Liber Primus Kilkenniensis*, 11.
15. *Annals*, 36.
16. *Polychronicon* in Horrox, 62; Gwynn, 'The Black Death', 34 and Walsh, *Richard FitzRalph*, 292; Barnes, *History*, 440.
17. Horrox, 53-4.
18. Hollingsworth, *Historical Demography*, 362-3; Horrox, 34-5.
19. Biraben, *La peste*, i. 157-161; Ziegler, *The Black Death*, 82.
20. Shrewsbury, *History*, 49.

21. Russell, 'Late ancient and med. population', 101-7, 110-112; and 'Population in Europe', 25-70; Pounds, *Historical Geography*, 329, 350-351; Gottfried, *The Black Death*, 42-76; Keen, *English Society*, 79; Jordan, *The Great Famine*, 129ff.
22. Cited Smith, 'Demographic developments', 50, n.69; Jordan, *The Great Famine*, 128, n.14.
23. Otway-Ruthven, 'The character of the Anglo-Norman settlement', 75-84; Russell, 'Late thirteenth-century Ireland', 500-512; Hollingsworth, *Historical Demography*, 269-70.
24. MacNiocaill, 'Socio-economic problems', 18-19; Houston, *Population History*, 122.
25. Hollingsworth, *Historical Demography*, 385.
26. Graham, 'The towns of med. Ireland', 41; McEneaney, 'Mayors and merchants', 153 and n.44.
27. 'The Entrenchment of New Ross', reprinted in Seymour, *Anglo-Irish Literature,* 23-8; cf. Shields, 'The Walling of New Ross'; Mullally, 'Hiberno-Norman literature', 333; Bliss & Long, 'Literature in Norman French and English', 718-9.
28. Graham, 'Urbanisation in the high Middle Ages', 136; *Med. Irish Settlement*, 32.
29. Postan, 'Med. agrarian society in its prime', 561.
30. Gen. Office MS 192; Chancery Miscellanea, C 47/10/22 (2) m.2.
31. Twohig, 'Archaeological heritage'; Houston, *Population History*, 122.
32. Otway-Ruthven, 'The med. Irish town', cited O'Brien, 'Med. Youghal', 355 and 349 *passim*.
33. Holmes, (ed.), *Oxford Illustrated History of Med. Europe*, 264.
34. *Cal. Anc. Rec.*, ii. 132-5, part iii, No. 11; iv., 235. *Statutes, John-Henry V*, 374-396.
35. Curtis, *Med. Ireland*, 213-9; Nicholls, 'Two islands, one street', and 'Gaelic economy', 491.
36. *Cal. Pat. Rolls 1358-61*, 492-3, 501; *Cal. Close Rolls 1360-64*, 163; Lydon, *Lordship* , 207; O'Brien, 'Med. Youghal', 353-5; MacNiocaill, 'Socio-economic problems', 17, 13.
37. Pounds, *Historical Geography*, 339-40; Rorig, *The Med. Town*, 115.
38. Lydon, 'Richard II's expeditions to Ireland', 137; O'Brien, 'Politics, economy and society', 125; Cosgrove, 'The emergence of the Pale', 552-3 and *Late Med. Ireland*, 33ff.
39. *Roll of the Proceedings of the King's Council*, No. 5, 8-9.

40. *Cal. Anc. Rec.*, i.30.

41. Cited Green, *The Making of Ireland*, 131-2; Gilbert, *Viceroys of Ireland*, 331.

42. *Facsimiles of National Mss of Ireland*. III, xxxix; cf. *Cal. Anc. Rec.*, i.322; *Cal. Pat. Rolls*, 1420-36, 64.

43. *Chronicon*, in Horrox, 79-80.

44. Gen. Office MS 192; Chancery Miscellanea, C.47/10/22 (2) m.2.

45. Sweetman, 'Excavations at Shop Street, Drogheda, Co. Louth', 198.

46. Walsh, C., *Archaeological Excavations at Patrick, Nicholas and Winetavern Streets, Dublin*, 121.

47. *Cal. Pat. Rolls 1374-7*, 207; *Cal. Pat. Rolls 1385-9*, 495, 521-2; *Rot. Pat. et Claus. Cal.*, 111-4, 118.

48. Bradley, 'Med. towns of Tipperary', 52; Barry, *Archaeology*, 176.

49. O'Brien, 'Politics, economy and society', 124.

50. Jennings, B., 'Brussels MS 3947', 75; *Cal. Carew MSS*, v. 475.

51. Nicholls, *Gaelic and Gaelicised Ireland*, 122.

52. *Chronicon*, in Horrox, 80 .

53. Beresford & Hurst (eds.), *Deserted Med. Villages*, 8, 11-17, 21; Saltmarsh, 'Plague', 24.

54. Hall, *et al.*, 'Med. agriculture', 16-25; Crawford, E. 'William Wilde's tables of Irish famines', 6.

55. O'Conor, *Med. Rural Settlement*, 47-8.

56. Otway-Ruthven, 'The med. Irish town', cited O'Brien, 'Med. Youghal', 355.

57. Glasscock, 'The study of deserted med. settlements ', 293-7, and 'Moated sites', 168-174; Otway-Ruthven, *Med. Ireland*, 225-308, and 'The med. county of Kildare', 184; Graham, *Anglo-Norman Settlement*, 16-17, 126-9; Simms, K., 'The Norman invasion', 74-96; *Red Book of Ormond*, 19, 64-6; Westropp, 'The manor of Bunratty', 14-15; Barry, 'The people of the country', 115-6 and *Archaeology*, 80-81, 87-92, 168-79.

58. Feehan, J., *Laois*, 370-1, cited Barry, *Archaeology*, 177.

59. Gwynn, 'The Black Death in Ireland', 33.

60. *Cal. Pat. Rolls 1350-54*, 253; O'Brien, 'Politics, economy and society', 127, and 'Med. Youghal', 363.

61. *Cal. Close Rolls 1361-4*, 299; *Cal. Close Rolls*, v.219; Cosgrove, 'The emergence of the Pale', 551-2.

62. *Cal. Pat. Rolls*, 1350-54, 253; *Cal. Close Rolls 1349-54*, 376; Gen. Office, Excerpts from the Plea Rolls, MS 193.

63. O'Brien, 'Med. Youghal', 355-6; McNeill, *Anglo-Norman Ulster*, 91.

64. Gen. Office MS 192; Chancery Misc., C.47/10/22 (2) m.2; *Cal Pat. Rolls 1350-1354*, 117; *Cal. Close Rolls 1354-60*, 76; *Cal Pat. Rolls 1354-58*, 87.

65. *Cal. Pat. Rolls 1374-7*, 309; *ibid., 1385-9*, 495; *ibid., 1391-6*, 203; *ibid., 1399-1401*, 400.

66. *Cal. Close Rolls 1349-54*, 376; 'Miscellanea of the Chancery', No. 23 (12); *Roll of the Proceedings of the King's Council*, No. 77, 80; *Cal. Pat. Rolls 1385-9*, 492.

67. *Cal. Anc. Rec.*, i. Nos 34, 36, 37, 40, 42, 53, 59, 60.

68. d'Alton, *History of Drogheda*, ii. 90ff; *Cal. Doc. Ire.*, ii. 199-200, 297, 430, 494-5, 505, 520-3; *ibid.*, iii. 277-8; *Cal. Pat. Rolls 1370-74*, 132; *ibid.*, 1374-7, 255; O'Brien, 'Med. Youghal', 372-3.

69. Graham, 'Towns of med. Ireland', 46; Barry, *Archaeology*, 171.

70. Gwynn, 'The Black Death', 34.

71. McEneaney, 'Merchants and Mayors', 164; d'Alton, *History of Drogheda*, ii. 93; Hardiman, *History of Galway*, 55.

72. Gransden, *Historical Writing*, ii. 172-3.

73. Neely, *Kilkenny*, cited Barry, 'Late med. Ireland', 114; McEneaney, 'Mayors and merchants', 167.

74. Cosgrove, *Late Med. Ireland*, 95.

75. Curtis, *Richard II in Ireland*, 125-6; *Roll of Proceedings of the King's Council*, 162.

76. MacNiocaill, 'Socio-economic problems', 7-22 and Na Buirgéisí, ii. 394-5; Lydon, *Lordship*, 242, 260.

77. Cf. Down, 'Colonial society', 490.

78. Beresford, *New Towns of the Middle Ages;* Du Boulay, *An Age of Ambition*, 45.

CHAPTER 6: THE CHURCH AND THE BLACK DEATH

1. Cf. Hand, *The Church in the English Lordship*, 3-13, 31-3; Watt, *The Church in Med. Ireland*, 184-6, 189-92; Empey, 'The sacred and the secular', 146-7.

2. *The Church and the Two Nations*, 2; Walsh, K., 'The clerical estate', 363-5.

3. Clyn, *Annals*, 17.

4. Watt, *The Church and the Two Nations*, 197, also 183ff.

5. *Chart. St Mary's, Dublin*, i. No. 253, 275; *Cal. Pat. Rolls 1330-34*, 552; *Reg. Swayne*, 4-5. *CPL*, ii.

27; *Cal. Doc. Ire. 1302-7*, 237-44.

6. Harris, *Collectanea*, 320-1; *Cal. Doc. Ire. 1293-1301*, No. 94; *CPL*, i. 494; *Cal. Doc. Ire. 1302-7*, 310, 316; *CPL*, ii. 260, 306.

7. *Cal. Close Rolls 1323-7*, 363; *Cal. Ormond Deeds*, No.692.

8. Richardson & Sayles, *Irish Parliament*, 52-3, 111-8; Lydon, 'The Irish Church and taxation', 158-65; 'Cal. of Liber Ruber', 166-74.

9. *CPL*, iii. 290, 339, 312, 279.

10. Byrne, 'List of Bishops', 264-332. See also *CPP*, i.331; Burke, *History of the Catholic Archbishops of Tuam*, 44; Flood, 'The episcopal succession of Tuam', 630-37; 'Frag. Annals', 153.

11. Hatcher, *Plague*, 26.

12. 'Frag. Annals', 153; *CPP*, i. 331.

13. Rennison, *Succession List of the Dioceses of Waterford and Lismore*, 59, 42.

14. *CPP* i. 287, 331, 346.

15. Clyn, *Annals*, 36;

16. *CPP* i. 207; Nicholls, *Gaelic and Gaelicised Ireland*, 73-6, 91.

17. Rennison, *Succession List*, 32; *Black Book of Limerick*, 145; Gleeson, *A History of the Diocese of Killaloe*, 361.

18. *CPL*, iii. 290; *CPP*, i. 412; *Fasti of St Patrick's Cathedral*, 60, 68-9, 150ff; *Reg. de Kilmainham*, xii; Gwynn & Hadcock, *Med. Religious Houses*, 74.

19. Gwynn, 'The Black Death', 37-8; Gwynn & Hadcock, *Med. Religious Houses*, 4.

20. Shrewsbury, *History*, 55; Hatcher, *Plague*, 26; Ziegler, *The Black Death*, 235-6.

21. Barry, *Archaeology*, 167, 145.

22. Gwynn & Hadcock, *Med. Religious Houses*, 6; 'Brussels MS 3410', 192ff.

23. Ziegler, *The Black Death*, 273-4; Watts, *Epidemics*, 32; Horrox, 68, 66, 76.

24. *Annals*, 37; Fitzmaurice & Little, *Materials*, 141; Moorman, *History*, 351 n.6.

25. *Reg. de Kilmainham*, xii.

26. 'Annals of Nenagh', 161; *CPP*, i. 565, 511; Gwynn & Hadcock, *Med. Religious Houses*, 214.

27. Platt, *King Death*, 7.

28. *Cal. Inq. Misc.* iii (1348-77), No. 636.

29. Ravi, *A Med. Parish*, 99; Hatcher, *Plague*, 26.

30. 'Charters of Duiske'; *Chart. St Mary's*, i. 378-82; *Reg. Hospital of St John the Baptist*, xx-xxi.

31. Martin & de Meijer, 'Irish material', 81; Stalley, *Cistercian Monasteries*, 21-7; Leask, *Irish Churches*, iii. 6-7; Gwynn & Hadcock, *Med. Religious*

Houses, 9, 118-9, 265; Barry, *Archaeology*, 147, 153, 166; Lydon, *Lordship*, 109.

32. *Chronicon* in Horrox, 78-9.

33. Horrox, 57.

34. *CPP*, i. 19, 119, 462, 467, *passim*; Gwynn, 'The medieval university of St Patrick's Dublin', 199ff, and 'Anglo-Irish church life', 30.

35. Gwynn, 'Richard FitzRalph', 399; *CPP*, i. 467.

36. *CPP*, i. 207, 193, 444, 462, 461, 445.

37. *CPP*, i. 469; *CPL*, iii. 432; *CPL*, iv. 12; Connolly, 'Irish material in the class of Ancient Petitions', 32; Ministers' Accounts SC8/93/4601; *Reg. Swayne*, 1-2; Walsh, *FitzRalph*, 192.

38. Hennessy, 'Parochial organisation', 68-70; *De Annatis Hiberniae*, 177, *passim*.

39. *CPL*, iii. 283.

40. Moorman, *History*, 344, 351-2; *CPP*, i. 461, 445.

41. Martin & de Meijer, 'Irish material', 64; *Cal. Pat. Rolls 1348-50*, 114.

42. See, for example, Wales in Cowley, *The Monastic Order in South Wales*, 268-9.

43. *CPL*, iii. 432; 'Cal. Liber Ruber', No. 21; Walsh, *FitzRalph*, 299; *CPP*, i. 444.

44. *CPL*, vi. 441, vii. 212; *De Annatis Hiberniae*, Ulster, 123, 299.

45. *Cal. Pat. Rolls 1354-8*, 91; Fitzmaurice & Little, *Materials*, 160; Connolly, 'Irish material in the class of Ancient Petitions', 35.

46. *Chart. of Llanthony Prima and Secunda*, ii. 311.

47. *Cal. Fine Rolls*, vii. 109; 'Cal. of liber albus' in 'Cal. of liber niger and liber albus', Nos. 6, 61; 'Cal. of register of Archbishop Fleming', No. 133; *Cal. Close Rolls 1360-64*, 102.

48. *Statute Rolls, Ireland: Henry VI*, 96-8; *CPL*, vi. 280.

49. *CPP*, i. 461-2; *CPL*, v. 598, x. 463; Gwynn & Hadcock, 195.

50. *CPL*, v. 74; *CPL*, vii. 181; *CPL*, ix. 470.

51. Fitzmaurice & Little, *Materials*, 197ff.

52. *CPL*, vii. 180-181, 128, 276; vi. 157; iv. 448; viii. 22; *CPL*, vi. 411; vii. 261; vi. 66, 316, 314; iv. 448; vi. 218; *CPP*, i. 468, 444, 330; *Liber Primus Kilkenniensis*, 18.

53. *Chart. of Llanthony Prima and Secunda*, ii. 289ff.

54. Horrox, 68.

55. *CPP*, i. 76; Gwynn, 'Richard FitzRalph', vi. 86, 87; Walsh, *FitzRalph*, 298, 314-5, 324; *Reg. Swayne*, 8, 17.

56. *CPP*, i. 76, 206, 444, 461, 466.

57. Gwynn, 'Richard FitzRalph', vi. 84 and 85ff; cf., Gwynn, 'Archbishop FitzRalph and

George of Hungary', 562-3; Walsh, *FitzRalph*, 329-331, 337.

58. *Reg. Swayne*, 82, 150-51; TCD MS E.3.16, cited Watt, *Church in Med. Ireland*, 182.

59. Heuser, *Kildare-Gedichte*, 155-6; Seymour, *Anglo-Irish Literature*, 111, 113.

60. Fitzmaurice & Little, *Materials*, 158-9, 225; Moorman, *History*, 341ff.

61. Horrox, 75.

62. Walsh, 'The clerical estate', 373 and *FitzRalph*, 213-4, 304, 323, 334; cited Moorman, *History*, 347.

63. Barry, *Archaeology*, 147, 166, 151, 195; Rae, 'Architecture and sculpture', 763-7.

64. Empey, 'The sacred and the secular', 151.

65. Rae, 'Architecture and sculpture', 751-2.

66. Watt, *Church in Med. Ireland*, 193; Gwynn & Hadcock, *Med. Religious Houses*, 7, 9, 263-6; De Breffny & Mott, *Churches and Abbeys*, 99; Fitzmaurice & Little, 'Materials', xxx-xxxii, 169, 186-7, 194-7, 203; Watt, *Church in Med. Ireland*, 199ff.; Moorman, *History*, 417-28, 560ff.

67. *Statutes Ireland, John-Henry V*, 445.

68. Platt, *Abbeys and Priories of Med. England*, 180.

69. Gwynn & Hadcock, *Med. Religious Houses*, 236; Martin, 'Irish Augustinian reform', 230-264.

70. Rae, 'Architecture and sculpture', 776.

71. *Statutes Ireland, John-Henry V*, 434.

72. Barry, *Archaeology*, 194-5.

CHAPTER 7: THE EFFECTS ON THE GOVERNANCE OF IRELAND

1. Richardson & Sayles, *Administration of Ireland*, 88; Cosgrove, 'Chief Governors of Ireland', 473; Burke, *History of the Lord Chancellors*, 13; Wood, 'The office of Chief Governor of Ireland'; Gwynn, 'The Black Death', 38-41.

2. Richardson & Sayles, *Administration of Ireland*, 95-6, 102, 106-112; 28; Brand, 'Chancellors and Keepers of the Great Seal', 500-508.

3. Berry, 'Catalogue of Mayors'; Hill, 'Mayors and Lord Mayors of Dublin', 549-50.

4. Berry, 'Sheriffs of the County Cork', Part i. 45; Butler, 'The sheriffs of the liberty of Tipperary,' 120-23 and 'The seneschals of the liberty of Tipperary', 297; d'Alton, *History of County Dublin*, 47.

5. *AU*, ii. 491; *AC*, 303; *Ann. Clon.*, 297; *A. L. C.*, ii. 5; *Frag. Annals*, 153.

6. *ALC*, ii. 23; *Ann. Clon.*, 301; *AU*, ii. 513; *AC*, 32; *CPP*, i. 461-2.

7. Excerpts from the Plea Rolls, MS 193; *Cal. Anc. Rec.*, i. 139.

8. Richardson & Sayles, *Irish Parliament*, 239; Cosgrove, 'Parliaments in Ireland', 593-608.

9. Connolly, 'Pleas held before the Chief Governors', 120-126.

10. *Cal. Close Rolls*, 292.

11. Otway-Ruthven, *Med. Ireland*, 267ff, 280ff.

12. These areas included most of Ulster, Clare, western Leix and Offaly, Cavan, Leitrim and Roscommon, the Wicklow mountains and adjoining valleys. Cf. Nicholls, *Gaelic and Gaelicised Ireland*, 12ff; Orpen, *Ireland*, iv. 261-2; Curtis, *Med. Ireland*, 149ff.; Empey, 'Conquest and settlement', 5-31.

13. Orme, *Ireland*, 112.

14. Curtis, 'Unpublished letters', 296; Lydon, *Lordship*, 207.

15. *Rot. et Pat. Claus. Hib.Cal*, 56: Nos. 30, 31, 62; 62: Nos. 98, 108, 111; 63: Nos. 127, 116, 117.

16. *Cal. Pat. Rolls 1354-8*, 563-4; *Cal. Close Rolls 1369-74*, 420; cf. Clarke, M.V., 'William of Windsor in Ireland', 191; Lydon, *Lordship*, 229-230.

17. McEneaney, 'Mayors and merchants', 162ff; Mac Niocaill, 'Socio-economic problems', 10-15.

18. Keen, *English Society*, 93-4.

19. Otway-Ruthven, *Med. Ireland*, 251, also 106; Duffy, S., *Ireland in the Middle Ages*, 143-4.

20. Simms, K., 'The Norman invasion', 83.

21. *Parliaments and Councils*, i.20; Otway-Ruthven, 'The partition of the deVerdun lands', 417; *Cal. Dowdall Deeds*, x.

22. *Cal. Fine Rolls 1356-68*, 308; *Irish Hist. Doc.*, 60-61; Cosgrove, *Late Med. Ireland*, 19ff; Lydon, *Lordship*, 201-6.

23. *Med. Ireland*, 271; Lydon, 'A land of war', 241-3.

24. Clyn, *Annals*, 30.

25. Spenser, *A View of the Present State of Ireland*, 18.

26. *Statutes, John–Henry V*, 332-63; *Cal. Close Rolls 1341-2*, 509-16.

27. Gwynn, 'The Black Death', 32; *Parliaments and Councils*, i.20; *Chronicon*, Horrox, 82.

28. Otway-Ruthven, *Med. Ireland*, 267; Frame, *English Lordship in Ireland*, 132-9.

29. Irwin, *The Middle East*, 137; Watts, *Epidemics*, 27-8; Fossier, 'The great trial', 273.

30. Frame, R., 'Two kings in Leinster', 165 and *passim*; cf. Lydon, 'Medieval Wicklow: a land of war', 175-7.

31. Nicholls, *Gaelic and Gaelicised Ireland*, 160-1, 133-5; Lydon, 'A land of war', 240-74; Simms, K., 'The Norman invasion', 82ff.

32. Cf. Empey, 'The Anglo-Norman community in Tipperary and Kilkenny', 457-64.

33. Cf. Nicholls, 'Development of lordship', 157-96; O'Brien, 'Politics, economy and society', 114-9.

34. Nicholls, 'Development of lordship', 194-5.

35. Genicot, 'Crisis: from the Middle Ages to modern times', 700.

36. Frame, 'Two kings in Leinster', 175.

37. *Parliaments and Councils*, i. 19-22.

38. *Cal. Fine Rolls 1356-68*, 308.

39. *Roll of the Proceedings of the King's Council,* 264.

40. Richardson & Sayles, 'Irish revenue', 90; Lydon, 'Edward II and the revenues of Ireland', 41.

41. Richardson & Sayles, 'Irish revenue', 93-7, 100; Otway-Ruthven, 'The medieval county of Kildare', 199.

42. Connolly, P., 'The financing of English expeditions', 105.

43. Frame, 'Two kings in Leinster', 174-5, and 'Military service in the lordship of Ireland', 120; cf. *Colonial Ireland*, 111-135.

AFTERMATH

1. Clyn, *Annals,* trans. Horrox, 83.

2. *AFM*, iv. 962, 1045; v., 1439; *Cal. Ann. Rec.*, i.139; ii. 100-104, 419-420, 424; iii.118-9, 536-8; ALC, ii. 229; SPD, 11. iii. 38-9; Crawford, 'William Wilde's tables of Irish famines', 20ff; Shrewsbury, *History*, 433ff. See Kelly, *The Great Dying*, 188-206.

3. McNeill, *Plagues and Peoples*, 159, 326; Bewley, 'An account of the Biological Club'.

4. Zinsser, H., *Rats*, 69.

5. McNeill, *Plagues*, 170.

6. Zinsser, *Rats*, 43.

7. Livi-Bacci, *A Concise History*, 54.

8. Biraben, *La peste*, i. 17-20.

9. www.cdc.gov/plague (Division of Vector-Borne Infectious Diseases, Centers for Disease Control and Prevention, USA).

10. Biraben, *Les hommes*, ii. 185.

Select Bibliography

PRO, LONDON
Chancery Miscellanea: C 47/10/18, 19, 22, 23.
Ministers' Accounts: SC 6/1237/ 3, 8-11, 14, 23, 24, 25, 29, 30; 1238/10-15, 21-4, 32; 1239/14, 16, 18, 20.

GENEALOGICAL OFFICE, DUBLIN
Excerpts from the Plea Rolls, MS 192-194.

TRINITY COLLEGE, DUBLIN
MS H. 2.15 (Seanchas Mór)

PRO, DUBLIN
Memoranda Rolls, Vol. 26.

PRIMARY PRINTED SOURCES

Annals of Clonmacnoise, ed. D. Murphy (Dublin, 1896).
Annals of Connacht AD 1224-1544, ed. A.M. Freeman (Dublin, 1944).
Annals of Innisfallen, ed. S. Mac Airt (Dublin, 1951).
Annals of Ireland (Annales Hiberniae) by Friar John Clyn and Thady Dowling, Chancellor of Leighlin, ed. R. Butler (Dublin, 1849).
Annals of the Kingdom of Ireland by the Four Masters, from the Earliest Period to the Year 1616, ed. J.G. Donovan, 7 vols. (Dublin, 1848-51).
Annals of Loch Cé: A Chronicle of Irish Affairs, 1014-1590, ed. W.H. Hennessy, 2 vols. (London, 1871).
Annals of St Mary's Abbey, Dublin, Chartularies of St Mary's Abbey, Dublin, Vol. 2 (London 1884).
Annals of Ulster, 431-1541, ed. W.M. Hennessy and B. MacCarthy, 4 vols. (Dublin, 1887-1901).
Miscellaneous Irish Annals, AD 1114-1437. Ed. S.Ó Hinnse (Dublin, 1949).
Annals of Nenagh, ed. D.F. Gleeson, Anal. Hib., 12 (1943), 155-164.
Annals of Christ Church Dublin, ed. A.Gwynn, Anal. Hib., 16 (1949), 324-9.
Account Roll of the Priory of the Holy Trinity, Dublin, 1337-1346, ed. J. Mills (Dublin, 1891).

De Annatis Hiberniae: A Calendar of the First-fruits' Fees levied on Papal Appointments to Benefices in Ireland, AD 1400-1535, i. Ulster, ed. M.A. Costello and A. Coleman (2nd ed. Maynooth, 1912).
Black Book of Christ Church, ed. A. Gwynn, Anal. Hib., 16 (1946).
Black Book of Limerick, ed. J. McCaffrey (Dublin, 1907).
'Brussels MS 3947: Donatus Moneyus, De Provincia Hiberniae S. Francisci', ed. B. Jennings, Anal. Hib., 6 (Nov. 1934), 12-138.
'Brussels MS 3410 – a chronological list of the foundations of the Irish Franciscan province', ed. J.Moloney, Anal. Hib., 6 (Nov. 1934), 192-202.
Calendar of the Ancient Records of Dublin, ed. J.T. Gilbert, 19 vols. (Dublin, 1889-1944).
Calendar of Archbishop Alen's Register, c.1172-1534, ed. C. McNeill (Dublin, 1950).
Calendar of the Carew MSS, ed. J. Brewer, and W. Bullen, 6 vols. (London 1867-73).
Calendar of Close Rolls, 1272-1500, 45 vols., ed. Tresham (London, 1892-1963).
Calendar of Documents Relating to Ireland, 1171-1307, ed. H.S. Sweetman, 5 vols. (London, 1875-86).
Cal. Dowdall Deeds, ed. McNeill and J. Otway-Ruthven (Dublin 1960).
Calendar of Entries in the Papal Registers Relating to Great Britain and Ireland, Papal Letters, Vols.1-X1V (1198-1492), ed. Bliss, Johnson, Twemlow (London, 1897-1960).
Calendar of Entries in the Papal Registers relating to Great Britain and Ireland. Petitions to the Pope, 1, 1342-1491, ed. Bliss (London, 1896).
Calendar of Inquisitions Post Mortem (London, 1904-74).
Calendar of the Justiciary Rolls of Ireland 1295-1314, ed. Mills and Griffith, 3 vols. (Dublin, 1905-14).
Calendar of Inquisitions Miscellaneous (London, 1916)
'Calendar of the Liber Niger and Liber Albus of Christ Church, Dublin', ed. H. J. Lawlor,

PRIA., 27C (1908-9), 1-93.

'Calendar of the Liber Ruber of the Diocese of Ossory', ed. H.J. Lawlor, *PRIA*, 27C (1908), 159-208.

Calendar of Ormond Deeds, 1172-1603, 6 vols., ed. E. Curtis (Dublin, 1932-43).

Calendar of Patent Rolls (London, 1891-1971).

'Calendar of the Register of Archbishop Fleming', ed. H.J. Lawlor, *PRIA*, 30C (1912), 94-190.

Calendar of State Papers and Letters Domestic Series, 2 vols., ed. Brewer, J.S. (London, 1830-34).

Cambrensis, G., *Topography of Ireland*, ed. J.J. O'Meara (Dundalk, 1951).

Chartularies of Llanthony Prima and Secunda, ed. E. St J. Brooks (Dublin, 1953).

'Charters of the Cistercian Abbey of Duiske in the County of Kilkenny', ed. C.M.Butler and J.H. Bernard, *PRIA*, 35C (1918-20), 1-188.

Chartularies of St Mary's Abbey Dublin with the Register of its House at Dunbrody and Annals of Ireland, 1162-1370, ed. J.T. Gilbert, 2 vols. (London, 1884-6, 1965).

'Chronicle of Pembridge', *Anal. Hib.,* 16 (March 1946).

Facsimiles of National Mss of Ireland, ed. J. Gilbert (London, 1874-84).

Fasti of St Patrick's Cathedral, Dublin, ed. H.J. Lawlor (Dublin, 1930).

Fragmentary Annals from the West of Ireland, ed. E.G. Gwynn, *PRIA*, 37C (1921-4), 149-157.

Harris, 'Collectanea de rebus Hibernicis', ed. C. McNeill, C., *Anal. Hib.*,V1 (Nov. 1934), 284-450.

Historic and Municipal Documents of Ireland, 1172-1320, ed. J.T. Gilbert (London, 1870).

Irish Historical Documents 1172-1922, ed. E. Curtis and R.B. McDowell (London, 1943).

Liber Primus Kilkenniensis, ed. C. McNeill (Dublin 1931); trans. A.J. Otway-Ruthven (Kilkenny, 1961).

'Miscellanea of the Chancery', ed. J. Hogan, *Anal. Hib.*, 1 (March 1930), 179-218.

Parliaments and Councils of Medieval Ireland, ed. H.G. Richardson and G.O Sayles (Dublin, 1947).

Red Book of the Earls of Kildare, ed. G. MacNiocaill (Dublin, 1964).

Red Book of Ormond, ed. N.B.White (Dublin, 1932).

Registrum de Kilmainham, 1326-1350, ed. C. McNeill (Dublin, 1932).

Register of the Hospital of St John the Baptist, ed. E. St John Brooks (Dublin, 1936).

Register of John Swayne, Archbishop of Dublin and Primate of Ireland, ed. D.A. Chart (Belfast, 1935).

Roll of the Proceedings of the King's Council in Ireland, ed. J. Graves (London, 1877).

Rotulorum Patentium et Clausorum Cancellariae Hiberniae Calendarium, ed. E. Tresham (Dublin, 1828).

'Some unpublished texts from the Black Book of Christ Church, Dublin', ed. A. Gwynn, *Anal. Hib.*, 16 (1946), 281-337.

Statutes and Ordinances and Acts of the Parliament of Ireland: King John to Henry V, ed. H. F. Berry (Dublin, 1907).

Statute Rolls, Ireland: Henry VI, ed. H.F. Berry (Dublin, 1910).

SECONDARY SOURCES

GENERAL

Bailey, M., '*Per impetum maris*: natural disaster and economic decline in eastern England, 1275-1350' in Campbell, B. (ed.), *Before the Black Death: Studies in the 'Crisis' of the Early Fourteenth Century* (Manchester & N.Y., 1991*)*, 184-208.

Ballard, A., 'The Black Death' in Vinogradoff, P. (ed.), *Oxford Studies in Social and Legal History*, Vol.V (Oxford, 1916), 181-216.

Barkai, R., 'Jewish treatises on the Black Death (1350-1500): a preliminary study', in French, R. et al., *Medicine from the Black Death to the French Disease* (N.Y., 1998), 6-25.

Barnes, J., *The History of that Most Victorious Monarch, Edward III* (Cambridge, 1688).

Bean, J.M.W., 'Plague, population and economic decline in England in the Later Middle Ages', *Economic History Review*, 2nd ser., 15 (1962-3), 423-37.

Beresford, M.W., *New Towns of the Middle Ages* (London, 1967).

—, and Hurst, J.G., (eds.), *Deserted Medieval Villages* (London, 1971).

Bernard, J., *Le sang et l'histoire* (Paris, 1983).

Biraben, J.-N., *Les hommes et la peste en France et dans les pays européens et mediterranéens*, 2 vols. (Paris, 1975), i. *La peste dans l'histoire*; ii. *Les hommes face à la peste*.

Bowsky, William, (ed.), *The Black Death: A Turning Point in History?* (New York, 1978).

Bridbury, A.R., 'The Black Death', *Economic History Review*, 2nd ser., 26 (1973), 557-92.

Campbell, A.M., *The Black Death and Men of Learning* (New York, 1931)

Campbell, Bruce, 'Population pressure, inheritance and the land market in a fourteenth-century peasant community' in R.M.Smith (ed.), *Land, Kinship and Life-Cycle*, (Cambridge, 1984), 87-134.

Carmichael, A., *Plague and the Poor in Renaissance Florence* (Cambridge, 1986).

Castiglioni, A., *A History of Medicine*, trans and ed. E.B. Krumbhaar (New York, 1958).

Cohn, S.K., *The Black Death Transformed: Disease and Culture in Early Renaissance Europe* (London, 2002).

Cowley, F. G. *The Monastic Order in South Wales, 1099-1349* (Cardiff, 1977).

Crawford, R., *Plague and Pestilence in Literature and Art* (Oxford, 1914).

Deaux, George, *The Black Death, 1347* (London, 1969).

Dols, M.W., *The Black Death in the Middle East* (Princeton, 1977).

—, 'Al-Manbiji's "Report of the Plague": a treatise on the plague of 764-65/1362-64 in the Middle East', in Williman (ed.), *The Black Death: The Impact of the Fourteenth-Century Plague* (Binghamton, N.Y., 1982), 64-72

Du Boulay, F.R.H., *An Age of Ambition: English Society in the Late Middle Ages* (London, 1970).

Duby, G., *Rural Economy and Country Life in the Medieval West*, tr. C. Postan (London, 1968).

—, *The Age of Cathedrals* (Chicago, 1980).

Duffy, E., *The Stripping of the Altars: Traditional Religion in England 1400-1580* (New Haven, 1982).

Fossier, R. 'The great trial' in *The Cambridge Illustrated History of the Middle Ages*, vol.iii: 1250-1520, ed. Fossier (Cambridge, 1987).

French, R., *Practical Medicine from Salerno to the Black Death* (Cambridge, 1994).

Froissart's Chronicles, ed. J. Jolliffe , trans. Geoffrey Brereton (Harmondsworth, 1968).

Gasquet, F.A., *The Great Pestilence* (London,1893).

Genicot, L., 'Crisis: from the Middle Ages to modern times' in *The Cambridge Economic History of Europe, i. The Agrarian Life of the Middle Ages* (Cambridge, 1966), 660-741.

Gottfried, R.S., *The Black Death: Natural and Human Disaster in Medieval Europe* (N.Y. & London, 1983).

—, 'The Black Death' in Strayer *et al.*, *Dictionary of the Middle Ages* (N.Y., 1983), Vol.ii, 257-67.

Gransden, A., *Historical Writing in England, ii. c.1307-early 16th century* (London, 1982).

Harvey, B.F., 'Introduction: the "Crisis" of the Early Fourteenth Century' in Campbell (ed.), *Before the Black Death: Studies in the 'Crisis' of the Early Fourteenth Century* (Manchester & N.Y., 1991), 1-24.

Hatcher, J., *Plague, Population and the English Economy 1348-1530* (London 1977), reprinted in Anderson (ed.), *British Population History from the Black Death to the Present Day* (Cambridge, 1996), 15-93.

'Mortality in the fifteenth century: some new evidence', in *Economic History Review*, 2nd Ser. (1986), 19-38.

Hecker, J.F.C., *The Black Death, Epidemics of the Middle Ages*, trans. and ed. B.G. Babington (1859, reprinted Lawrence, Kansas, 1972).

Heer, F., *The Medieval World* (London, 1962).

Herlihy, D., *The Black Death and the Transformation of the West*, ed. S.K. Cohn, Jr. (Cambridge, Mass., 1997).

Hirst, L., *The Conquest of Plague: A Study of the Evolution of Epidemiology* (Oxford, 1953).

Hollingsworth, T.H., *Historical Demography* (London, 1969).

— and Hollingsworth, M.F., 'Plague mortality rates by age and sex in the Parish of St Botolph's without Bishopsgate, London 1603', *Population Studies*, 25 (1971).

Holmes, George (ed.), *The Oxford Illustrated History of Medieval Europe* (Oxford, 1988).

—, *The Estates of the Higher Nobility in Fourteenth Century England* (Cambridge, 1957).

Horrox, Rosemary (ed. and trans.), *The Black Death* (Manchester, 1994).

Houston, R.A., *The population history of Britain and Ireland 1500-1750* (1992), reprinted in Anderson (ed.), *British Population History from the Black Death to the Present Day* (Cambridge, 1996), 99-190.

Huizinga, J., *The Waning of the Middle Ages* (London: Peregrine Books, 1965).

Ibeji, M., 'The Black Death: the blame', www.bbc.co.uk/history/blackdeath

Irwin, R., *The Middle East in the Middle Ages: The Early Mamluk Sultanate 1250-1382* (London, 1986).

Jordan, W.C., *The Great Famine: Northern Europe in the Early Fourteenth Century* (Princeton, 1996).

Keen, M., *English Society in the Late Middle Ages: 1348-1500* (Harmondsworth, 1990).

Knowles, D., *Religious Orders in England, ii. The End of the Middle Ages* (Cambridge, 1955).

Kohn, G.C., *Encyclopedia of Plague and Pestilence* (Ware, 1998).

Kosminsky, E., *Studies in the Agrarian History of England in the Thirteenth Century* (Oxford, 1927).

Lamb, H.H., *Climate, History and the Modern World* (London, 1982).

Leff, G., *Medieval Thought: St Augustine to Ockham* (London, 1958).

Lerner, R.E., 'The Black Death and western European eschatological mentalities' in Williman (ed.), *The Black Death* (Binghamton, N.Y., 1982), 77-105.

Levett, A.E., 'The Black Death on the estates of the See of Winchester' in P. Vinogradoff (ed.), *Oxford Studies in Social and Legal History*, V (Oxford, 1916), 13-180.

Livi-Bacci, M., *A Concise History of World Population* (2nd ed., Oxford, 1997).

Lunn, P., 'Nutrition, Immunity and Infection' in Schofield, R., Reher, D., Bideau, A., (ed.), *The Decline of Mortality in Europe* (Oxford 1991), 131-45.

Mate, Mavis, 'The agrarian economy of south-east England before the Black Death: depressed or buoyant?' in Campbell, B. (ed.), *Before the Black Death: Studies in the 'Crisis' of the Early Fourteenth Century* (Manchester & N.Y., 1991), 79-109.

McNeill, W., *Plagues and Peoples* (Oxford, 1977).

Meiss, M., *Painting in Florence and Siena after the Black Death* (New York, 1964).

Miller, E. and Hatcher, J., *Medieval England: Rural Society and Economic Change 1086-1348* (London, 1978).

Moorman, J.R., *A History of the Franciscan Order from its Origin to 1517* (Oxford, 1968).

Morris, C., 'The plague in Britain', *The Historical Journal*, 14, no. 1 (1971), 205-224.

Nicholas, D., *Medieval Flanders* (London & N.Y., 1992).

Nohl, J., *The Black Death, A Chronicle of the Plague Compiled from Contemporary Sources (London, 1961).*

Nutton, V., 'The seeds of disease: an explanation of contagion and infection from the Greeks to the Renaissance', *Medical History* 27 (1983), 1-34.

Ottaway, Patrick, *Archaeology in British Towns: From the Emperor Claudius to the Black Death* (London & N.Y., 1992).

Paterson, R., '*Yersinia* seeks pardon for the Black Death', *Lancet Infectious Diseases*,Vol.2. 6 (2002), 323.

Perremond, A. 'The attenuation of mortality crises and the decline of mortality' in Schofield, R., Reher, D. and Bideau, A., *The Decline of Mortality in Europe* (Oxford, 1991), 18-37.

Platt, C., *The Abbeys and Priories of Medieval England* (London, 1984).

—, *King Death: The Black Death and its Aftermath in Late Medieval England* (London, 1996).

Polzer, J., 'Aspects of the fourteenth-century iconography of death and the plague' in Williman (ed.), *The Black Death: The Impact of the Fourteenth-Century Plague* (Binghamton, NY., 1982), 107-129.

Postan, M.M., 'Some economic evidence of declining population in the later Middle Ages', *Economic History Review*, 2nd Ser., 11 (1950), 221-46.

—, *The Medieval Economy and Society: An Economic History of Britain 1100-1500* (London, 1972).

—, 'Medieval agrarian society in its prime: England' in *The Cambridge Economic History of Europe*, i. *The Agrarian Life of the Middle Ages*, 2nd ed., (Cambridge, 1966), 549-632.

Potts, W.T.W., 'History and blood groups in the British Isles', in *Medieval Settlement*, ed. P.H.Sawyer (London, 1976), 236-53.

Pounds, N.J.G., *An Historical Geography of Europe, 450 BC-AD 1330* (Cambridge, 1973).

Raoult, D., *et al.*, 'Suicide PCR/*Yersinia pestis* as cause of the Black Death', *Proceedings National Academy of Science, USA*, 97.23 (7 Nov. 2000), 12800-12803.

Razi, Z., *Life, Marriage and Death in a Medieval Parish: Economy, Society and Demography in Halesowen 1270-1400* (Cambridge 1980).

Robo, Etienne, *Medieval Farnham: Everyday Life in an Episcopal Manor* (Farnborough, 1980).

Rorig, F., *The Medieval Town* (London, 1967).

Rotberg, R.I. and Rabb, T.K., *Hunger and History* (Cambridge, Mass., 1985).

Russell, J.C., 'Late ancient and medieval population', *Transactions of the American Philosophical Society*, 48, 3 (Philadelphia, 1958).

—, *British Medieval Population* (Albuquerque, 1948).

—, 'Population in Europe 500-1500', in Cipolla, C. (ed.), *Fontana Economic History of Europe: The Middle Ages* (London 1972), 25-70.

Saltmarsh, 'Plague and economic decline in England in the later Middle Ages', *Cambridge Historical Journal*, VII (1941).

Schofield, R.S., 'The geographical distribution of

wealth in England, 1334-1649', *Economic History Review*, 2nd ser., 18 (Dec. 1965), 483-510.

—, Reher, D. and Bideau, A., *The Decline of Mortality in Europe* (Oxford, 1991).

Scott, S. and Duncan, C.J., *Biology of Plagues: Evidence from Historical Populations* (Cambridge, 2001).

Shrewsbury, J.F.D., *A History of Bubonic Plague in the British Isles* (Cambridge, 1970).

Smith, R. M., 'Demographic developments in rural England, 1300-1348: a survey' in Campbell, B. (ed.), *Before the Black Death: Studies in the crisis of the early fourteenth century* (Manchester & N.Y., 1991), 25-77.

Simpson, W.J., *A Treatise on Plague* (Cambridge, 1905).

Swanson, R.N., *Church and Society in Late Medieval England* (Oxford, 1989).

Titow, J.Z., *English Rural Society, 1200-1350* (London, 1969).

Trevalyan, G.H., *English Social History* (London, 1942).

Twigg, *The Black Death: A Biographical Reappraisal* (London, 1984).

Van Bath, B.H. Slicher, *Agrarian History of Western Europe, AD 500-1850*, tr. O. Ordish (London, 1965).

Van Werveke, H., 'De Zwarte Dood in de Zuidelijke Nederlanden (1349-1351)', *Mededelingen van de koninklijke Vlaams academie voor wetenschappen, letteren en schone kunsten van België*, xii. 3 (Brussels, 1951).

Walter, J. and Schofield, R., 'Famine, Disease and Crisis: Mortality in Early Modern Society' in Walter and Schofield (eds.), *Disease and the Social Order in Early Modern Society* (Cambridge, 1989), 1-73.

Watts, S., *Epidemics and History: Disease, Power and Imperialism* (New Haven, 1999).

Wenzel, S., 'Pestilence and Middle English literature: Friar John Grimestone's poems on death' in Williman (ed.), *The Black Death: The Impact of the Fourteenth-Century Plague* (Binghamton, NY, 1982), 131-159.

Ziegler, P., *The Black Death* (London, 1969).

Zinsser, H., *Rats, Lice and History* (Boston, 1965).

IRELAND

Aalen, F.H.A.,'The origin of enclosures in eastern Ireland', in N. Stephens and R.E. Glasscock (eds.), *Irish Geographical Studies in honour of E. Estyn Evans* (Belfast, 1970).

d'Alton, J., *History of Drogheda* (Dublin, 1844).

Bardon, J., *A History of Ulster* (Belfast, 1992).

Barry, T.B., *The Archaeology of Medieval Ireland* (London, 1987).

—, ' "The people of the country...dwell scattered": the pattern of rural settlement in Ireland in the later Middle Ages' in *Settlement and Society in Medieval Ireland: Studies Presented to F. X. Martin OSA*, ed. J. Bradley (Kilkenny, 1988), 345-360.

—, 'Late medieval Ireland: the debate on social and economic transformation, 1350-1550' in B.J. Graham and L.J. Proudfoot (eds.), *An Historical Geography of Ireland* (London, 1993), 99-122.

—, 'The last frontier: defence and settlement in late medieval Ireland' in Barry, Frame and Simms (eds.), *Colony and Frontier in Medieval Ireland: Essays Presented to J.F.Lydon* (London, 1995), 217-228.

Berry, H.F., 'Catalogue of Mayors, provosts and bailiffs of Dublin city, AD 1229-1447', *PRIA*, 28C (1910), 47-61.

—, 'Sheriffs of the County Cork, Henry III to 1660', *JRSAI, 25* (1905), 39-48.

Bewley, G., 'An account of the Biological Club', *Irish Journal of Medical Science*, 6th Ser. (1960).

Bliss, A.'Language and Literature' in Lydon (ed.), *The English in Medieval Ireland* (Dublin, 1984), 27-45.

—, and Long, J.,'Literature in Norman French and English to 1534' in *NHI*, ii. 708-36.

Bradley, John,'The medieval towns of Tipperary' in Nolan, W. and McGrath, T.G. (eds.), *Tipperary: History and Society* (Dublin, 1985), 34 -59.

—, 'The medieval tombs of St Canice's Cathedral' in Barry, Bradley and Empey (eds.), *A Worthy Foundation: The Cathedral Church of St Canice, Kilkenny* (Mountrath, 1985), 49-103.

Briand, P., 'The formation of a parish: the case of Beaulieu, County Louth', in Bradley (ed.), *Settlement and Society in Medieval Ireland* (Kilkenny, 1988), 261-275.

Burke, C., *The History of the Lord Chancellors of Ireland, 1186-1874* (Dublin, 1879)

Burke, O., *History of the Catholic Archbishops of Tuam* (Dublin, 1882).

Butler, T.,'The sheriffs of the liberty of Tipperary,' *The Irish Genealogist*, 3, No. 4 (July 1959).

—,'The seneschals of the liberty of Tipperary', *The Irish Genealogist*, 2, No.10 (July 1953).

Byrne, F.J., 'Bishops 111-1534' in Moody, Martin, Byrne (eds.), *A New History of Ireland* (Oxford, 1984), ix. 264-332.

Carney, James, *The Irish Bardic Poet* (Dublin, 1967).

—, 'Literature in Irish, 1169-1534' in *NHI*, ii. 688-707.

Carrigan, *History and Antiquities of the Diocese of Ossory* (Dublin, 1905).

Clarke, M.V., 'William of Windsor in Ireland, 1369-76', *Fourteenth-Century Studies* (Oxford, 1937).

Colfer, W., 'Anglo-Norman settlement in Co. Wexford' in Whelan (ed.), *Wexford: History and Society* (Dublin, 1987), 65-101.

Colledge, Edmund, (ed.), *The Latin Poems of Richard Ledrede, OFM, Bishop of Ossory, 1317-1360* (Toronto, 1974).

Connolly, P., 'The financing of English expeditions to Ireland, 1361-1376' in J. Lydon (ed.), *England and Ireland in the Later Middle Ages* (Dublin, 1981), 104-121.

—, 'Pleas held before the Chief Governors of Ireland 1308-76', *Irish Jurist,* xviii (1983), 101-131.

—, 'List of Irish Material in the Class of Chancery Files (Recorda) (C260) in the Public Record Office, London', *Anal. Hib.* 31 (1984), 1-18.

—, 'Irish material in the class of Ancient Petitions', *Irish Jurist,* 18 (1983), 3-106

Cosgrove, Art, *Late Medieval Ireland, 1370-1541* (Dublin, 1981).

—, (ed.), *A New History of Ireland. ii. Medieval Ireland 1169-1534* (Oxford, 1987).

—, 'The emergence of the Pale, 1399-1447' in *NHI*, ii. 533-556.

—, 'Ireland beyond the Pale 1399-1460' in *NHI*, ii. 569-590.

—, 'Parliaments in Ireland 1264-1800' in Moody, Martin, Byrne (eds.), *A New History of Ireland,* ix (Oxford, 1984), 593-608.

—, 'Chief Governors of Ireland 1172-1534' in Moody, Martin, Byrne (eds.), *A New History of Ireland*, ix (Oxford, 1984), 469-485.

Crawford, E. M., 'William Wilde's Tables of Irish Famines 900-1850' in Crawford (ed.), *Famine: The Irish Experience 900-1900* (Edinburgh, 1989), 1-30.

Cullen, *Life in Ireland* (London and N.Y., 1968).

Curtis, Edmund, *A History of Medieval Ireland* (2nd ed. London, 1938).

—, 'Unpublished Letters from Richard II in Ireland, 1394-5', *PRIA*, 37 C (1921-4).

—, 'Rental of the manor of Lisronagh, 1333, and notes on 'Betagh' tenure in medieval Ireland', *PRIA*, 43C (1935-7), 41-76.

—, *Richard II in Ireland* (Oxford, 1927).

De Breffny, B. and Mott, G. *The Churches and Abbeys of Ireland* (London, 1976).

Down, K., 'Colonial society and economy in the high Middle Ages' in *NHI*, ii. 439-490.

Duffy, S., *Ireland in the Middle Ages* (Dublin, 1997).

Dunlevy, M. 'The medical families of medieval Ireland' in Doolin, W. and Fitzgerald, O. (eds.), *What's Past is Prologue* (Dublin, 1952), 15-22.

Edwards, K.J., Hamond, F.W., Simms, A., 'The medieval settlement of Newcastle Lyons, Co. Dublin: an interdisciplinary approach', *PRIA*, 83C (1983), 351-76.

Empey, C.A., 'The sacred and the secular: the Augustinian priory of Kells in Ossory 1193-1541', *IHS*, 24, (Nov. 1984), 131-51.

—, 'The Norman period, 1185-1500' in Nolan, W. and McGrath, T.G. (eds.), *Tipperary: History and Society* (Dublin 1985), 71-91.

—, 'Conquest and settlement: patterns of Anglo-Norman settlement in north Munster and south Leinster' in *Irish Economic and Social History Journal,* 13 (1986), 5-31.

—, 'The Anglo-Norman community in Tipperary and Kilkenny: change and continuity' in *Keimelia: Studies in Medieval Archaeology and History in Memory of Tom Delaney,* ed. G. Mac Niocaill and P. Wallace (Galway, 1988), 457-464.

Falkiner, C.L., 'The Hospital of St John of Jerusalem in Ireland', *PRIA*, 26C (1906-7), 275-317.

Fitzmaurice, E.B. and Little, A.G., (ed.). *Materials for the History of the Franciscan Province of Ireland, 1230-1450* (Manchester, 1920).

Flood, W.H. Grattan, 'The episcopal succession of Tuam, 1152-1595', *IER.*, XXVII, 5th series, No.6 (Jan. 1926), 630-637.

Frame, R., *English Lordship in Ireland, 1318-1361* (Oxford, 1982).

—, *Colonial Ireland, 1169-1369* (Dublin, 1981).

—, 'Military service in the lordship of Ireland 1290-1360: institutions and society on the Anglo-Gaelic frontier' in R. Bartlett and A. Mac Kay (ed.), *Medieval Frontier Societies* (Oxford, 1989), 101-126.

—, 'War and peace in the medieval lordship of Ireland,' in J.F. Lydon (ed.), *The English in Medieval Ireland* (Dublin, 1984).

—, 'Two kings in Leinster: The Crown and the MicMhurchadha in the fourteenth century' in Barry, Frame and Simms (ed.), *Colony and Frontier in Medieval Ireland* (London, 1995), 155-176.

Gilbert, J.T., *Viceroys of Ireland* (Dublin, 1865).

Glasscock, R. E., 'The study of deserted medieval settlements in Ireland' in Beresford, M. and Hurst, J.G.(ed.), *Deserted Medieval Villages* (Guildford and London, 1971), 297-301.

—, 'Moated sites and deserted boroughs and villages: two neglected aspects of Anglo-Norman settlement in Ireland' in Stephens, N. and Glasscock, R.E., (eds.), *Irish Geographical Studies in Honour of E. Estyn Evans* (Belfast, 1970), 162-177.

Gleeson, D. F., *A History of the Diocese of Killaloe* (Dublin, 1962).

—, 'A fourteenth-century Clare heresy trial', *IER*, 5th series, 89. No. I (Jan. 1958), 36-42.

Graham, B.J., *Medieval Irish Settlement: A Review* (Norwich, 1980).

—, *Anglo-Norman Settlement in Ireland* (Athlone, 1985).

—, 'Economy and town in Anglo-Norman Ireland' in J. Bradley (ed.), *Settlement and Society in Medieval Ireland: Studies Presented to F.X. Martin, OSA* (Kilkenny, 1988), 241-260.

—, 'The definition and classification of medieval Irish towns' in *Irish Geography* 21 (1988), 20-32.

—, 'The towns of medieval Ireland', in Butlin, R.A., (ed), *The Development of the Irish Town* (London, 1977), 28-60.

—, 'The High Middle Ages: *c.*1100 –*c.*1350' in Graham and Proudfoot (eds.), *A Historical Geography of Ireland* (London, 1993), 58-98.

Green, A.S., *The Making of Ireland and its Undoing, 1200-1600* (London 1908).

Gwynn, A., 'The Black Death in Ireland', *Studies, 24* (1935), 25-42.

—, 'Richard FitzRalph, Archbishop of Armagh', *Studies*, 22 (1933), 389-405, 591-607; 23 (1934), 395-411.

—, 'Archbishop FitzRalph and George of Hungary', *Studies*, 24 (1935), 558-72.

—, 'The medieval university of St Patrick's Dublin', *Studies*, 27 (1938), 199-212, 437-54.

—, 'Anglo-Irish church life: fourteenth and fifteenth centuries', *History of Irish Catholicism.* ii. Part iv. (Dublin and Sydney, 1968).

—, and Hadcock, R.N., *Medieval Religious Houses: Ireland* (London, 1970).

Hall, D.N., *et al.*, 'Medieval agriculture and settlement in Oughterard and Castlewarden, Co. Kildare', *Irish Geography* 18 (1958), 16-25.

Harbison, P., *Guide to the National Monuments in the Republic of Ireland* (Dublin, 1975).

Hand, G.H., *English Law in Ireland, 1290-1324* (Cambridge, 1967).

—, 'The Church in the English Lordship 1216-1307', *History of Irish Catholicism*, ii. Part iii. (Dublin and Sydney, 1968).

Hennessy, M., 'Parochial organisation in medieval Tipperary', in *Tipperary: History and Society*, ed. Nolan, W. and McGrath, T.G. (Dublin, 1985), 60-70.

Heuser, W. (ed.), *Die Kildare-Gedichte* (Darmstadt, 1965).

Hill, J., 'Mayors and Lord Mayors of Dublin 1229-1447' in Moody, Martin, Byrne (eds.), *A New History of Ireland*, ix (Oxford, 1984), 548-551.

Hourihane, C., '"Holye Crossys": A catalogue of processional, altar, pendant and crucifix figures for late medieval Ireland', *PRIA*, 100C (2000), 1-85.

Houston, R.A., *The Population History of Britain and Ireland 1500-1750* (1992), reprinted in Anderson (ed.), *British Population History from the Black Death to the Present Day* (Cambridge, 1996), 99-190.

Hunt, J., *Irish Medieval Figure Sculpture 1200-1600* (2 vols., Dublin and London, 1974).

Hurley, M.F., 'Excavations in medieval Cork: St Peter's Market', *Journal of the Cork Historical and Archaeological Society*, 91 (1986), 1-25.

Kelly, M., *The Great Dying: The Black Death in Dublin* (Stroud, 2003)

Leask, H.G., *Irish Castles and Castellated Houses* (Dundalk, 1973).

—, *Irish Churches and Monastic Buildings*, 3 vols (Dundalk, 1955-60).

Logan, P., *The Holy Wells of Ireland* (Gerrards Cross, 1980).

Lucas, A.T., 'The Plundering and Burning of Churches in Ireland, 7th-16th Centuries' in O'Riain (ed.), *North Munster Studies: Essays in Commemoration of Monsignor Moloney* (Limerick, 1967), 172-229.

Lydon, J.F., *The Lordship of Ireland in the Middle Ages* (Dublin, 1972).

—, 'The impact of the Bruce Invasion, 1315-27' in *NHI*, ii. 275-302.

—, 'A land of war' in *NHI*, ii. 240-74.

—, 'Richard II's expeditions to Ireland', *JRSAI*, 93 (1963), 135-149.

—, 'Edward II and the revenues of Ireland in 1311-12', *IHS.*, 14, No. 53 (March 1964).

—, 'The Irish Church and taxation in the fourteenth century', *IER*, C III (March 1965), 158-165.

Lyons, M.C., 'Manorial administration and the manorial economy in Ireland, *c.*1200-*c.*1377', unpublished PhD dissertation, Trinity College Dublin (1984), 2 vols.

—, 'Weather, famine, pestilence and plague in Ireland, 900-1500' in *Famine: The Irish Experience*, ed. E. M.Crawford (Edinburgh, 1989), 31-74

Mac Arthur, W.P., 'The identification of some pestilences recorded in the Irish annals', *Irish Historical Studies*, 6. No. 23 (March 1949).

McEneaney, E., 'Mayors and Merchants in Medieval Waterford 1169-1495', in Nolan and Power (ed.), *Waterford: History and Society* (Dublin, 1992), 150-172.

McGrath, F. S.J., *Education in Ancient and Medieval Ireland* (Dublin, 1979).

MacKenna, L., 'Some Irish Bardic Poems', *Studies*, 16 (1927), 24 (1935) 41 (1952).

Mac Leod, C., 'Some late medieval wood sculptures in Ireland' in *JRSAI*, 77 (1947), 53-62.

Hourihane, "'Holy Crossys"', 33.

MacNeill, M., *The Festival of Lughnasa: A Study of the Survival of the Celtic Festival of the Beginning of Harvest* (Dublin,1982).

McNeill, T.E., *Anglo-Norman Ulster: The History and Archaeology of an Irish Barony, 1177-1400* (Edinburgh, 1980).

Mac Niocaill, Gearóid, *Na Buirgéisi, xii-xv aois*, 2 vols. (Dublin, 1964).

—, 'Socio-economic problems of the late medieval town' in D. Harkness and M. O'Dowd (eds.), *The Town in Ireland* (Belfast, 1981), 7-21.

Marlborough, Henry, *The Chronicle of Ireland, Ware's Ancient Irish Histories* (Dublin. 1809).

Martin, F.X., O.S.A., 'The Irish Augustinian reform movement in the fifteenth century', in Watt, Morall, Martin (eds.), *Medieval Studies Presented to A. Gwynn* (Dublin, 1961), 230-264.

—and de Meijer, A., O.S.A., 'Irish material in the Augustinian general archives, Rome, 1354-1624', *Archivium Hibernicum*, 19 (1956), 61-134.

Maxwell, C., *Irish History from Contemporary Sources*, 1509-1610 (London, 1923).

Mills, J., 'Tenants and agriculture near Dublin in the fourteenth century', *JRSAI*, 21 (1891), 54-163.

—, 'Notices of the Manor of St Sepulchre, Dublin in the fourteenth century', *JRSAI*, 9 (1889), 37-41.

—, 'The Earl of Norfolk's estates in Ireland', *JRSAI*, 22 (1892), 53-84.

Mitchell, F., *The Irish Landscape* (London, 1977).

Morton, Grenfell, *Elizabethan Ireland* (London, 1971).

Mullally, 'Hiberno-Norman literature and its public', in Bradley (ed.), *Settlement and Society in Medieval Ireland* (Kilkenny, 1988), 327-343.

Murphy, J.E., 'The religious mind of the Irish bards' in Ó Riain (ed.), *Féilscríbhinn Eoin Mhic Néill* (Dublin,1940), 82-6.

Nicholls, K., *Gaelic and Gaelicised Ireland in the Middle Ages* (Dublin, 1972).

—, *Land, Law and Society in Sixteenth-Century Ireland*. O Donnell Lecture (Cork, 1976).

—, 'Gaelic society and economy in the high Middle Ages' in *NHI*, ii.397-438.

—, 'The development of lordship in County Cork, 1300-1600' in O'Flanagan, P. and Buttimer, C.G., *Cork: History and Society* (Dublin, 1993), 157-211.

—, 'Anglo-French Ireland and after', *Peritia*, I (1982), 370-403.

—. 'Merchant families prosper' in 'History of Cork', *Cork Examiner*, 6 March 1985.

—, 'Two islands, one street' in 'History of Cork', *Cork Examiner*, 13 March 1985.

O Brien, A.F., 'Medieval Youghal: the development of an Irish seaport trading town *c.*1200 to *c.*1500' in *Peritia* 5 (1986), 346-378.

—, 'Medieval politics, economy and society: the development of Cork and the Irish south-coast region *c.*1170 to *c.*1583' in O Flanagan, P. and Buttimer, C.G., *Cork, History and Society* (Dublin 1993), 83-154.

O'Conor, K., *The Archaeology of Medieval Rural Settlement in Ireland* (Dublin, 1998).

Ó Háinle, C., '*Congaibh Ort, A Mhacaoimh Mná* (DG 103): Content and Form' in *Eigse: A Journal of Irish Studies*, Vol. 32 (2000), 47-58.

Ó Lochlainn, C., 'Roadways in Ancient Ireland', in Ó Riain (ed.), *Féilscríbhinn Eoin Mhic Néill* (Dublin, 1940), 465-474.

Ó Rathile, T.F., *Dánta Grádha: An Anthology of Irish Love Poetry of the Sixteenth and Seventeenth Centuries* (Dublin, 1916).

O Riordáin, S. P. and Hunt, J., 'Medieval dwellings at Caherguillamore, Co. Limerick', *JRSAI*, 72 (1942), 37-63.

Orme, A.R., *The World's Landscapes: IV, Ireland* (London, 1970)

Orpen, G.H., *Ireland under the Normans*, 4 vols (Oxford, 1911-1920).

Otway-Ruthven, A.J., *A History of Medieval Ireland* (London, 2nd ed. 1980).

—, 'The organisation of Anglo-Irish agriculture in the Middle Ages', *JRSAI*, 81 (1951), 1-13.

—, 'The character of the Norman settlement in Ireland', in *Historical Studies*, 5 (1965), 75-84.

—, 'The medieval county of Kildare', *IHS*, 11 (1959), 181-99.

—, 'The partition of the de Verdun lands in Ireland in 1332', *PRIA*, 66C (1968). 401-55.

Plummer, C., 'Vita Sancti Moling' in *Vitae Sanctorum Hiberniae*, Vol. ii (Oxford, 1968), 190-205.

Pochin Mould, D.D.C., *Irish Pilgrimage* (Dublin, 1955).

Power, C. 'A medieval demographic sample' in *Excavations at the Dominican Priory of St Mary's of the Isle, Crosse's Green, Cork*, ed. M.F. Hurley and C.M. Sheehan (Cork, 1995), 66-83.

Quinn, D.B., *The Elizabethans and the Irish* (N.Y., 1966).

Rae, E. C., 'Architecture and Sculpture 1169-1603' in *NHI*, ii. 736-779.

Richardson, H.G. and Sayles, G.O., *The Irish Parliament in the Middle Ages* (Philadelphia, new ed., 1964

—, *The Administration of Ireland, 1172-1377* (Dublin, 1963).

—, 'Irish revenue, 1278-1384', *PRIA*, 62 C (1962), 87-100.

Richter, Michael, *Medieval Ireland: The Enduring Tradition* (Dublin, 1988).

Russell, J.C., 'Late thirteenth century Ireland as a region', *Demography*, 3 (1966), 500-512.

Ryan, M. (ed.), *The Illustrated Archaeology of Ireland* (Dublin, 1991).

Rynne, C., *The Archaeology of Cork City and Harbour* (Cork, 1993).

Sayles, G.O., 'The rebellious first earl of Desmond', in Watt, Morrall and Martin (eds.), *Medieval Studies Presented to Aubrey Gwynn S.J.* (Dublin, 1961), 203-229.

—, 'The legal proceedings against the First Earl of Desmond', *Anal. Hib.*, 23 (1966), 3-47.

Seymour, St-J. D., *Anglo-Irish Literature, 1200-1582* (Cambridge, 1929).

—, *Irish Witchcraft and Demonology* (Dublin, 1913).

Shaw, F., 'Medieval medico-philosophical treatises in the Irish language', in Ó Riain (ed.), *Féilscríbhinn Eoin Mhic Néill* (Dublin 1940), 144-157.

—, 'Medicine in Ireland in medieval times', in Doolin, W. and Fitzgerald, O. (eds.), *What's Past is Prologue: A Retrospect of Irish Medicine* (Dublin, 1952), 10-14.

Shields, H., 'The walling of New Ross: a thirteenth-century poem in French', *Long Room*, xii-xiii (1975-6), 24-33.

Simms, A. 'Continuity and change: settlement and society in medieval Ireland, c.500-1500' in W. Nolan (ed.), *The Shaping of Ireland: The Geographical Perspective* (Cork and Dublin, 1986), 44-65.

—, 'Core and periphery in medieval Europe: The Irish experience in a wider context' in W. J. Smyth and K. Whelan (eds.), *Common Ground: Essays on the Historical Geography of Ireland* (Cork, 1988), 22-40.

Simms, K., 'Nomadry in medieval Ireland: The origins of the creaght or caoraigheacht', *Peritia* 5 (1986), 379-91.

—, 'The Norman invasion and the Gaelic recovery' in Foster (ed.), *The Oxford Illustrated History of Ireland* (Oxford and New York, 1989), 53-103.

Spenser, Edmund, *A View of the Present State of Ireland*, ed. W.L. Renwick (Oxford, 1970).

Stalley, R.A., *The Cistercian Monasteries of Ireland* (London and New Haven, 1987).

—, *Architecture and Sculpture in Ireland 1150-1350* (Dublin, 1971).

—, 'Irish Gothic and English fashion' in Lydon, J. (ed.), *The English in Medieval Ireland* (Dublin, 1984), 65-86.

—, 'Gothic art and architecture' in Ryan (ed.), *The Illustrated Archaeology of Ireland* (Dublin, 1991), 172-174.

Sweetman. P. D., 'Excavations at Shop Street, Drogheda, County Louth', *PRIA*, 84C (1984), 171-224.

—, 'Archaeological excavations at Trim Castle, Co. Meath, 1971-74', *PRIA*, 78C (1978), 127-98.

Twohig, D.C., 'Archaeological heritage' in 'History of Cork', *Cork Examiner*, 27 March 1985.

Walsh, C., *Archaeological Excavations at Patrick, Nicholas and Winetavern Streets, Dublin* (Dublin and Dingle, 1997.

Walsh, K., *A Fourteenth-Century Scholar and Primate:*

Richard FitzRalph in Oxford, Avignon and Armagh (Oxford, 1981).

—, 'The clerical estate in later medieval Ireland: alien settlement or element of conciliation?', in Bradley, J.(ed.), *Settlement and Society in Medieval Ireland* (Kilkenny, 1988), 361-377.

Watt, J.A., *The Church and the Two Nations in Medieval Ireland* (Cambridge, 1970).

—, *The Church in Medieval Ireland* (Dublin, 1972).

Westropp, T.J., 'Early Italian maps of Ireland from 1300-1600 with notes on foreign settlers in Ireland', *PRIA,* 30 C (1912-13).

—, 'The manor of Bunratty', *JRSAI*, 47 (1917).

Whelan, K. (ed.), *Wexford: History and Society* (Dublin, 1987).

Wood, H., 'The office of Chief Governor of Ireland 1172-1509', *PRIA*, 36C (1921-24), 206-38.

List of Illustrations

1. *Xenopsylla cheopis* (Division of Vector-Borne Infectious Diseases, Centers for Disease Control and Prevention, USA)
2. New Ross. (Photo © D. Kelly)
3. Dalkey Harbour
4. Thath Molyngis. (Photo © D. Kelly)
5. St Moling's Well. (Photo © D. Kelly)
6. Corbel Figure, St Francis Church, Kilkenny (Hunt, i, 194)
7 Bambino of Ross. (Photo © D. Kelly)
8. Rice Tomb in Christ Church Cathedral, Waterford. (Photo © D. Kelly)
9 and 10. Detail of fourteenth-century Black Death burial pits from the site of the former Royal Mint at East Smithfield in London (By permission of the Museum of London Archaeology Service)
11. Effigy of William Goer and his wife, Margaret, in the churchyard of St Mary's Parish Church, Kilkenny (Photo © D. Kelly)
12. Tomb-Chest at St Erc's Hermitage, Slane, Co. Meath. (Photo © D. Kelly)
13. The Wicklow Mountains, the territory of the MicMhurchadha (Photo © D. O' Connell)
14. Beaulieu Cadaver (Photo © D. Kelly)
15. St Francis Abbey, Kilkenny. (Photo © D. Kelly)
16. Ennis
17. Youghal Town
18. St Peter's Churchyard, Drogheda
19. Rock of Cashel (Photo © D. Kelly)
20. St Lawrence's Gate, Drogheda (Photo © D. Kelly)
21. Black Abbey, Kilkenny. (Photo © D. Kelly)
22. Medieval Kilkenny (Photo © D. Kelly)
23. Duleek, St Mary's Chapel, Priory of the Augustinian canons. (Photo © D. Kelly)
24. Youghal Town Wall. (Photo © D. Kelly)
25. Tyone Priory, Nenagh. (Photo © D. Kelly)

Index

Index

If you are interested in purchasing
other books published by Tempus, or in case you have
difficulty finding any Tempus books in your local bookshop,
you can also place orders directly through our website

www.tempus-publishing.com

or from

BOOKPOST
Freepost, PO Box 29,
Douglas, Isle of Man
IM99 1BQ
Tel 01624 836000
email bookshop@enterprise.net